OPERATIONS RESEARCH SOCIETY
OF AMERICA

Publications in Operations Research

Number 3

PUBLICATIONS IN OPERATIONS RESEARCH

Operations Research Society of America

Editor

GEORGE SHORTLEY

Associate Editors

JOHN W. ABRAMS

RUSSELL L. ACKOFF

THOMAS E. CAYWOOD

CHARLES GOODEVE

WILLIAM J. HORVATH

B. O. KOOPMAN

JOHN F. MAGEE

HUGH J. MISER

THORNTON PAGE

E. W. PAXSON

WILLIAM J. PLATT

ANDREW SCHULTZ, JR.

JACINTO STEINHARDT

No. 1. QUEUES, INVENTORIES AND MAINTENANCE
Philip M. Morse

No. 2. FINITE QUEUING TABLES
L. G. Peck and R. N. Hazelwood

No. 3. EFFICIENCY IN GOVERNMENT THROUGH SYSTEMS ANALYSIS
Roland N. McKean

No. 4. A COMPREHENSIVE BIBLIOGRAPHY ON OPERATIONS RESEARCH
Operations Research Group, Case Institute

EFFICIENCY IN GOVERNMENT THROUGH SYSTEMS ANALYSIS

31350 *With Emphasis on Water Resources Development*

A RAND CORPORATION RESEARCH STUDY

By ROLAND N. McKEAN

THE RAND CORPORATION
SANTA MONICA, CALIFORNIA

NEW YORK · JOHN WILEY & SONS, INC.
LONDON · CHAPMAN & HALL, LIMITED

H II 1694
A 5
M 15 e

TO MY FAMILY

PREFACE

IT IS HOPED that this volume will be useful to various persons, regardless of their backgrounds, who have a common interest in applied economizing. Although a good deal of economic theory is involved, the study is not aimed primarily at professional economists. It is intended, of course, that the discussion be acceptable to specialists in economics. But the presentation is meant to be suitable for a somewhat wider and more heterogeneous audience—cost-benefit analysts, operations researchers, government personnel who are engaged in one way or another in evaluating alternative courses of action, those in academic circles who are interested in such evaluations, and persons in general who are concerned about economy in government.

The study is rather different from most of the work undertaken by The RAND Corporation, and its place in the organization's research program should be made clear. RAND is a private, non-profit corporation which does most of its research under contract with the United States Air Force. However, the Corporation sponsors and finances additional studies of its own choosing. This inquiry into the analysis of water-resource investments and civil government operations was undertaken as one of these additional studies. It seemed natural enough for a member of RAND to study the evaluation of alternative water-resource systems and other non-military courses of action: experience with comparisons of military systems (which have entailed the estimation of their gains and costs) could be applied, at least in part, to these non-military problems.

For various publications and for cooperation in general, I am greatly indebted to the Department of Agriculture, the Corps of Engineers, and the Department of the Interior. For suggestions or special materials, thanks are due to many individuals in government (or persons who were in government at the time the study was being prepared), particularly to Lyle E. Craine, formerly of the Department of Interior, and now on the faculty of the School of Natural Resources at the University of Michigan; the late Henry Erlanger, formerly of the Bureau of the Budget; Mark M. Regan of the Department of Agriculture, long associated with the staff of the Subcommittee on Benefits and Costs of the Federal Inter-Agency River Basin Committee; and Ira A. Watson of the Bureau of Reclamation. I also wish to thank Mr. F. Friend, formerly Chief, Planning and Reports Branch, and Mr. J. G. Jobes, Assistant Chief, Engineering Division, in the Los Angeles District of the Corps of Engineers, for the loan of mimeographed reports and for assistance given to me at the District Office; and Robert P. Beach and Joseph C. Wheeler of the Department of Agriculture for discussions and materials related to Chapter 13 on "Analysis in Connection with Performance Budgets."

I am also under obligation, for criticisms and suggestions, to numerous other persons, especially to Harold J. Barnett of Resources for the Future; G. Diran Bodenhorn of the University of Chicago; James M. Buchanan of the University of Virginia; Gershon Cooper of Dunlap and Associates, Inc.; Otto Eckstein of Harvard University; H. P. B. Jenkins of the University of Arkansas; Carl Kaysen of Harvard University; John V. Krutilla of Resources for the Future; Charles E. Lindblom of Yale University; Julius Margolis of the University of California at Berkeley; Harold W. Metz of the National Association of Electric Companies; Jerome W. Milliman of the University of California; Mary B. Novick of the University of California at Los Angeles; and Arthur Smithies of Harvard University.

I wish to convey special thanks to Sam H. Schurr, formerly of The RAND Corporation and now with Resources for the Future, for many discussions and suggestions, and to several members of The RAND Corporation—Armen A. Alchian (also of the University of California at Los Angeles), Alain C. Enthoven, Charles J. Hitch, Malcolm W. Hoag, and Norman M. Kaplan—who have read and criticized the entire manuscript. To others at RAND, I wish to make blanket acknowledgment, since a list of the individuals who have helped me, particularly in the Economics Division, would amount almost to a roster of personnel, and to single out a few might do more injustice than simply to say that I am under obligation to all.

ROLAND N. MCKEAN

Santa Monica, California
April, 1958

CONTENTS

Part 1

Introduction

Chapter 1

SETTING, SCOPE, AND PLAN
OF THE STUDY

"THE FEDERAL GOVERNMENT in fiscal 1954 absorbed about one-sixth of all the goods and services produced in this country. . . . All told, Federal government activities including trust fund operations [transfer payments] resulted in cash expenditures of about $72 billion."[1] To get the most that we can from the resources devoted to these activities is a matter of undisputed importance. One possible way to get more from these resources—that is, to increase efficiency—is to use systematic quantitative analysis in the comparison of alternative courses of action. However, in order for this use of analysis to make possible significant economies, improved analytical methods and wider application are both necessary. This study is an attempt to contribute to those two things, the improvement of analysis in government and the extension of its use. The inquiry deals specifically with the comparison of water-resource projects, and its purpose is partly to contribute to this particular application of analysis. But the comparison of alternative operations or policies of other sorts involves many of the same problems, and the broader purpose of the study is to assist in the general struggle for economy.

THE ROLE OF ANALYTICAL AIDS IN ECONOMIZING

It should go without saying that all decision-making persons or groups attempt to economize, in the true sense of the word. That is, they try to make the "most," as they conceive of the "most," of what-

[1] *Control of Federal Government Expenditures*, A Statement on National Policy by the Research and Policy Committee of the Committee for Economic Development, January 1955, p. 1.

ever resources they have. Business firms may have a comparatively clear-cut notion of what they mean by the most, while consumers and governmental units have much more difficulty in defining it. But all of them, unless they make their decisions by drawing straws, are trying to do something in the best way possible with the resources that are available. Even the church, in offering spiritual guidance, is concerned with economy, but economy at a high level. The attitude of the clergy is that while we are good at getting the most in day-to-day lower-level problems, we sometimes define "most" incorrectly by choosing the wrong high-level goals. Incidentally, it will be convenient, from time to time, to make this rough distinction between broad or high-level problems and narrower or lower-level problems.[2]

The Usefulness of Analytical Aids

In tackling problems of choice, people have always found it advantageous to think about the consequences of alternative policies rather than to choose among them by, say, flipping coins alone. To assist them in predicting those consequences, they use models of the real situation. These may be small-scale representations, such as a model airplane in a wind tunnel or a pilot industrial plant. They may be representations on paper—mathematical models which grow out of laboratory experiment, reasoning, or the observation of small-scale physical models. Or, finally, these models may be simple sets of relationships that are sketched out in the mind and not formally put down on paper. If a schoolboy considers different ways to throw a basketball, he figures that the ball, if thrown with a certain type of English and at a particular angle to the backboard, will probably rebound into the basket. If a sales manager compares different advertising campaigns, he uses certain relationships to help him estimate the consequences. If a person tries to gage the effects of tariffs, price controls,

---

[2] This distinction is the basis for another one that is often made. It is sometimes said that "economic problems" are concerned with picking the best allocation of given resources among *competing* uses, while "technological or engineering problems" are concerned with finding the best way of using given resources to achieve a *single* end [e.g., G. Stigler, *The Theory of Price* (New York: The Macmillan Company, 1946), p. 15]. But most engineering problems really involve the allocation of resources among competing uses, and thus are "economic problems," or else there is no choosing to be done. To find the best way to use a given stock of machine tools within a firm means to allocate them among competing uses. And the allocation involves the valuation of those competing uses. The distinction, and it is a convenient one, is really between problems of choice at different levels.

or monopoly, he makes use of some model of the economy. Or, to refer once more to the church's concern about high-level economy, if your minister advises you to mend your ways, he definitely has a model in mind.

Now in no case are these models photographic reproductions of reality. If they were, they would be so complicated that they would be of absolutely no use to us. So they abstract from a great deal of the real world. This does not mean that they are "bad" models, nor does it mean that they are "good." Whether or not one is better than another depends upon whether or not it gives better predictions (and, therefore, helps us to make better decisions) than another. This may be hard to determine, but it is the acid test of a model's quality.

The notion of models has been stressed because the term is widely used and because systematic thought about any problem of choice necessarily involves models, naive or otherwise. The alternative is to flip coins, draw straws, or rely on conjecture. Sometimes, of course, these are the only things one can do, but by and large good solutions to problems have been reached by means of thoughtful analysis, and that means through the use of models. All history shows—which means "I think," according to a rough translation by Frank H. Knight —that this is so. But seriously, most history *does* indicate that thought-taking is better than chance in solving problems.

The Development of Analytical Aids

Some of the most fundamental analytical aids have long been available, and could have been used in the past to much greater advantage than they were. Although refinements have occurred, e.g., in the handling of uncertainty, the main elements of the theory of choice have existed for a long time, in economic theory, mathematics, and certain branches of philosophy, for example. This sort of aid indicates at least what questions should be asked in comparing alternative courses of action, and even without other tools, raising the right questions can generate simple models that are powerful problem solvers.

The spectacular advances over the past fifty years, however, have pertained to other tools. One thing that has happened has been the rapid development of all the sciences so that it has become possible to say much more about the relationship of one event to another— about the effects, for example, of using prestressed concrete or higher octane fuel, or about the relationship between smog and combinations of sunshine, ozone, and gasoline fumes. As missing links in the chains of relationship were filled in, it became possible to predict more accurately the consequences of various actions. This development has sometimes necessitated, in problems of sufficient importance, the collaboration of teams of scientists and analysts in order to bring the knowledge of specialists to bear.

Along with the better understanding of scientific relationships has come more and better data. Or perhaps the data might be described as one facet of that better understanding. In any event, more facts are available about plastics, rainfall, markets, disease, national income, and so on. Also there have been refinements in the methods of statistical inference—for instance, in the use of small samples, sequential sampling, and experimental designs—and in techniques of computation and model-building, such as linear programming. Finally, electronic computers have come along to make it practicable to utilize all the other refinements. More complex models, which in some cases yield more useful predictions, can be employed; more numerous calculations to show results in a wider range of situations have become feasible. In fact, some persons believe that modern computers mark a massive technological breakthrough, so far as analysis is concerned, somewhat as the microgroove recording was a crucial breakthrough in the high-fidelity reproduction of music. However, it should be recognized that much of the most useful quantitative analysis of today is still done with a hand computer or even on the back of an envelope.

At the same time that these tools were being developed, new applications, or types of analysis, were emerging, and new terminology was being used to describe them. Originally, thoughtful analysis may have been called just that, or possibly "problem solving." In connection with problems which have attracted the attention of economists[3]—such

---

[3] It is surprising, incidentally, how little attention has been given by economists, especially by public-finance specialists, to efficiency in government. A good deal of work has been done to compare alternative means of getting revenue and alternative ways of handling the government's liabilities. With respect to expenditures it is sometimes suggested that, in principle, the government should allocate outlays so that the gains from an incremental dollar's expenditure are the same in every direction (including tax reduction). For the most part, however, economists have been *relatively* uninterested in the optimal allocation of government expenditures or (the same problem at a practical level) in comparisons of alternative purchases by government. This was noted several years ago by V. O. Key, Jr., who remarked that in their textbooks, public-finance experts ". . . generally dispose of the subject of expenditures with a few perfunctory chapters and hurry on to the core of their interest—taxation and other sources of revenue." ("The Lack of a Budgetary Theory," *American Political Science Review,* December, 1940, p. 1139.) In recent years, a few economists have stressed the importance of looking at expenditures: e.g., see Arthur

as those pertaining to the balance of payments, price level fluctuations, and possible improvements in general resource allocation—the comparison of alternative policies has been labeled simply "economic analysis." In the early decades of this century, there was a period of "scientific management" or "efficiency engineering" when F. W. Taylor focused attention on factory layout and time-motion studies. Through the years, the stop watch of the early studies has been supplemented by high-speed cameras and by other instruments for measurement and techniques for looking at problems. During roughly the same period, "financial analysis" caught on rapidly, as executives turned to accounting data and short-cut models to predict the effects of alternative management policies. Another development was "consumers' research," in which simple models spelled out some of the characteristics of competing products. For example, lawn sprinklers have been compared with respect to "evenness" by finding out how much water fell into various tin cans evenly spaced around the sprinklers. Also, in the comparison of possible locations, new products, or sales policies, "market research" became widely used.

During World War II, modern statistical techniques and knowledge from different sciences were used, sometimes with striking effectiveness, in the comparison of military tactics, such as various deployments of aircraft or ships. As these studies were used to assist in operational decisions, they became known as "operations research." Since the war, this general approach has been applied also to military development and procurement problems, which has meant peering further into the future, including a greatly expanded number of variables, examining a wider range of possible actions, and taking higher-level alternatives into account. The comparison of such enlarged systems of interrelated elements has often been called "systems analysis." For analysis to help business firms increase their profits, a variety of names, from operations research to capital budgeting, have been used during this past decade.[4]

Smithies, *The Budgetary Process in the United States*, Committee for Economic Development Research Study (New York: McGraw-Hill, 1955), and James M. Buchanan, "The Pure Theory of Government Finance: A Suggested Approach," *Journal of Political Economy*, December, 1949, pp. 496–505; and there were exceptions before World War II, such as Mable L. Walker, *Municipal Expenditures* (Baltimore: The Johns Hopkins Press, 1930).

[4] See various issues of *The Journal of the Operations Research Society of America;* Joel Dean, *Capital Budgeting: Top-Management Policy on Plant, Equipment, and Product Development* (New York: Columbia University Press, 1951).

For the most part, these various titles do reflect somewhat different types of analysis, the differences stemming largely from the character of the problems attacked. Yet at the same time these types exhibit a marked similarity: all of them are attempts to trace systematically at least part of the effects of alternative courses of action. Consequently, many of the methodological difficulties that are encountered in any one of these types are common to all.

Despite the encouraging developments of analytical tools and of new applications, it is clear that the role of such analysis must be that of an *aid* to the decision-maker, not that of a substitute for him. In the face of uncertainty about outcomes, for instance, operations research and kindred activities can assist, but not supplant, the exercise of judgment as to which policy is best. Perhaps it should also be mentioned that such analysis is no serious rival of the price mechanism and free enterprise in the organization of the private economy for technical reasons alone (quite apart from the merits of the price system as a decision-making process). Indeed, the best medicine for well-meaning central planners is perhaps a stiff dose of down-to-earth operations research on complex problems of the Federal government; such an experience would lay bare, more vividly than does meditation alone, the awesome difficulties that would be encountered (and the grim mistakes and concentration of power that would surely occur) in detailed central direction of the economy. But where the price mechanism and the action of competing firms do not attend to problems of choice—in *internal* decisions of a consumer, government unit, or firm—it is operations analysis that often has no practicable rival.

The Application of Analytical Aids in Government

In recent years, governmental units have turned increasingly to the quantitative comparison of the alternative policies that are open to them. For example, the military services have internal operations analysis sections or evaluation groups, and, in addition, the Departments of the Army, Navy, and Air Force hire independent organizations to perform such research.[5] As another case in point, some agencies have made progress in the use of work-measurement systems to help select the administrative policy that achieves a fixed task at lowest cost or the maximum output for a given cost. This type of analysis involves the selection of "work-units" (such as hearings

---

[5] See Florence N. Trefethen, "A History of Operations Research," in *Operations Research for Management*, ed. J. F. McCloskey and F. N. Trefethen (Baltimore: The Johns Hopkins Press, 1954), pp. 3–35.

completed, parcels shipped, applications examined) in terms of which to measure the output of accounting divisions, legal divisions, wrapping and shipping departments, licensing offices, and so on.[6] Private firms, such as mail-order houses, have long used work-measurement systems to help project personnel requirements in different departments at various times of the day, thus enabling them to shift some employees from time to time in such a way as to maximize the value of their services. In the last few years, the Department of Agriculture has turned to such a system to compare output at various regional offices and under various circumstances,[7] enabling officials to reduce the manpower required to perform a given task, to make sure that manpower is reduced when the task or workload declines, or to consolidate regional offices in response to altered workloads. State and local governments and numerous other agencies have also made use of work-measurement systems.

Another instance, the one to which much of our attention will be devoted in this study, is the use of "cost-benefit analysis" in the evaluation of water-resource developments, such as navigation, flood control, and soil-conservation measures. Even in the thirties the Bureau of Reclamation and Corps of Engineers worked up estimates of benefits and costs for numerous water-resource projects in order to facilitate their comparison. Since World War II, however, interest in cost-benefit analysis has heightened; the Department of Agriculture has completed similar analyses of several watershed-treatment programs, and the Federal Inter-Agency River Basin Committee has been reviewing current procedures and drawing up recommendations concerning future measurement of benefits and costs.[8]

NEED FOR SUCH ANALYSIS IN GOVERNMENT. But surely a great deal more can be done. The trend toward the greater use of quantitative analysis is a response to a very real need, one that is intensified by (a) the absence of any built-in mechanism which would lead to

[6] See the bibliography contained in *A Work Measurement System: Development and Use (A Case Study)*, Management Bulletin, Bureau of the Budget, March, 1950. For a good clear discussion of the main problems, see *Techniques for the Development of a Work Measurement System*, Bureau of the Budget, March, 1950.

[7] "Work-Measurement and Work-Status Reporting System: PMA Commodity Offices," unpublished working papers, loaned by Mr. Robert P. Beach, Budget Officer, Production and Marketing Administration, Department of Agriculture.

[8] *Proposed Practices for Economic Analysis of River Basin Projects*, Report to the Federal Inter-Agency River Basin Committee Prepared by the Subcommittee on Benefits and Costs, May, 1950.

greater efficiency, and (b) the spectacular growth in the size of government.

Absence of Price Mechanism, Profit Lure, "Natural Selection." For one thing, there is no price mechanism within government which points the way to high-level efficiency, that is, to the correct allocation of resources among "industries" or broad governmental functions. For another, there is no competitive force that induces lower-level efficiency—the adoption of methods and equipment which carry out each function at minimum cost. Because of the lure of profits and the threat of bankruptcy, private firms are under pressure to seek out profitable innovations and efficient methods. In this search they have often used, and are now using to an increasing extent, formal quantitative analysis.[9] But even if they do not, continued progress and increased efficiency still tend to come about, though less rapidly. After all, *some* firm is likely to discover more efficient methods through trial and error even if systematic analysis is absent, indeed even if the right questions are not asked. Subsequently, other firms copy the innovation; those that fail to do so (those who make inferior choices of methods) begin to suffer losses, and the process of "natural selection" tends to eliminate them.[10]

In government, however, there is no profit lure, and promotions or salary increases do not depend on profits. Most of the cost of poor decisions does not fall on those who make them. The incentive to seek profitable innovations and efficient methods is not a strong one. Experience in the Post Office Department may illustrate this point: a few postmasters with exceptional drive or motivation have introduced cost-cutting innovations even though this action brought no personal gain; yet there are no lures sufficient to cause these innovations to be imitated in other post offices of similar size and setup.[11]

Finally, the process of "natural selection," whose working depends upon the degree and type of rivalry, operates only weakly, if at all, to eliminate wasteful governments. The Federal government, for instance, competes only with the political party that is out of office,

[9] See various articles in *Operations Research for Management.*

[10] A. Alchian, "Uncertainty, Evolution, and Economic Theory," *Journal of Political Economy*, June, 1950, pp. 211–221. The prevention of mistakes by systematic analysis would be a cheaper path to progress than their correction by natural selection—*if* the former procedure were as effective as the latter.

[11] For evidence on this point, see Paul Douglas, *Economy in the National Government* (Chicago: University of Chicago Press, 1952), p. 127; and the *Task Force Report on the Post Office* prepared for the Commission on Organization of the Executive Branch of the Government, January, 1949, p. 17.

and survival in this competition depends upon many things other than efficiency in the use of resources. Thus, there are no forces which operate to reveal the cheapest methods of performing public functions and to induce or compel the government to adopt such methods.

It should be mentioned that in a few government activities, for example, the Military Sea Transport Service, simulation of the market mechanism is attempted. These activities are set up as businesses, provided with working-capital funds, and instructed to charge market prices for the output and to achieve maximum profits—often in the light of special constraints. At present, this institutional arrangement is not widespread, and one is justified in referring to the absence of the price mechanism in government. However, such simulation of the market is a policy which should be explored and evaluated.

Adoption of "Requirements Approach." In the absence of such forces and, to a considerable extent, of systematic analyses in terms of gains and costs, a procedure that might be called the "requirements approach" is used throughout much of the government. Officials inspect a problem pertaining to, say, defense, water usage, or medical care, and set up a "required" task, piece of equipment, or performance characteristic. Cost, i.e., whatever has to be sacrificed in order to obtain the requirement, is given little or no explicit consideration at this point: the requirement is somehow drawn up in the light of the need or payoff alone.[12] (Of course, some notion of cost, however imprecise, is implicit in the recognition of any limitation.) Then feasibility is checked: Can the performance characteristic, such as some designated speed or degree of reliability, be achieved? Can the necessary budget be obtained? Does the nation have the necessary total resources? If the program passes the feasibility tests, it is adopted; if it does not, some adjustments must be made. But the question—what are the payoffs *and the costs* of alternative programs? —may not be explicitly asked during the process of setting the requirement or deciding upon the budget.

The procedure is illustrated by the way in which programs are developed in the Department of Interior. Each of the seven Field Committees (for example, there is one for the Colorado River-Great Basin Region) is instructed to prepare an "optimum program" which is "... formulated on the basis of regional needs. It takes into account all practical limitations (such as availability of manpower, laboratory

---

[12] Indeed, the situation is still worse; as will be indicated in Chapter 2, "requirements" are often drawn up in the light of little or no idea of true potential payoffs.

facilities, etc.), *except limitations on funds* [italics added]. This program presents the optimum schedule which should be undertaken in the first year of the six-year program to meet the goals described in the narrative part of each functional chapter."[13]   Other programs which relate to alternative budget levels are also prepared in advance (a highly commendable procedure), but the "optimum" program, the one that is regarded as the requirement, is derived by disregarding fund limitations. In the end, higher officials *may* consider alternative programs in the light of their costs. But in all likelihood, major problems of choice will already have been disposed of before costs enter the picture.

The defects of this approach can be seen clearly if an analogy from the life of the consumer is introduced. Suppose the consumer mulls over his transportation problem and decides, "I need a Cadillac," without any information about the cost—that is, about the required outlay and hence about the goods and services that could be had for the same amount. An alternative purchase is a more modest automobile plus other items that could be purchased with the amount saved. But thousands of additional possibilities exist. There is ordinarily a wealth of choice, and to ignore the cost of a course of action is to ignore the possible worth of all these other actions.

This requirements approach appears to be prevalent at various levels of decision-making. Requirements are often set by looking at "need" without regard to cost not only when selecting broad programs but also when choosing the means of carrying them out. With this approach, it is not unnatural for a military service to procure, for example, all-hair wrestling mats even though they cost about twice as much as the half-hair-half-wool mats that are used in most gymnasiums.[14] Specifications for ping-pong balls that take up five and a half pages of single-spaced typing may also stem from too much emphasis on "requirements" and too little on cost.[15]

Importance of Economy in Government. All of this—the absence of the price mechanism and competitive forces, and the prevalence of the requirements approach—was comparatively unimportant thirty years ago when Federal expenditures were about three billion dollars, but it is an extremely serious matter now that the national government

---

[13] "Instructions on the Preparation of Regional Program Reports," attached to a memorandum to all Field Committee Chairmen from the Office of the Secretary, U.S. Department of the Interior, January 7, 1953.

[14] Douglas, *op. cit.*, p. 175.

[15] *Ibid.*, p. 173.

alone disburses more than 70 billion dollars per year. The point is sometimes emphasized by the following type of comparison: during the two years 1953–1954, the Federal government disbursed roughly the same amount (about 140 billion dollars) that was spent in the entire 140-year period from 1789 to 1929. (And during the 15 years from 1939 to 1954, Federal outlays have amounted to almost 800 billion dollars.) Such comparisons are meaningful only in a very limited sense, for changes in the price level are left out of account, but they certainly show that our national government uses and transfers a lot of resources.

The present-day importance of economy in government is also suggested by the amount of attention which it is finally getting. A few years ago the Hoover Commission examined various aspects of government economizing, and now the second Commission has brought out its reports. Senator Paul Douglas has written extensively about the urgency of economizing.[16] Not too long ago, the Rockefeller committee on reorganization sent its recommendations to the President,[17] and Rockefeller funds set up a permanent "Hoover Commission."[18] There have been several recent studies of budgetary procedures and possible improvements.[19] Also, the Rockefeller committee has urged that the scale of work by the Bureau of the Budget in the field of government reorganization, budgetary procedure, and administrative management be increased. This list of efforts is not at all exhaustive, but it suggests a growing concern about efficiency in government.

NEED FOR BETTER ANALYSIS. Thus, because of government's lack of a competitive market mechanism and because of its tremendous expansion, formal analysis of alternative actions may be especially rewarding in the public sphere. But mere quantity of analysis is unlikely to be particularly rewarding. Although the potential gains from "good" operations analysis may be greater in government than in

[16] *Ibid.*

[17] A committee on reorganization, with particular emphasis on the Defense Department, chaired by Nelson A. Rockefeller. Just prior to the appointment of this committee, the Citizens Advisory Commission on Manpower Utilization in the Armed Services, headed by David Sarnoff, presented its report to Defense Secretary Wilson.

[18] *New York Times,* April 24, 1953, p. 1.

[19] One study, under the direction of Dr. Harold Metz, has been made by the Brookings Institution; Dr. Arthur Smithies, under the auspices of the Committee on Economic Development, has completed the volume on the budgetary process that was mentioned earlier; another study is Dr. Frederick C. Mosher's *Program Budgeting: Theory and Practice* (New York: Public Administration Service, 1954).

private industry, the likelihood of social losses from "bad" analysis is also greater, chiefly for two reasons: (1) the process of "natural selection" does not penalize the government that bases decisions on inferior analyses—e.g., comparisons which, however systematic in other respects, use inappropriate criteria or conceal crucial uncertainties; (2) the problem of choosing appropriate criteria, which will be examined later, is even more difficult in the analysis of many governmental operations than in the analysis of business operations. In the latter, one can usually take the ultimate objective to be the maximization of the present value of expected profits, and then judge whether criteria in particular problems are consistent with the over-all objective. For these reasons, firms can often use relatively poor criteria, such as the minimization of unit costs, in a way that leads them to genuine economies. In the analysis of government operations, however, the over-all objective is so complex, and the "firm" so big and compartmentalized, that it may be more difficult to select appropriate criteria that are consistent with over-all objectives or to use poor criteria judiciously. Therefore it is not mere analysis, but *careful* analysis, that is so urgently needed to assist decision-making in government.

Indeed the bulk of this inquiry is devoted to pitfalls and the means of avoiding them. If these pitfalls are not avoided, quantitative comparisons can do more harm than good: ". . . there is an arguable case for the view that it is better than spurious definiteness, that final decisions actually use judgment rather than implicitly following benefit-cost ratios calculated by different agencies in different ways."[20] This comment (which could apply equally well to types of analysis other than cost-benefit) is surely an understatement if careless estimates are to be carelessly used. Hence it is *better* quantitative analysis which holds the promise of greater economy.

It is also worth noting that additional criticism and independent analysis are especially needed. It would be helpful if outside researchers (for example, those in universities) devoted more time to the painstaking comparison of alternative government actions at various levels. It would be a good thing, so far as quality of analysis is concerned, if staff agencies within government engaged in mutual criticism to a greater extent. In fact, without competition and criticism, staff agencies may not do much good, for they labor under cer-

[20] J. M. Clark, E. L. Grant, and M. M. Kelso, "Secondary or Indirect Benefits of Water-Use Projects," Report of Panel of Consultants to Michael W. Straus, Commissioner, Bureau of Reclamation, June 26, 1952 (mimeographed), p. 12.

tain handicaps: they have special allegiances,[21] they may develop goals of their own, and they may confuse lines of authority.[22] "Agencies which are under the necessity of competitive survival, with high principles but with equally high desires to develop in size and in significance, cannot be expected to appraise the validity of undertakings in the most abstract and impartial manner."[23]

OUTLOOK FOR THE USE OF ANALYTICAL AIDS. Questions are often, and quite properly, raised about the practical usefulness of analytical aids in the solution of government problems. First, *would* their use have any impact, given the welter of political considerations? Despite the pessimistic views that are sometimes expressed, there is every reason to believe that more and better analysis would influence policy-makers. Pork-barrel aims, local pressures, log-rolling, empire-building —in short, political considerations both good and bad—are obviously powerful forces, often decisive ones, in the shaping of decisions at all levels. Yet one reason that these forces are so powerful is that decision-makers are rarely presented with analyses in terms of economic criteria. If these are unavailable (or unreliable), then why not press for a special interest, or flip a coin, or adopt some "off-beat" criterion? If, however, the effects of different policies on economic efficiency are made apparent, it becomes at least a little harder to neglect this consideration. The pressures shift; the cost of making uneconomic choices becomes real.

This is not to say, of course, that cogent analysis would promptly carry the day or that it ought to do so if this implied the nullification of independent judgments or of checks and balances. The point here is merely that sound analyses are seldom completely disregarded by policy-makers. Wherever specific studies have had something to contribute, they have usually (not always, to be sure) had some impact on policy. A reading of Congressional hearings on appropriations suggests to me that by and large the departments *do* struggle to achieve something more than, say, departmental security, and Congress and the Agencies *do* grope for sensible allocations of the budget among programs. The trouble is mainly that proper criteria are slippery and the problems difficult.[24] The risk that log-rolling

21 Douglas, *op. cit.*, pp. 68–69.

22 See Herbert A. Simon, "Staff and Management Controls," *Annals of the American Academy of Political and Social Science,* March, 1954, pp. 95–103.

23 *Principles of a Sound National Water Policy,* Prepared under the Auspices of the National Water Policy Panel of Engineers Joint Council, July, 1951, p. 22.

24 For a revealing account of the headaches of budget allocation, see *The Forrestal Diaries,* ed. W. Millis (New York: Viking Press, 1951), pp. 492–530.

officials will ignore "good" analysis is not too great, probably not as great as the risk that they will be receptive to "bad" analysis or mere assertion.

A second question that arises is the following: could such analysis really play a substantial role? The answer is certainly yes. It could play a most important role because many government operations appear to be susceptible to this sort of analysis. (It should be recalled that quantitative analysis, such as operations research, is referred to; there is obviously a vital role for thought-taking in general as opposed to mere hunch, in every problem of choice.) The possibilities will be considered in some detail at the end of this study. At this point, it will suffice to say that opportunities for quantitative analysis are numerous in activities that account for over three-quarters of current disbursements. In order for such opportunities to exist, there must be (a) alternative ways to carry out tasks or programs, and (b) meaningful quantitative indicators of gain and of cost. According to the survey that is to be described in the final chapter, these conditions are fulfilled in most defense activities and in at least half of the non-defense programs. Indeed, in programs accounting for perhaps one-fifth of the non-defense budget, gains can probably be given meaningful price tags and measured in terms of dollars so that activities which carry out rather dissimilar functions can be compared directly. To be sure, there are some activities, such as those pertaining to foreign policy, which appear to offer little opportunity for the measurement of gains and costs. But other sectors of the Federal budget—such as the natural-resource programs, the Post Office Department, transportation programs, and the provision of health services—are promising from the standpoint of applying quantitative analysis.

COST-BENEFIT ANALYSIS AND WATER-RESOURCES POLICY

An important example of the application of formal quantitative analysis to non-military problems is cost-benefit analysis, which is used in the shaping of water-resource programs. It is an important application from several points of view. First, current and anticipated expenditures on water-resource activities come to a substantial amount of money. Each year from one to two billion dollars are spent on water-resource development by the Federal government alone. Over the next generation, such expenditures might well be from seventy to one hundred billion dollars.[25]

[25] *A Water Policy for the American People,* Vol. 1 of The Report of the President's Water Resources Policy Commission (Washington, D.C.: U.S. Government Printing Office, 1950), p. 93.

Second, there is a great deal of controversy about the preparation of the analyses, the way they are used, and the programs that are formulated. The debate is heated, and gives rise to publications with such intriguing titles as Muddy Waters, Big Dam Foolishness, and The Battle that Squanders Billions.[26] The Hoover Commission has raised numerous doubts about the efficiency with which outlays have been spent or are scheduled to be spent. In the Congressional hearings on appropriations for fiscal 1956 there was disagreement on questions about the Upper Colorado River Basin Project:[27] would the gain from each of the ten proposed dams exceed its cost? How would the project affect the amount of power and water that would be available from Hoover, Davis, and Parker dams in the lower Colorado River? And, of course, questions arose about "intangibles," e.g., how much importance should be attached to the inundation of part of Dinosaur National Monument?

Third, cost-benefit analyses are analytical aids the study of which is relevant to the use of quantitative analysis in connection with other problems. Such study is pertinent above all else to the systematic scrutiny of still other water-resource projects, such as component measures that are not now subjected to analysis, drainage of marshlands, subsurface storage, reclaiming of water from sewage, or direct use of sea water.[28] Experiences with cost-benefit are pertinent to special studies that may be called for from time to time; for example, a bill was introduced some time ago by Senator Monroney to provide for a special comparison of alternative ways to achieve flood-control.[29] The lessons of cost-benefit analysis are relevant also to operations research for private firms, the most direct connection being to the comparison of net profits to the agricultural firm from different operations.[30] Finally, whatever can be learned from cost-benefit has some

[26] Arthur Maass, *Muddy Waters* (Cambridge, Mass.: Harvard University Press, 1951); Elmer T. Peterson, *Big Dam Foolishness* (New York: Devin-Adair Co., 1954); Leslie A. Miller, "The Battle that Squanders Billions," *Saturday Evening Post*, May 14, 1949, pp. 30–31.

[27] *Business Week*, February 12, 1955, pp. 56–62.

[28] See "Methods Other Than Saline Water Conversion for Increasing Supplies of Water," in James C. DeHaven, Lynn A. Gore, and Jack Hirshleifer, *A Brief Survey of the Technology and Economics of Water Supply* (RAND Corporation, Report R-258-RC, October, 1953), pp. 35–46.

[29] *Congressional Record*, Vol. 98, Part 1, 82nd Congress, 2nd Session, February 14, 1952, p. 975.

[30] An early study which brings out this connection is *Value and Cost of Water for Irrigation in the Coastal Plain of Southern California*, by Frank Adams and Martin R. Huberty (Bulletin No. 43 in the South Coastal Basin Investigation, Division of Water Resources, State of California Department of Public Works,

applicability to the comparison of alternative actions in other governmental activities. The general methodological problems are much the same, and in some cases even the problems of model construction are similar. For instance, estimation of damage reduction due to flood-control projects is not wholly unlike the estimation of potential damage reduction attributable to certain defense operations.

History of Cost-Benefit Analysis

Early legislation pertaining to water-resource activities of the government—for example, the Reclamation Act of 1902 and the Navigation-Improvement Act of 1824—provided for surveys and engineering reports to be made for each proposal. The subsequent development of "economic evaluations" in terms of cost-benefit estimates took place gradually, but a number of specific dates stand out. The River and Harbor Acts of 1927 and 1928 authorized the Corps of Engineers to prepare what have become known as "308" reports.

The "308" surveys constituted the most complete and comprehensive studies of the river basins of the United States made up to that time to present an inventory of their water-resource problems and potentialities. The plans were general in nature and, together with the estimates of project costs, were based largely on available data supplemented by reconnaissance surveys. They were not originally intended to be a basis for authorizing Federal improvements; although the reports set forth specific plans of improvement and projects, they generally did not include recommendations for construction by the Federal Government. The "308" reports were, however, the best available data on such improvements and were used by Congress as a basis for subsequent legislation for flood control and for the Tennessee Valley Authority. They also provided a backlog of specific projects for accomplishment with Federal funds for emergency relief during the depression in the early 1930's; formed the major source of information for the National Resources Planning Board in 1934; and are still in use by all Federal agencies concerned with water-resource development.

The River and Harbor Act of August 30, 1935, authorized the Chief of Engineers to keep the "308" studies up to date to take into account changes in economic factors and accumulated engineering data. . . . Experience gained in carrying out the "308" surveys, and procedures devised in preparing general plans for water-resource development, were to exert a strong influence over subsequent planning activities of the Corps of Engineers.[31]

The idea that benefits should be measured, and that they should

---

1933). The report had a direct bearing upon both the worth of irrigation ventures from the government's point of view and the profitability of alternative crops and practices from the farmers' points of view.

[31] *Annual Report of the Chief of Engineers, U.S. Army, 1951* (Washington, D.C.: U.S. Government Printing Office, 1952), Part 1, Vol. 3, p. 229.

exceed costs in order for a project to be justified, became widespread in the thirties. The Flood Control Act of 1936 authorized new surveys by the Corps of Engineers and required the Department of Agriculture to estimate benefits and costs of certain watershed treatment programs. It also established "the principle of comparing benefits to whomsoever they may accrue with the estimated costs."[32] Between 1936 and 1939, the Chief of Engineers issued to the District Offices numerous instructions about the preparation of cost-benefit analysis, and set about getting, in cooperation with the Weather Bureau, much-needed hydrological and meteorological data.[33] As for the Bureau of Reclamation, the 1939 Reclamation Project Act provided for authorization of irrigation and related improvements if total cost could be either repaid (by users of water for irrigation) or properly charged to non-reimbursable functions, such as flood control, navigation, or preservation of wildlife.

As the result of such directives and legislation, the Corps of Engineers, Department of Agriculture, and Department of the Interior's Bureau of Reclamation—hereinafter referred to as the Agencies—were required to use benefit-cost evaluation in some situations, and they elected to do so in others. The advisability of coordinating their procedures soon became apparent, and led to a "tripartite" agreement in 1939 and a quadrupartite agreement, which included the Federal Power Commission, in 1943.[34] This led in turn to the Federal Inter-Agency River Basin Committee, whose membership included the Department of Commerce and, later, the Public Health Service of the Department of Health, Education, and Welfare.

The purpose of cost-benefit analysis, as it developed, was and is to *help* determine both the size of the Agencies' budgets, or the number of projects, and the particular projects that are to be undertaken. The criterion that is used to indicate the relative merits of different proposals is the *ratio* of benefits to cost. According to "The Green Book," "the ratio of benefits to cost reflects both benefit and cost values and is the recommended basis for comparison of projects."[35]

[32] *Proposed Practices for Economic Analysis of River Basin Projects*, Report to the Federal Inter-Agency River Basin Committee Prepared by the Subcommittee on Benefits and Costs, May, 1950, p. 61.

[33] *Annual Report of the Chief of Engineers . . . , 1951*, pp. 232–233.

[34] *Ibid.*, p. 233.

[35] *Proposed Practices for Economic Analysis . . .* , p. 14. This report to the Federal Inter-Agency River Basin Committee by the Subcommittee on Benefits and Costs is frequently called "The Green Book," and it will sometimes be referred to here by that name.

If this ratio is higher than unity, a project is said to be economically justified. If there are many projects with comparatively high ratios, there is a better chance than would otherwise exist of getting a comparatively large budget. Also, of course, the selection of specific projects for construction, first by the Agencies and the Budget Bureau and finally by Congress, depends upon this ratio: in general, the higher the ratio, the more favorably a project is looked upon. Later, more will be said about this criterion; here the aim is simply to describe briefly how cost-benefit analysis is supposed to work.[36]

Naturally, this ratio is not regarded as the only piece of information which is relevant to these decisions. This is clearly recognized by the Agencies which prepare and use the analyses[37] and by Congressmen, who also use them in reaching their decisions. "The establishment of any fixed figure of a ratio with a minimum below which a project would be assured of rejection and a second level above which a project would be assured of acceptance appears to place an unwarranted emphasis on the validity and accuracy of such an index. The benefit-cost ratio . . . can be accepted as only one measure of the national and public worth of a project."[38] Nonetheless, cost-benefit analyses clearly play an important role in the determination of budgets and in the selection of particular projects.

Room for Improvement of Cost-Benefit Analyses

The Agencies and others have generated many excellent suggestions about the preparation and use of cost-benefit analysis, and a good deal of progress has been made. However, feasible improvements have by no means been exhausted. There is still much to be said, for instance, about the general methodological problems—those pertaining to such matters as criteria, time streams, and uncertainty—problems which come up in connection with any type of analysis. And there is ample room, too, for better treatment of the special measurement problems. This is suggested rather vividly by the variations that

[36] For some abbreviated samples of cost-benefit analysis and comments thereon, see "Specific Projects," in *Economic Evaluation of Federal Water Resource Development Projects,* Report to the Committee on Public Works, House of Representatives, by Mr. Jones of Alabama from the Subcommittee to Study Civil Works, 82nd Congress, 2nd Session (Washington, D.C.: U.S. Government Printing Office, 1952), pp. 20–44.

[37] *Proposed Practices for Economic Analysis* . . . , p. 3.

[38] *Economic Evaluation of Federal Water Resource Development Projects,* p. 54.

exist from one Agency to the next in estimation procedures.[39]   The Green Book, which is surely the greatest step forward thus far, emphasizes the possibility of doing better: "While this report affords a basis for considerable improvement in economic analysis of river basin developments, as the state of our knowledge and experience develops, and as testing of the recommendations becomes possible, further refinement and improvement of the suggested techniques and recommendations in this report should become possible."[40]

PLAN AND PURPOSE OF THE STUDY

In the present inquiry, some general methodological problems in the analysis of alternative actions are taken up first; and in order that the generality of these problems may be appreciated, illustrations are taken from various activities, such as business, military planning, and water-resource development.   In this portion of the study, attention is given to the devising of criteria, the selection of the alternatives to be compared, the treatment of intangibles and uncertainty and what is implied about criteria, and, finally, methods of taking time streams into account.

Next, some special problems in the analysis of water-resource projects are examined.   Major topics include the criterion questions that come up in this particular application of analysis, and several special difficulties of measurement or valuation.   For the most part, the study deals with the translation of certain initial physical effects of projects into later impacts and thence into dollar estimates.   That is, little or no effort is devoted to questions about the basic physical data—to questions about the accuracy of the hydrologic data, the effect of channel clearance upon stream flow, the effect on crop yields of applying two acre feet of water per year to a specified acre of land.   These are vital questions in individual analyses, but they are outside the scope of this study.

Case studies of two analyses prepared by Federal Agencies are then presented.   Again, queries about the physical models are largely neglected, for the main purpose of the case studies is neither to criticize the analyses that were made by the Agencies nor to arrive

---

[39] See Table 2, "Comparison of the current practices of the participating agencies in measurement of tangible benefits and costs," in *Proposed Practices for Economic Analysis . . .* , pp. 74–81.

[40] *Ibid.,* pp. 3–4.

at a revised evaluation of those particular projects. The purpose is rather to bring out and clarify the methodological suggestions offered in the earlier chapters, and to show how they might be implemented.

Finally, having discussed the methodological problems of analysis in general, and of one application in particular, the study explores the potential use of analysis to increase efficiency in other government activities. The application of similar principles and techniques in connection with performance budgets is illustrated, and opportunities for making quantitative comparison, both between broad programs and within programs, are surveyed.

Perhaps it should be pointed out that the inquiry's objective is not to criticize the past work of any particular Agency or of these Agencies collectively. Nor is there any such drastic objective as the one which General Pick, formerly Chief of Engineers, once mentioned: ". . . We do not get mad with people because they criticize. One of the reasons is because we do not accept the criticism as being of a personal nature, but rather an attempt to discredit the organization to such an extent that it would cause the organization to be done away with."[41] To be sure, faultfinding is expressed or implied here and there in the study, but the objective is one which is held by the Agencies themselves: to draw up some constructive suggestions for the preparation and use of cost-benefit analysis. In addition, as stated before, the more general aim is to stimulate the increased use of better analysis in connection with other government activities.

[41] *Study of Civil Works,* Hearings before the Subcommittee to Study Civil Works of the Committee on Public Works, House of Representatives, 82nd Congress, 2nd Session (Washington, D.C.: U.S. Government Printing Office, 1952), Part 1, p. 81.

Part 2

Some General Problems of Analysis

Chapter 2

THE CRITERION PROBLEM

COST-BENEFIT ANALYSIS, like the other types of research discussed in Chapter 1, is intended to help us choose among alternative means to our ends. In this case, the principal alternatives to be compared are different investments or actions relating to resource development. They may be additions to projects such as extra elevators for the Carlsbad Caverns or larger navigation locks at Bonneville. The alternatives may be similar, such as certain irrigation projects in the West, or quite dissimilar, such as water-shed treatment in the Connecticut Valley and a multiple-purpose dam at Hungry Horse, Montana. Whatever the particular problem, it is fairly obvious that, in choosing among alternative means to our ends, we need to scan the ends themselves with a critical eye. Philosophers and theologians remind us frequently that scientific developments may be extremely efficient in achieving certain ends but that these ends may be the wrong ones—ends that are selected almost unconsciously or at least without sufficient critical thought We may be like the man "who, by running very fast, succeeds in jumping aboard the wrong train."[1]

Indeed, philosophers are themselves subject to such errors. For instance, even Dr. Leys (the author of the preceding quotation) seems to board a train without much deliberation when he laments "the sad history of the American forests." He writes, "It is a case of almost sheer thoughtlessness. During the early period of exploration and settlement, the North American continent offered what seemed like an inexhaustible supply of timber. As immigrants poured in from Europe, wood was used both for fuel and for construction with little

---

[1] Wayne A. R. Leys, *Ethics for Policy Decisions: The Art of Asking Deliberate Questions,* p. 8, copyright 1952 by Prentice-Hall, Inc., Englewood Cliffs, N.J.

worry about future supplies. In fact, great tracts of woodland were cleared for farming and the standing timber was sometimes regarded as a nuisance."[2] Maybe, upon careful analysis, it would appear to be a particularly "sad history." The evidence provided, however, is mostly that immigrants traded timber for heat, houses, and cropland in order to obtain consumption goods and productive equipment. Mere *use* of resources at a high rate is not patently wasteful—unless our value judgments are those of a miser. On the other hand, it is not necessarily foolish to preserve some resource, or to use it up at a low rate. The purpose here is neither to condemn nor defend our early treatment of forests but to emphasize that the ends implicit in such pronouncements, even in books on ethics, need critical examination.

But to say that we should scrutinize our ultimate ends carefully in deciding upon the best course of action is much too vague. Suppose we wish to choose between two used cars or two irrigation projects. Merely to name and list the things we ultimately value (such as growth, approval, security, freedom, leisure, goods) is not enormously helpful in solving the problem. It is wise to think about such a list, for it may prevent us from choosing some absurd project that does not provide *any* of these things, but in most situations the list provides little counsel. One reason is the tremendous gap between the direct consequences of an irrigation project and the ultimate aims that might be listed—or the gap between gas consumption, wheel base, and new seat covers, on the one hand, and leisure, security, and approval, on the other. This gap has to be at least partially bridged in order for policy implications to emerge. Another reason is the necessity of trading part of one desideratum for some of another, sacrificing faster "pick-up" for improved fuel consumption or giving up a little security for a little more freedom.

The point can be brought out by referring to a recent report on the Missouri Basin. It was stated there that

. . . the over-all objective of resource development should be to enhance economic opportunity for the people of the basin, improve their welfare, and enlarge their contribution to the Nation. The program goals necessary to achieve this objective in line with the foregoing principles are as follows:
. . . Erosion and resulting sediment must be reduced to a minimum, and the productivity of the soil must be protected and improved. . . . The lands should be so managed that they will make their optimum contribution in alleviating the impact of drought and in reducing flood waters. . . . Each

[2] Wayne A. R. Leys, *Ethics for Policy Decisions: The Art of Asking Deliberate Questions*, p. 20, copyright 1952 by Prentice-Hall, Inc., Englewood Cliffs, N.J., reprinted by permission of the publisher.

watershed unit should be planned and developed as rapidly as possible. . . . In developing irrigation, reasonable costs and suitable land should be the prime consideration. . . . Full development of the basin's water resources should require the adoption of adequate pollution control measures.[3]

It should be recognized that the enumeration of these goals, while it may be pertinent, does not serve as a guide to specific action. The goals mean, if anything, that it would be nice to have minimum erosion, "optimum" flood control, low cost, and "adequate" pollution control; also it would be nice to have them "as rapidly as possible." But while good intentions are sometimes reputed to be excellent paving materials, in themselves they do not pave the way to preferred action.

CRITERIA

Hence, in choosing among alternatives, we do more than to list things which it would be nice to have. Explicitly or implicitly, we adopt criteria or tests of preferredness. They fit into the process of choosing somewhat as follows. One step in this process is predicting the consequences of alternative actions—a step which, as indicated earlier, involves the use of sets of relationships called models. Another vital step is distinguishing preferred combinations of consequences from less desirable ones. This step entails the use of criteria. Thus, after having the features of different cars spelled out, the chooser has to decide what is the best combination of features. He may want a car that has maximum power while meeting specific constraints on other aspects of performance and on cost. If so, that is his criterion. Or he may compare the features of different cars subjectively and reach his decision. If so, the criterion is never made explicit, but it is presumably the maximization of some dimly perceived preference function (given the chooser's limited resources).

A hard-and-fast line between the problems of prediction or measurement and those of criteria is difficult to draw. Changing the manner of measuring some consequence could be regarded as changing the criterion, at least the real content and meaning of the criterion. Hence, unless restrained by convention, the criterion problem could swallow up practically all aspects of the comparison of alternative courses of action. At the other extreme, we might say that the criterion is maximum satisfaction, and from there on the whole difficulty would be the measurement of satisfaction. The measurement problem could

---

[3] *Missouri: Land and Water,* The Report of the Missouri Basin Survey Commission (Washington, D.C.: U.S. Government Printing Office, 1953), pp. 64–65.

then embrace practically everything. Nonetheless, a rough distinction can be made between determining the criterion's general form and making the actual measurements;[4] and therefore certain difficulties of devising criteria can be sorted out for special scrutiny.

In some comparisons, the term "criterion" may appear to be a misnomer. For sometimes the analyst can unravel only *some* of the consequences of alternative actions and exhibit these consequences to decision-makers as is done in consumers' research. In fact, this may well be the most useful function, generally speaking, of analysis. Insofar as this is true, a partial criterion (comparison in terms of selected consequences) may be used. There is then no problem of devising a definitive test, but there is the closely related problem of deciding *what* consequences the decision-maker should know about. In other situations, however, the analyst may be able to trace all of the significant effects and learn enough about the decision-makers' wants to evaluate those effects. In these instances, quantitative analysis per se may be used to pick out preferred courses of action. Insofar as this is the case, a definitive test of preferredness is necessary, and the criterion problem is the devising of that test. Most of the discussion will relate directly to the criterion problem faced in the latter situations, but the statements pertain indirectly to the selection of partial criteria, that is, of selected effects which are relevant to the comparison of alternative actions.

THE NECESSITY OF USING "PROXIMATE" CRITERIA

Ideally we should choose that course of action which, with available resources, maximizes something like the "satisfaction" of an individual, the profits of a firm, the "military worth" of the defense establishment, or the "well-being" of a nation. If possible, we should like to ascertain the total amount of these magnitudes under each of various alternative policies. Then we would pick the policy that yielded the most satisfaction, the greatest military force, or the most national well-being (depending upon whether the "chooser" was an individual,

---

[4] The valuation of the predicted consequences is sometimes broken out as another separable aspect of the choosing process, so that the steps are (1) prediction of consequences, (2) valuation of consequences, and (3) application of a criterion. This sort of breakdown has not been followed in organizing most of this study, although some aspects of valuation are considered separately in Part III.

a military service, or a government, respectively). But this prescription helps little more than saying that we want the best. Nobody knows precisely how satisfaction, military worth, and national well-being are related to the observable outcomes of various courses of action. We have not the models or the wit to translate those outcomes into such terms. In practical problem solving, therefore, we have to look at some "proximate" criterion which serves, we hope, to reflect what is happening to satisfaction, profits, or well-being. Actual criteria are the practicable substitutes for the maximization of whatever we would ultimately like to maximize.

In comparisons of military operations or equipment, for instance, what is desired is the course of action which would contribute most to the winning of the war or toward our national security. Since it is impossible to measure achievements in these terms, it is necessary to adopt indirect but workable criteria that appear to be consistent with ultimate aims.

The point can be illustrated in connection with water-resources development. A 4½ mile submarine cable across Puget Sound has been proposed as a means of transmitting hydro-power to the naval defense area in Kitsap County, Washington. It is said to be cheaper than the 90 miles of land transmission lines that would otherwise be necessary.[5] If the two means were compared, the criterion might be the transmission of a specified annual load at minimum cost, or perhaps the performance of certain defense functions at minimum cost. In any event, practicable tests for preferred policies would be linked only indirectly with ultimate criteria.

SUBOPTIMIZATION AND CRITERIA[6]

As noted, proximate rather than ultimate tests would have to be used no matter what problem of choice might be considered. Thus the door is opened to erroneous criteria. But the door is really swung wide (in fact, one might say that the welcome mat is put out) by another fact of life: the fact that problems of choice must be broken down into component pieces or subproblems.

[5] *House Hearings on Interior Appropriations for 1953,* 82nd Congress, 2nd Session, Part 4, pp. 1501–1502.

[6] For many of the points presented in this chapter, see Charles J. Hitch, "Suboptimization in Operations Problems," *Journal of the Operations Research Society of America,* May, 1953, pp. 87–99.

Meaning and Inevitability of Suboptimization

Let us examine this difficulty in some detail. A firm or government cannot possibly have one man or one committee examine *all* its problems of choice simultaneously and pick each course of action in the light of all the other decisions. It is inevitable that decision-making be broken into chunks. Almost necessarily the task is divided among various persons along hierarchical lines, some of the broader policy choices being made by "high-level" officials or groups, and others being delegated to "lower levels." Incidentally, no connotation of greater or lesser significance should be associated with these terms "higher" and "lower" levels. They are used merely to indicate that the division of labor in decision-making can be viewed in terms of successive hierarchical levels.

Similarly analysis-making must be broken into chunks, since it is impossible for a single analysis to examine all problems of choice simultaneously. Thus comparisons of alternative courses of action always pertain to a *part* of the firm's or government's problem. Other parts of the over-all problem are temporarily put aside, possible decisions about some matters being ignored, specific decisions about others being taken for granted. The resulting analyses are intended to provide assistance in finding optimal, or at least good, solutions to subproblems: in the jargon of systems analysis, they are "suboptimizations."

Table 1 may help to show precisely what is meant by suboptimization and, in the light of subsequent discussion, what kind of difficulties are involved. In "subproblem 1," when the head of the sales department, or some management committee, decides how much money should be devoted to various means of increasing sales, what should be done depends in part upon decisions at other levels. That is, the best allocation of the sales budget depends partly upon the way the whole firm's budget is allocated and partly upon the way direct-mail campaigns and other sales efforts are carried out. Nonetheless, decisions at all these levels will not be made simultaneously. To be sure, the right hand will not be completely ignorant of what the left hand, the thumb, and the shoulder are doing or of how they are affected. But the allocation of the sales department's budget may be made more or less independently of decisions about production, research, expansion, and specific materials for a direct-mail campaign. In connection with the selection of specific sales letters and folders (subproblem 2), the allocation of the sales budget, a "higher-level"

TABLE 1

SUBOPTIMIZATION ILLUSTRATED

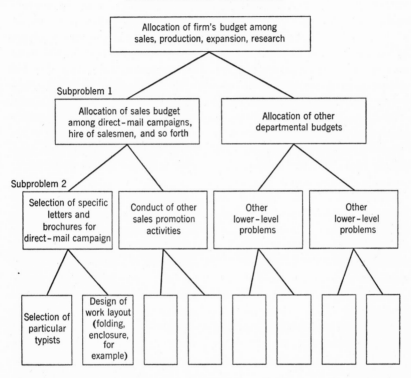

choice, and the selection of the specific work layout prior to mailing, a "lower-level" choice, will probably not be decided upon at the same time. The choice which is a central problem at one level will be taken as given, or perhaps even ignored, at another. Similarly, analysis intended to assist the management inevitably looks at pieces of the firm's problem, with many other facets of the over-all problem temporarily "fixed" or else neglected, because of the sheer size and complexity of the firm's operations.

The Advantages

Now piecemeal analysis and decision-making have their advantages. For one thing, as problems are broken down into smaller chunks, more detail can be taken into account by decision-makers or by researchers. In large firms, a degree of decentralization greater than that which is inevitable is usually believed to be desirable so that the "man on the spot" can decide about many matters.[7] In analysis, somewhat similarly, considerable breakdown of a firm's or government's problem may be desirable so that the models used in estimating outcomes can be "on the spot," that is, less aggregative and more accurate in their predictions than global or firm-wide models would be. Furthermore, better hedging against uncertainty *may* result from breaking the big problems into smaller pieces. The difficulties that stem from inherent uncertainties will be discussed mostly in a later chapter, but a few words are in order here. If decision-making is decentralized to a considerable extent, it may help hedge against the possibility of getting stuck with lopsided or downright pernicious views at the top. For instance, in civil government some separation of powers and dispersal of authority are important, partly as a hedging device. And in analysis, a degree of suboptimization *may* mean, for some problems, less risk of tying all analytical results to a "bad" criterion, say one involving a spuriously specific objective in which inherent uncertainty is neglected.

Note, however, that the scope of analysis does not have to coincide with, or imply anything about, the scope of authority in decision-making. Take the case of government. Analysis of a problem from the standpoint of the whole economy may be relevant to decisions within some Agency, even though, fortunately, no single authority runs the whole executive-legislative-judicial process. Note also that nothing has been said about the appropriate degree of suboptimization. All that has been stated is that the breakdown of problems makes some aspects of analysis more manageable and has some advantages.

The Danger: Inconsistency with Higher-Level Criteria

On the other side of the fence, there is a real danger inherent in piecemeal analysis, one whose importance can scarcely be overemphasized. We shall discuss this hazard at some length because it is probably not as widely appreciated as are the difficulties inherent in biting off too big a chunk of the problem. This danger is that

[7] This may not only take advantage of the man-on-the-spot's familiarity with the details of a problem but also constitute a more desirable decision-making process anyway, getting more persons in the habit of using ingenuity and taking responsibility. Indeed, this is of major importance from the viewpoint of the whole economy.

the criteria adopted in lower-level problems may be unrelated to higher-level criteria. As mentioned before, proximate criteria would have to be used in any case; but since problems must be considered a piece at a time, a whole hierarchy of proximate criteria comes into play, and potential inconsistencies are abundant.

For example, consider the problem of selecting a sales folder in Table 1. This problem is somewhat removed from top-level choices and aspirations. In these circumstances, maximum customer response per thousand folders mailed may seem like a plausible criterion, and it may lead to a very handsome brochure. But one should not expect it to lead to maximum profits, which would presumably be the higher-level test, because the exhorbitant cost of a sales folder that would truly maximize response might outweigh the increased revenues attributable to it. As an example from the military sphere, suppose that the military requires 90 per cent reliability in the functioning of its weapons systems. Bows and arrows may pass such a test with flying colors, yet hand grenades may accomplish much more at the same cost, even if half of them are duds. Perhaps 90 per cent (or 50 per cent or 99 per cent) has some intuitive appeal, but this gives little assurance that it is a sensible "requirement." The point is that even plausible criteria for choosing lower-level policies may not harmonize with higher-level tests, that is, may not be in agreement with what we really wish to do. Earlier it was suggested that "requirements" are sometimes set without looking explicitly at costs. Because of the fact that problems must be taken up piecemeal, there is danger that they will be set without looking critically at payoffs either. And the achievement of a blindly selected "requirement" (even at minimum cost!) is likely to be inconsistent with higher-level aims.

The difficulty also arises in water-resource development. Suppose the test of the proper flood-control proposal at the design level is "storage of any conceivable runoff" in a designated river valley—virtual certainty that no flooding will occur. The minimum cost of achieving such an extreme objective may turn out to be very great indeed, far in excess of the estimated benefits of the dam. In this case, the Agency, or the Congress, will probably turn down the project in favor of some other activity. Yet if the criterion at the design level is consistent with that of the Agency (say maximum benefits obtainable with a given budget), a dam intended to achieve a more modest objective may be thoroughly justified. In other words, some additional flood protection may be worth the cost, though virtually complete protection—say a probability of .99 that a flood will not occur during the next century—may cost more than it could possibly be worth.

SOME COMMON CRITERION ERRORS

Thus the fact that proximate criteria and piecemeal analysis cannot be avoided leaves the door open to mistakes in the selection of criteria. In general, these errors involve inconsistency between the tests that are selected in analyzing lower-level problems and the tests that are applicable at higher levels. However, some of the mistakes that occur most frequently have special characteristics so that they can be put into categories and given particular emphasis.

Maximizing Gain While Minimizing Cost

The consequences of an action fall into two types: (1) those positive gains which we like to increase, or the achievement of objectives, and (2) those negative effects which we like to decrease, or the incurrence of costs. Neither type by itself can serve as an adequate criterion: the maximization of gains without regard to cost or resource limitation is hardly a helpful test, and the minimization of cost regardless of other consequences of the alternative actions is nonsense. Hence both gains and costs must appear in criteria but, as will be seen, they can make their appearance in various ways.

One ubiquitous source of confusion is the attempt to maximize gain while minimizing cost or, as a variant, the attempt to maximize two types of gain at once. Such efforts are made, or at least talked about, in connection with all manner of problems. For example, according to one writer, the purpose of analysis is ". . . to assure that we are getting the most power for the least dollars when creating a new airborne weapon system. . . ."[8] Or consider the following broad criterion that allegedly guided one military operation: "The Germans' triumphant campaign . . . was inspired by the idea of . . . achieving the unexpected in direction, time, and method, preceded by the fullest possible distraction and followed by the quickest possible exploitation along the line of least resistance to the deepest possible range."[9]

[8] "Application of Operations-Research Techniques to Airborne Weapon System Planning," *Journal of the Operations Research Society of America,* August, 1953, p. 198.

[9] B. H. Liddell Hart, *Strategy, The Indirect Approach* (New York: Frederick A. Praeger, 1954), p. 240.

As for an illustration from business, a financial house once planned to use operations research to select investments, and its test was to be "maximizing yield while simultaneously minimizing risk." In water-resources problems we are said to be ". . . working for maximum [flood] protection at minimum expense."[10] Even the London *Economist* slips in connection with the comparison of investment projects in India. "Above all, in choosing between possible schemes, the Indian planners never admit to using the simple test: which will be more profitable? Which, in other words, will give the maximum increase in the national income for the minimum use of real resources?"[11]

Actually, of course, it is impossible to choose that policy which simultaneously maximizes gain and minimizes cost, because there is no such policy. To be sure, in a comparison of policies A and B, it may turn out occasionally that A yields greater gain, yet costs less, than B. But A will not also yield more and cost less than all other policies C through Z; and A will not maximize yield while minimizing cost. Maximum gain is infinitely large, and minimum cost is zero. Seek the policy which has that outcome, and you shall not find it.

It may seem that proposals to use such tests are harmless bursts of poetry, since it is impossible to use such a criterion in concrete cases. When the analyst buckles down to the comparison of specific alternatives, he simply cannot apply this kind of test. Just try to select the store at which you can maximize the amount of aspirin purchased while simultaneously minimizing the amount of money spent. Nonetheless, this type of criterion error should be taken seriously, for it can lead to some wild compromise criteria. If a person approaches a problem with the intention of using such a criterion, he is confused to begin with; then when he finds that it will not work, he may fasten upon *any* sort of constraint on gain or cost which converts this impossible test into a feasible one.

Overlooking Absolute Size of Gain or Cost

One common procedure is to pick that policy which has the highest ratio of "effectiveness," or achievement of objective, to cost. In that circumstance, the maximization of this ratio is the criterion. Note that the terms "effectiveness" and "achievement of objectives" mean positive gains, or the achievement of tasks that it is desirable to carry out. In order to examine this criterion, let us look at the comparison

10 *Study of Civil Works,* Part 2, p. 325.
11 *The Economist,* July 30, 1955, p. 400.

of alternative military weapons. These could be anything from various anti-tank weapons to different bombers, but suppose it is the latter. Let the ability to destroy targets, in the relevant circumstances, be the measure of effectiveness. Suppose next that a B-29 system, already on hand and relatively easy to maintain, would be able to destroy 10 targets and would entail extra costs of $1 billion—a ratio of 10 to 1—while System X would destroy 200 targets and cost $50 billion, a ratio of 4 to 1. Does it follow that we should choose the B-29 system, the one with the higher ratio? The answer is surely no, for it might merely be a system which would invite and lose a war inexpensively. To maximize the *ratio* of effectiveness to cost may be a plausible criterion at first glance, but it allows the absolute magnitude of the achievement or the cost to roam at will. Surely it would be a mistake to tempt the decision-maker to ignore the absolute amount of damage that the bombing system could do.

To bring this point closer home, suppose two dwellings are being compared. Let us accept floor space as a suitable measure of effectiveness, or positive gains. How does the ratio of effectiveness to cost perform as a criterion? Home A has 1,500 square feet and costs $18,000, the ratio being 1 to 12; B has 2,800 square feet and costs $28,000, a ratio of 1 to 10. Is B an obvious choice? Clearly one has to be concerned about the scale, the absolute amount of space the house will provide and the absolute amount of money it will cost. The ratio conceals the vital question: Is B's extra 1,300 square feet worth an extra $10,000?

Without constraints on either total level of effectiveness or total budget, then, the ratio of the two may point to extreme solutions, to nearly zero or to almost infinite effectiveness and cost. Of course, common sense and empty pocket books prevent us from paying attention to such a ratio at the extremes. But what is its significance in the middle ground that is not ruled out by common sense? Suppose one feels that he can pay from $15,000 to $20,000 for a house. Does the ratio take on meaning in these circumstances? The absurdity of the choice to which the ratio might lead is then bounded, and perhaps the chances of its pointing to the "correct" choice are increased, simply because the ratio is partially confined. In these circumstances, then, does the ratio take on real meaning? It does not. In fact, the only way to know what such a ratio really means is to tighten the constraint until either a single budget or particular degree of effectiveness is specified. And at that juncture, the ratio reduces to the test of maximum effectiveness for a given budget, or else a specified effectiveness at minimum cost, and might better have been stated that way at the outset.

Of course, if the ratios did not alter with changes in the scale of achievement (or cost), the higher ratio would indicate the preferred system, no matter what the scale. That is, if the ratio of achievement to cost were 10 to 1 for the B-29 system and 4 to 1 for System X at *all* levels of achievement, then the B-29 system would be "dominant." For it would destroy 500 targets at the $50 billion level of cost, clearly a better performance than that of System X. But to assume that such ratios are constant is not permissible some of the time and hazardous the rest of the time. In the comparison of the two houses, whose floor space is fixed, it is not permissible to assume that each house can have various sizes. In the other illustration, the assumption of constant ratios would obviously be wrong, because with larger scales of activity, it would be necessary to buy more B-29's instead of merely using the ones on hand. Moreover, whatever one's belief about the constancy of the ratio, the straightforward test of maximum effectiveness for a given budget (or, alternatively, minimum cost of achieving a specified level of effectiveness) reveals just as much as the ratio—and seems much less likely to mislead the unwary.[12]

It might be observed that ratios are sometimes handy devices for ranking a list of possible actions when (1) the scale of activity is fixed, and (2) the actions are not interdependent (more on this point later). Thus the rate of return on stocks and bonds (the ratio of annual net return to the cost of the investment) is a convenient aid in ranking securities. Then, *with a fixed investment fund,* the set of securities that yields the greatest return for that fund can be quickly determined. Again, no one would want to maximize the rate of return; an investor might in that case confine himself to one small but golden opportunity, say 500 per cent on a $5 investment. Also, *some* types of benefit-cost ratio, such as the internal rate of return, or the value of future net benefits divided by the amount of investment cost, may be useful in precisely the same manner. Note, however, the limited conditions under which such ratios can be used.

Setting Wrong Size of Gain or Cost

As just suggested, a criterion in which the budget or level of effectiveness is specified has the virtue of being aboveboard. The test's

---

[12] For examples of ratios used as criteria, see Charles Kittel, "The Nature and Development of Operations Research," *Science,* February 7, 1947, pp. 152–153. For more on the hazards of using ratios as criteria, see Hitch, *op. cit.,* pp. 94–95.

limitation, the fact that it relates to a particular level of cost or achievement, is perceivable with the naked eye. This fact indicates, however, that although avoidance of ratio tests is a step in the right direction, our troubles are not over. For if an erroneous or irrelevant scale of gain or cost is taken as given, the test is unlikely to result in good policy decisions.

In choosing the bombing system, let us suppose that the test is minimum cost of achieving the ability to destroy 10 targets. In these circumstances, the hypothetical B-29 system is better than System X. In contrast, if the criterion is minimum cost of achieving an ability to destroy 200 targets, System X is better. Clearly it makes a difference which scale of gain, i.e., effectiveness, is stipulated, and it would be possible to fix upon the wrong scale.

If the analyst is instructed to specify a particular level of effectiveness, no alternative procedure is open to him, and there is no problem of choosing this aspect of the criterion. If he has leeway, however, and chooses the scale uncritically, he is using what was described earlier as the requirements approach. In other words, he is picking the desired task or level of achievement without inquiry into the sacrifices of other achievements which would be entailed. What he can do to choose the right scale will be discussed a little later. The thing to be noted here is that this sort of criterion error is always a threat in piecemeal analysis.

This mistake also threatens if the cost instead of the gain is to be stipulated. Consider once again the firm and its sales-promotion program. The best brochure for a direct-mail campaign, given a budget of $5,000, is unlikely to be the best one if the direct-mail budget is $100,000. Of course, if the budget is already definitely set by higher-level decision, the best the analyst can do is to take the predetermined amount as given. However, if the budget is subject to change, perhaps on the advice of the analyst, his test should not take as given a budget that is uncritically determined.

Neglecting Spillovers

In economics, impacts of one firm's action upon other firms' gains or costs are referred to as "external economies and diseconomies." For example, an oil well that forces brine into the underground water supply may reduce the fertility of adjacent farmlands. Within firms or governmental units, similarly, the action of one department may affect the gains or costs of other operations. (This would be the case, for instance, if the oil-producing firm owned the farmlands.) The term "spillovers"[13] will be used here, chiefly because it is short, as a general title covering all such effects.[14]

In comparing alternative policies or actions, it is easy to adopt a criterion which leads to the neglect of spillover effects. For example, a classic piece of operations research may have ignored some impacts on activities other than the one that was directly under examination. In this frequently cited example of successful analysis, alternative arrangements for washing and rinsing mess-kits were compared. The analyst used as his test of preferredness the minimization of the number of man-hours required to do the job, given a total of four tubs. The optimal arrangement, according to this test, turned out to be the use of three tubs for washing and one tub for rinsing. One writer tells us how the mess sergeant may have viewed the work of this analyst:

Yeah, I remember that guy. He had some screwball idea that the mission of the Army was to eliminate waiting lines. Actually I had it all figured out that two was the right number of rinse tubs. With everyone rinsing in one tub the bacteria count would get way past the critical level. But we switched to one rinse tub while he was around because the old man says he's an important scientist or something and we got to humor him. Had damn near a third of the outfit out with the bellyache before we got the character off the reservation. Then we quick switched to three rinse tubs and really made a nice line. "Nothing like a good line to get the men's legs in condition," the old man says.[15]

The purpose of using this example is not to disparage this particular piece of analysis, which may have been quite useful. The point is simply to suggest how easy it is, in the comparison of *any* policies, to neglect spillover effects.

It can also happen in business. In a department store's study of Wednesday-night openings, the gains attributed to opening were at first identified as the receipts from *total* Wednesday-night sales.[16] In

---

[13] The term "spillover costs" and a helpful discussion of those that arise from congestion are contained in J. M. Buchanan's article, "The Pricing of Highway Services," *National Tax Journal,* June, 1952, pp. 97–106.

[14] Argument pertaining to "external economies and diseconomies" and "secondary benefits"—spillovers which are of special concern to cost-benefit analysis—will be discussed in Chapters 8 and 9, respectively

[15] From A. M. Mood's Review of P. M. Morse and C. E. Kimball, *Methods of Operations Research,* in the *Journal of the Operations Research Society of America,* November, 1953, p. 307.

[16] H. C. Levinson, "Experiences in Commercial Operations Research," *Journal of the Operations Research Society of America,* August, 1953, p. 225

comparing the alternatives, to open on Wednesday night or not to open, the test would have been: choose the policy that yielded maximum net receipts, meaning Wednesday-night receipts minus Wednesday-night costs. In a later study, it was recognized that the night operation would affect the gains, and possibly costs, of other operations, namely, daytime sales. The test used in the first study was wrong, because it ignored these spillover impacts.

Water-resource measures, too, are likely to involve spillover costs and gains. Upstream retention structures and revegetation measures may affect the flood protection that can be attributed to main-stem dams and levees. A hydroelectric installation is likely to affect the firm kilowatt-hour output of private and government installations in the same river basin. Multiple-purpose projects that alter the flows of streams may influence the chemical content of industrial and domestic water supplies. Criteria for the selection of water-resource projects should not be designed in such a way that these effects are neglected.

In retrospect, it may appear that setting the wrong absolute size of the gain or cost is a special case of neglecting spillovers. And in fact it is, because the uncritical stipulation of a requirement (a budget or level of effectiveness, for example) leaves out of account the effects of that requirement on the achievement of other tasks. It is a special case, however, which seems to be worth separate presentation. It may also appear that the neglect of spillovers is a defect of the model rather than of the criterion, since the end result is failure to *measure* gains and costs properly. Nonetheless, it seems appropriate to treat it as a criterion error, because, as the examples suggest, it is often the selection of the criterion which leads to this error.

Using Wrong Concepts of Cost or Gain

Similarly, the manner in which cost and gain are defined seems to be a matter of measurement; yet these definitions too are pertinent in a discussion of criterion errors, because wrong concepts of cost and gain may grow out of, or be inextricably bound up with, the adoption of erroneous criteria.

For example, in a wartime study of alternative ways to destroy enemy shipping, the criterion adopted was the ratio of enemy ships sunk (the gain) to allied man-years of effort (the cost).[17] Now our

---

[17] Kittel, *op. cit.,* p. 152.

concern in this section is not with the hazards of such a ratio test,[18] but rather with the nature of these concepts of gain and cost.

NEGLECT OF HIGHER-LEVEL GAIN. First, let us consider "ships sunk" as a measure of gain. If the analysts were instructed to consider only ship destruction, then this was the only measure they could use. If they were not so restricted, however, this may have been an unfortunate conception of the gain, for shipping could be destroyed, e.g., bottled up, by actions such as mine-laying, which would not necessarily sink many ships. The criterion adopted would have prejudiced the case against such maneuvers.

NEGLECT OF VALUABLE INPUTS. Next, let us examine the costs of these ship-sinking operations. Costs are the consequences which have negative values, or in other words they are the sacrifices which have to be made in order to conduct the operation. In the above-mentioned study, man-years of effort—which included those used in construction of vessels and equipment, training, operations, and replacements— appear to be a somewhat dubious measure of these sacrifices. One reason is that man-years, although important in wartime (and in peacetime), were not the only items given up. Thus a method of destroying enemy shipping that used comparatively little manpower, even though it required extremely valuable equipment and skills, had a spurious advantage over a method that utilized relatively worthless equipment and much labor. In effect the test ignored inputs other than man-years as if they were free.

In extreme cases, this sort of procedure may be correct. Since the cost of one course of action is whatever has to be sacrificed, that cost depends upon what alternatives are genuinely possible. If, for example, the only courses of action that can be considered are different ways for unskilled laborers to use given equipment to carry out a specified task, the only thing of value which is being sacrificed is the labor. Alternative uses for the other inputs are not to be considered, and hence they *are* free goods. The analysis becomes a time-and-motion study, and a suitable test is the achievement of the specified task with the minimum expenditure of man-hours.

In general, however, the use of man-hours, a "critical material," or

[18] The operation that maximized the *ratio* of ships sunk to allied effort might be a trivial operation sinking one ship or a gigantic effort destroying vast quantities of shipping and requiring the bulk of our resources. There is little assurance that the operation picked solely on the basis of this *ratio* would contribute the most toward victory.

any other single input to represent cost is likely to be wrong. Other valuable inputs are usually involved. To ignore these other inputs is to pretend that their use involves no sacrifice, whatever the quantity employed. Another plausible procedure, to put a specific constraint on the amount of each input that is to be used, is in most instances equally misleading. Such a constraint pretends that this particular amount of the input is free, i.e., that we could not devote any of that amount to another use, and furthermore that we have not the choice of acquiring extra amounts of the input. Sometimes the choices open to us are limited in this fashion; but placing specific constraints on all inputs usually distorts the list of alternatives that is truly admissible, and hence distorts the cost of the actions that are in fact examined.

What, then, is the right way to measure cost? For the present, it will simply be asserted that the use of money costs is better than the use of other feasible measures when there is time to acquire more inputs and reallocate resources. The applicability of dollar costs to business problems of choice is clear enough. Their applicability to the comparison of national policies will be examined in connection with the selection of water-resource projects.[19] In brief, however, in a reasonably competitive system, prices tend to reflect costs, i.e., the worth of inputs in other uses or, to put it differently, the gains that must be given up if the inputs are withdrawn from present uses. And price tags enable us to consider varying the amount of each input, unveiling relevant alternatives and hence costs that would be concealed by specific constraints.

In considering potential errors in these concepts, we have focused attention mostly on the analysis of military problems. Perhaps it should be noted that in business, too, misleading notions of cost or gain can arise. For instance, suppose that the test of efficiency in rolling steel bars is the minimum number of substandard lengths, which are complete rejects, in carrying out a specified job of rolling.[20] The easy way for operators to minimize the short bars is to make them all too long, which then increases the amount of trimming that has to be done. To minimize the number of complete rejects is to ignore the costs of trimming—to act as if trimming were a free service.

INCLUSION OF "SUNK" COSTS. Consider once again the costs counted in the search for the best way to destroy enemy shipping. These costs included man-years of effort used in the construction of

19 Chapter 7.
20 Sir Charles Goodeve, "Operational Research as a Science," *Journal of the Operations Research Society of America*, August, 1953, pp. 169–170.

ships, equipment, and submarines—many of which were already built and on hand. Yet the sacrifice entailed by the use of existing equipment was really its value in other operations, not the original or historical cost of constructing it.

This point is an important one in connection with various problems of choice. Suppose the Bureau of Reclamation, alarmed at losses of water through seepage and evaporation, considers alternative methods of conveying water to certain irrigation districts. Canals with a particular type of lining are already in place. Should the Bureau "be fair" to each policy it considers (canals with different linings, different pumping facilities, different arrangements to utilize gravity) by costing each "from scratch"? In other words should the original cost of the existing facilities be included? No, it should not. The canals' value in alternative uses is the value that is sacrificed. If they have no alternative use and no scrap value, then the cost of incorporating them into various irrigation systems *now* is zero. If they have a scrap value that must be sacrificed, then that value is the relevant cost. It is only the *extra* or incremental cost (not historical or "from scratch" cost) entailed by each particular one of the alternatives that is relevant to their comparison.

This is a correct view whether it pertains to choices within business firms, households, or government. Sometimes it is urged that businessmen do not in fact think in terms of extra costs and gains,[21] particularly when the alternatives that are being compared are to produce another unit of output or not to produce it. However, insofar as firms succeed in maximizing profits, they are *in effect* guided by incremental costs and gains.[22] That is, they are getting the same result they would have obtained if they had been so guided. Moreover, when management formally compares alternatives of other types—alternative investments, facilities, or managerial policies—their analyses usually *are* in terms of incremental costs and gains.[23]

Cost-benefit analysis in water-resource development is on a sound footing in this respect, so far as statements on methodology are concerned. The general principle, repeatedly expressed, is to measure

[21] See R. A. Lester, "Marginalism, Minimum Wages, and Labor Markets," *American Economic Review,* March, 1947, pp. 135–148; H. M. Oliver, Jr., "Marginal Theory and Business Behavior," *American Economic Review,* June, 1947, pp. 375–383.

[22] Milton Friedman, *Essays in Positive Economics* (Chicago: The University of Chicago Press, 1953), p. 15.

[23] See Horace C. Levinson, "Experiences in Commercial Operations Research," *Journal of the Operations Research Society of America,* August, 1953, pp. 220–239.

costs and benefits *with and without* each project—to isolate the extra costs and gains attributable to each project.[24]   This is not to say that the relevant alternatives, e.g., different sizes of each project, are always examined.   But with respect to the alternatives that are examined, the official views are that extra costs, not historical costs, should be counted.

ALLOCATION OF JOINT COST IN MULTI-PRODUCT VENTURE.   Here we shall look at the costing of water-resource investments, but the point is applicable to the costing of various alternatives.   Consider for a moment a multiple-purpose dam of a particular size.   Suppose its full cost is $100 million; the cost of the extra capacity and features that are included for power generation amount to $30 million; the costs due solely to irrigation (consisting again of extra capacity and facilities) amount to $30 million.   The two $30 million dollar amounts will be called "separable costs"; if either the power or the irrigation functions were dropped from the plan, $30 million would be lopped off the project's cost.   The remainder, $40 million, will be called "joint cost."

According to one view, each function should be allocated an equitable share" of the "joint costs,"[25] that is, those costs that do not arise solely because of any one function such as irrigation, power, flood control, or navigation.   As a consequence, there have arisen endless controversies, numerous formulae for allocating these costs,[26] and startling discrepancies in estimates.   For instance, two allocations of cost for the identical main stem dam (Fort Peck) are as follows:[27]

ALLOCATION OF CONSTRUCTION COST
(Thousands of dollars)

			Purpose		
Agency	Power	Irrigation	Flood Control and Navigation	Recreation	Total
Corps of Engineers	$82,200	$29,400	$ 44,653	$380	$156,633
Bureau of Reclamation	35,268	0	121,365	0	156,633

[24] *Proposed Practices for Economic Analysis of River Basin Projects*, pp. 9–11; *Annual Report of the Chief of Engineers, U.S. Army, 1951* (Washington, D.C.: U.S. Government Printing Office, 1952), Part 1, Vol. 3, p. 39.

[25] See the exhibits and discussions in *Study of Civil Works*, Part 3, pp. 406–426, 436–437; and Bureau of the Budget Circular No. A-47, December 31, 1952, pp. 10–11.

[26] *Proposed Practices for Economic Analysis* . . . , pp. 53–57.
   I am indebted to Ralph Turvey for discussions of this topic.

[27] *Missouri: Land and Water*, p. 92.

Former Secretary of Agriculture Brannan supported such "full costing" (the term usually used in business accounting) : "The Department believes that the costs of multiple-purpose reservoir projects should be allocated on a basis which properly recognizes the added costs of including each separable function and a fair share of the joint costs."[28] Sometimes, it is urged that even the *separable* costs be allocated on an "equitable" basis among purposes and projects. In brief, it is urged that the project that looks good should support the project that looks bad. Most persons, however, recognize this procedure as a straightforward subsidy, whether they favor or oppose it.[29]

But let us turn once more to the amount which was defined above as joint cost. Suppose the $40 million in the case of the $100 million multi-purpose dam was allocated by means of some formula. Assume that the formula bestowed half of the $40 million for each purpose so that power now appeared to cost $50 million and irrigation $50 million. If the value of benefits from irrigation were $70 million and that from power $40 million (a total of $110 million), should we declare the power facilities unjustified or declare the entire project unjustified? Surely we could only say that the present value of the *total* benefits should be not less than $100 million, the present value of benefits from power output not less than $30 million, and that from irrigation not less than $30 million. An entrepreneur launching a multi-product firm would presumably think along these lines. Also, economic theory indicates that the costs of multiple products ought to be treated in this manner.[30]

If a formula for allocation is intended to show how costs actually

---

[28] *Study of Civil Works,* Part 2, p. 198.

[29] The State of Montana favored the procedure according to a letter from John W. Bonner, Governor of Montana, to Michael W. Straus, Commissioner of the Bureau of Reclamation, dated June 15, 1949: "We have reached the time when we cannot build any more [irrigation] projects and expect the land to repay the full construction cost. This subsidy [from power projects] should be made available to all projects within the basin and on the same basis regardless of whether they are built by a Federal or State agency." (Bureau of Reclamation, *The Columbia River,* Vol. 1, 1950, House Document 473, 81st Congress, 2nd Session, p. 59.)

On the other hand, Secretary Brannan said: "The Department of Agriculture is opposed to the use of a basin account or any other device which would have the effect of supporting the inclusion of any program component which can be separately evaluated in a project or program which on its own merits is not justified." (*Study of Civil Works,* Part 2, p. 200.)

[30] George J. Stigler, *The Theory of Price* (New York: The Macmillan Company, 1946), p. 307.

respond when one purpose is eliminated, then it is an attempt to get better estimates of separable, or incremental, costs. But a formula that is supposed to hand out "fair shares" of joint costs does not contribute to good decisions. Inability to allocate *all* costs meaningfully among joint products is often a fact of life, not a sign of disgrace or laziness. The extra cost of *adding on* a function or a feature can be calculated, or the total cost of the combination of features can be calculated—but not a meaningful total cost for one feature when undertaken jointly with the others. Incidentally this view, although often ignored in the analysis of multi-purpose projects,[31] is nonetheless accepted by a good many persons interested in water-resource development. For instance, in one section of the report by the Engineers Joint Council, it is stated that ". . . allocation of costs of such [multiple-purpose] projects to the several purposes usually lacks significance."[32]

APPROPRIATE CRITERIA

So much for potential errors in the devising of tests for preferred policies. What of a constructive nature can be said about the selection of criteria? Clearly, there is no all-purpose criterion, for the appropriate test depends upon what alternatives are open to the decision-maker, upon what aspects of the situation must be taken as given, and even upon what kind of measurements are feasible. Nonetheless a few general observations about suitable criterion-forms can be made.

Maximum Gains Minus Costs

If gains and costs can be measured in the same unit, to maximize gains minus costs is certainly an acceptable criterion-form—the equiv-

---

[31] There is one danger in general acceptance of the correct view: that *genuinely separable* costs will be treated as joint costs and not allocated to any purpose. This would be similar to the basin account, in which separable costs can be allocated to whatever purpose can stand the allocation and still appear justified.

[32] *Principles of a Sound National Water Policy*, The National Water Policy Panel of Engineers Joint Council, July, 1951, Appendix VIII, p. 184. However, the general recommendation in this report was that the costs of jointly-used facilities be allocated according to the proportionate use of capacity by each purpose (pp. 192–193).

Among the others who have long opposed the allocation of truly joint costs is Joseph S. Ransmeier, *The Tennessee Valley Authority, A Case Study in the Economics of Multiple Purpose Stream Planning* (Nashville: Vanderbilt University Press, 1942).

alent of making the most out of whatever actions can be taken. Suppose the possible courses of action are to put available resources to one of three uses, to be called A, B, and C. Now the gains that could have been obtained by using the resources in B and C are what have to be given up when we use the resources in A. These sacrifices are the *costs* of devoting the inputs to use A, the costs of obtaining the gains from A. When costs are viewed in this way, i.e., as gains that must be given up, it is easy to see that to maximize gains minus costs is the same as maximizing total gains. If A yields 100 units of gain, B yields 75 units, and C 50 units, A is the use that maximizes gains minus costs (100 minus 75), and it is the use that yields the greatest total gain in the circumstances. Note again that this sort of test is a possibility only when gains and costs are commensurable. It can be used in the comparison of business firms' actions and certain government policies but usually not in the analysis of military activities.

Either Gain or Cost Fixed

In any situation there are constraints. The decision-maker can borrow additional funds only at higher rates of interest, only a limited number of actions are open to him, there are only twenty-four hours in his day. In many analyses, a constraint is that a particular scale of gain or cost is fixed. This may be done when gain and cost are commensurable, as in the case of a firm comparing different ways to use a given investment budget. And it should be done, as a rule, when costs and gains are incommensurable. In such a situation, naturally, it is impossible to maximize gains minus costs; what would be the meaning of the ability to destroy ten targets minus one billion dollars? The next-best procedure appears to be to "set" either the costs or gains, seeking the way to get the most for a given cost, or to achieve a specified objective at least cost.

These two criterion-forms are equivalent, if the size of either gain or cost is the same in the two tests. If the test of maximum gain for a $5 budget points to the policy which yields a gain of 10, then the test of minimum cost to achieve a fixed gain of 10 will point to the same policy—the one which achieves the gain of 10 at a cost of $5. The two tests also yield equivalent information if calculations are carried out for many different scales of cost and gain. The choice between these two criterion forms depends largely upon whether it is gain or cost which can be fixed with the greater degree of "correctness."

This leads us to the big question: how does one determine the right achievement or budget to fix? If the achievement or budget is set uncritically, the procedure degenerates into the "requirements approach." For example, it might be taken as given that we "need" all-hair wrestling mats, or, in the case of the bombing system, a capability of destroying ten targets; and the analysis, if any, would seek the cheapest way to achieve that "requirement." What can be done to improve upon this approach?

As a starter, several tasks or scales of effectiveness can be tried, and several budget sizes can be assumed. If the same system is preferred for all tasks or budgets, that system is dominant. In the bombing-system example, the best bomber (though not the right scale or capability) is then determined. If the same course of action is not dominant, the use of several tasks or budgets is nevertheless an essential step, because it provides vital information to the decision-maker.

Note, however, that the decision-maker, in order to make use of the analysis, must still select the scale of the task or budget. He is presumably helped in reaching this decision by the information about the cost of achieving different tasks or the potential achievements with different budgets. But he has to draw on further information in order to set the right task or budget. He has to ask what task or budget, as the case may be, is consistent with higher-level criteria. Is a capability of destroying ten targets too much or too little in view of the over-all aims of the defense program? Or, to return to an earlier business example, is $100,000 a sensible direct-mail budget in view of the test of the firm's entire sales-promotion program?

Clearly the analyst will be more helpful if he can answer these questions than if he merely estimates the results for a variety of budgets or tasks. As a matter of fact, he must try to answer these questions if he is even to hit upon a reasonable range of tasks or budgets. He cannot experiment with all possible scales of achievement or cost, because the computations would be too expensive and voluminous to provide any net assistance. Hence the analyst can and should do more than try several tasks or budgets (the procedure which was labeled a "starter"). He should make some inquiry into higher-level criteria and into their relationship to possible lower-level tests. He may even convert the analysis into a higher-level suboptimization. At *some* higher-level, of course, the criterion must be taken as given—i.e., to carry out the higher-level task at minimum cost, or to get the most out of the higher-level budget. But this acceptance of a task or budget as given at some high level is skies apart from setting "requirements" uncritically all the way up and down the line.

Some Complications Yet to be Considered

Here in Part II, most of the discussion pertains to problems of choice in general. Consequently, not much is said about matters which relate to special cases. The meaning of cost and gain from the viewpoint of the whole economy, a concept that is defined in "welfare economics," will be discussed in Part III in connection with the special problem of choosing water-resource projects. Difficulties of valuation and measurement will also be taken up with reference to that particular application of analysis.

Furthermore, several complications in the criterion problem which have been ignored thus far will be introduced in subsequent chapters. One complication is the fact that costs or gains which occur in different time periods are not of equal value. Another crucial aspect of the criterion problem is uncertainty. There are also "intangible" considerations—those which cannot be translated into the same units in terms of which the other gains or costs are expressed. If enough weight is attached to these considerations, the relationship between the estimates of gain and cost cannot reveal the preferred policy. Even in industry, intangibles may carry a great deal of weight. One businessman used to advertise that he bought high and sold low, declaring that his wife was rich and it was more fun that way. But, as indicated, intangibles and certain other complications will be considered later.

Chapter 3

THE APPROPRIATE ALTERNATIVES

BEFORE WE TURN to any of the complications just mentioned, we shall consider briefly the question: what alternatives ought to be compared? The discussion of the criterion problem led up to this question by indicating a connection between criteria and the alternative courses of action that should be considered. As we have seen, the appropriate concepts of cost and gain depend upon the level of optimization and the alternative policies that are admissible. Also, the appropriate level of optimization and the alternatives that should be compared depend in part upon the search for a suitable criterion. Of course, what alternatives should be compared is a vital question in any case; no matter what the criterion, it will not reveal the proper course of action if that course has not been considered among the possible policies. Hence the design of the alternatives to be compared is critical from various points of view.

RELEVANT CONTEXT IN EACH SYSTEM

If policies A and B are to be compared, they have to be fitted into appropriate contexts. Thus, if the policies are the procurement and use of machines A and B, each machine has to be fitted into a context that may include other currently used equipment, various decisions and operations in the firm, relevant man-made features such as roads and communications networks, and such relevant natural features as climate. The term "system" is used here to embrace the context plus the policy; and in order to compare policies A and B, it is really necessary to compare the gains and costs of a system that includes A with those of a system that includes B.

A course of action can be combined with many possible contexts, some encompassing more "given" features than others, some encompassing operations at higher levels than others. In other words, the analyst has the option of comparing systems that differ considerably in scope. What level of optimization—what scope of system—should he choose? To examine this question more fully, let us consider another hypothetical military example. Suppose his assignment is to select the best electronic gun-sight for fighter aircraft. He might fit the sights into a small weapons system, a specific fighter, and score them according to the number of bull's-eyes made in attacking a tow target. Would this criterion be closely related to the real task? Not necessarily. The sights might be heavy enough to affect the plane's speed or maneuverability. The number of tubes in the electronic equipment would affect the reliability and "maintainability" of the weapons system. Furthermore, performance in combat situations might not be taken sufficiently into account in comparing the number of hits in a tow target.

Next, he might fit each gun-sight into a fighter plane in combat (on paper) with an enemy aircraft. Would it be in accordance with higher-level aims to put this particular emphasis on victory in individual duels? If a high cost was permitted, the best gun-sight in a duel of one against one would turn out to be an extremely expensive one, making it necessary to sacrifice numbers or range. The electronic gear might cause too many aborts or keep too many planes on the ground. From the standpoint of numerical superiority, the amount of combat, and other aspects of the whole fighter operation, this gun-sight might be a poor choice indeed. If the cost had to be low, the sight that maximized the chance of winning duels might still leave the fighter completely outclassed and might be a foolish choice in terms of the whole fighter operation. At this level, it is difficult to tell whether or not a budget (or a specified task) is consistent with carrying out the real job most effectively. In this problem, accordingly, the analyst might turn to still larger systems analyses and fit the gun-sights into planes, the planes into fighter groups, the groups into relevant military operations. In this way he could ask what tasks or budgets (or uncertainties about them) make sense in view of the whole military operation and of political realities.

However, although larger systems analyses make part of the criterion problem more manageable, they become more cumbersome and more aggregative. Unfortunately, there are no rules about how to balance the advantages and disadvantages. The discussion here, while intended to be constructive, provides no blueprint. About all that can be said is that the appropriate level of optimization and scope of the systems will surely vary from one problem to the next. But only good judgment, based on familiarity with over-all operations and awareness of the criterion problem, can prescribe the scope of the systems that should be compared in any particular analysis. Naturally, this goes for water-resource systems as well as others. Again, there are no pat answers, though the systems that are being compared should usually extend beyond the sites of individual projects.

RELEVANT COURSES OF ACTION

Another pitfall to guard against is failure to consider the right actions in the process of comparison and selection. No matter how much thought is devoted to criteria selection and model-building, analyses will be of little aid if the "wrong" policies are compared. Moreover, the devising of possible actions is usually up to the analyst, at least in part. It is practically always a general problem, not the list of alternatives, which is presented to him. When a company calls in management consultants, it does not usually ask, "Which of the following methods of running our plant is the best?" It is much more likely to pose a more general problem, such as, "How can we increase the profitableness of our plant?"

Actions That Differ in Nature

As consumers, we have all experienced an occasional failure to consider the policy that might in fact have been the preferred one. After exhaustively comparing several camping outfits, and finally buying one, we realize that we should have considered rental in order to find out, first of all, if camp life lived up to our expectations. This sort of omission is also a threat in the analysis of other problems of choice. It is a source of concern at the outset, when relevant courses of action are being thought up and, at the same time, the field is being narrowed down. It is also a source of concern throughout the analysis, when better modifications or mixtures of these policies can still be devised. Often the best time to devise improvements is after the analysis of one set of alternatives is under way—that is, after more and more has been learned about the particular problem.

To illustrate the difficulty, suppose the subproblem which is sliced off is to determine the best method of transporting a firm's output to the West Coast. If we confine our analysis to methods of transport, we may be blinding ourselves to alternatives which happen to involve broader problems, such as establishing a plant on the West Coast or shifting our marketing effort. At first glance, the solution may appear to be simple: just make sure that all courses of action that are "close substitutes" are considered. But this is more easily said than done, because it is seldom obvious whether or not two policies are substitutes. They may be substitutes, even though dissimilar in physical appearance and in specific function. Indeed, if sufficiently broad problems of choice are carved out, *all* of the various things which a firm, a government, or an individual buys, or might buy, are substitutes in the sense that they are alternative objectives of expenditure which may contribute to the buyer's ultimate satisfaction. Bookkeepers and overhead cranes, Voice of America and the Forest Service, all are alternatives, competing for the disbursing officials' checks. Hence, we have to work hard and imaginatively at designing and redesigning possible courses of action.

With respect to water-resource development there is undoubtedly some danger of omitting superior courses of action from the analyses. More attention should probably be given to drainage projects,[1] water-pollution control, diversion of water to industrial use, and the growth of foods in sea water as alternatives to irrigation developments. Quantitative analysis of the use of existing transmission lines through "wheeling" contracts with private utilities could be made more frequently. Again, there is no prescription that tells us just what to do in each analysis. What can be said is that although it is obviously impossible to examine *all* the possibilities, it is of the greatest importance, in looking at subproblems, to keep asking: are there additional alternatives that might be better than any of those we are about to compare? Are there modifications of those courses of action, or mixtures of them, that might be better? Whatever the scope of the problem that is initially chosen, the design of the alternatives to be

---

[1] The following statement implies the use of a rough and incomplete criterion, but it is suggestive: ". . . there is an opinion that worn-out eroded lands and also certain lands of natural low fertility can be put into satisfactory production on the basis of capital investment of not to exceed $50 an acre; that wet lands can be cleared and drained and made ready for cultivation at a cost of from $50 to $100 per acre; while the cost of supplying water to dry lands under the irrigational procedure, for the better remaining possible projects, will be on the order of $200 to $500 per acre." (*Principles of a Sound National Water Policy*, p. 23.)

evaluated is a vital aspect of analysis. Clearly, it is unwise to waste effort in the measurement of costs and gains from policies that are hopelessly out of the running. It is perhaps even more serious to waste resources by the recommendation of a policy that is merely the best of a bad lot.

Actions That Differ in Scale

It has been stressed that in some problems it is advisable to compare rather broad systems. This does not mean, however, that all parts of the systems to be compared must be completely different from each other. The equipment, organization, and procedures may be identical in most parts of the rival systems; the parts that differ—those that are being varied—from one system to the next may be relatively small pieces of equipment or methods of carrying out a comparatively small task. Or the differences may be relatively small increments in the size of some facility or in the scale of some operation, for example, the addition of one salesman as compared with the addition of two salesmen. It is the system, not the variations, that must sometimes be fairly large in order for us to define gains and costs, and hence pick criteria, intelligently.

In water-resource development, for instance, it is often urged that the only way to perceive the real job is to fit the projects into river-basin or even regional systems.[2] But each of the broad systems need not be entirely different, such as treatment of the Pecos River Watershed versus treatment of the Grand-Neosho Watershed. Important also is the comparison of various combinations of measures within the same basin. Thus the alternatives that are being considered should embrace several combinations of components, such as existing features of the watershed plus the planting of extra forests, existing features plus forests plus terraces, and then all these components plus channel-improvement. Also, the proposals considered should include several sizes, such as 50,000 miles of terraces, 100,000 miles of terraces, and so on. In the context of the river basin and given the other components, we should ask: what are the extra costs and extra benefits attributable to each major feature or to each major increment in size? Only in this way can we see whether or not uneconomic features or

[2] *A Water Policy for the American People,* the Report of the President's Water Resource Policy Commission, Vol. 1 (Washington, D.C.: U.S. Government Printing Office, 1950), pp. 4–5, 9; Arthur Smithies, *op. cit.,* p. 348.

uneconomic additions in size are riding on the coattails of the truly profitable parts of a proposal.[3]

It is to be emphasized that component parts cannot be analyzed outside of the system of water-resource measures, for it *is* necessary to recognize interdependencies in calculating benefits and costs. Moreover, these systems may need to be rather large in scope. But it would be a serious error if only large variations in the possible courses of action were considered.

INTERRELATIONSHIPS AMONG THE COURSES OF ACTION

Attention has been called to the interrelationships between a course of action and its context, including such things as natural features, other operations, and decisions at other levels. Partly because of these interrelationships, it has been suggested that rather broad systems must often be compared. That is, in order to compare proposals A, B, and C, we really have to compare rest-of-the-system-plus-A, rest-of-the-system-plus-B, and rest-of-the-system-plus-C. It is also possible that the proposed actions, A, B, and C, are themselves interrelated, so that the results of A depend partly upon whether or not B is in existence. Indeed, some of the alternatives whose relevance was stressed in the previous section—projects that differ in size or have modified features—are almost sure to be interrelated. Different-sized ventures are mutually exclusive, an extreme type of interdependence. If action A, the construction of a two-story building on a particular site, is adopted, the gains and costs of action B, the construction of a one-story building on the same site, become zero, because action B is impossible. Other projects may have a less extreme interrelationship in which the adoption of A does not make B impossible, but does affect B's cost and/or payoff.

This interdependence poses no difficulty, other than increasing the computational burden, if different combinations of A, B, and C are tried, as was urged in the previous section. However, suppose we try to evaluate A without B and C, B independently of A and C, and C independently of the other two. Comparison will still be satisfactory if only one of the three proposals is to be undertaken. But sometimes two are to be chosen, or projects are to be ranked for future reference,

[3] The desirability of thinking in terms of "separable segments or increments" is recognized in the Green Book (*Proposed Practices for Economic Analysis . . .*, p. 5).

with a view to proceeding down the list as far as the budget will go. In these circumstances, there may be trouble ahead, because as soon as one of the projects is to be constructed, the other evaluations may change.

Suppose we compare a watershed (including whatever measures exist or are taken for granted) plus a reforestation project, the watershed plus a forest-fire control program, and the watershed plus downstream levees. Suppose further that the reforestation project turns out to be best, and it is to be carried out. Perhaps the downstream levees are second-best according to the initial analysis. Will they continue to be second-best? Not necessarily, because reforestation will reduce the worth of the levees (a "competing" project) and increase the worth of forest-fire control (a "complementary" project).

In other words, strictly speaking, our conclusions pertain only to systems actually compared, and not necessarily to modifications of these systems. Occasionally we may use the comparisons of A, B, and C (each fitted into the system) as a basis for ranking them. We may accordingly assume that there are no significant interrelationships between the proposals and adopt the first two as though the gains and costs of each project did not depend on decisions about the others. However, this might be a serious mistake. When projects are interrelated, the correct procedure is to compare the systems that are actually being considered: A, B, C, A plus B, B plus C, A plus C, A plus B plus C. There is no correct independent ranking of projects that are themselves interdependent.

CONCLUSIONS

One conclusion is that one cannot make sweeping generalizations about the potential aid that analysis can provide or about the formulation of analyses in connection with particular problems of choice. This is necessarily so because there are no clear-cut rules for determining the list of actions that should be considered or the scope of the systems into which the actions should be fitted—just as there were no cut-and-dried rules for devising appropriate criteria.

As in the case of criteria selection, however, even if a tidy set of particular instructions cannot be drawn up, a few general precautions can be formulated.

First, the systems into which the possible actions should be fitted, and hence the level of optimization, must be decided upon hand-in-hand with the devising of criteria. The advantages and disadvantages of including additional parts of the systems should be consciously weighed. Second, ingenuity in the designing and redesigning of alternative courses of action is of great importance in operations research; the devising of the alternative policies to be compared cannot be undertaken prefunctorily. Third, in designing alternative policies, different scales of each project and different combinations of measures should not be neglected. The addition (or removal) of extra features or increments in size creates alternative courses of action that are highly relevant. Fourth, special regard must be given to interrelationships between the alternative courses of action if more than one of the actions may be taken or if those actions are to be ranked for future reference. Finally, the results or calculations must be interpreted and used critically, with constant awareness of the limitations that attach to piecemeal analysis.

Chapter 4

INTANGIBLES, UNCERTAINTY, AND CRITERIA

W E HAVE SEEN that at best the criterion problem is troublesome. The complications which are now to be introduced make the problem still less tractable, and indeed affect the very meaning that must be attached to the word criterion.

INTANGIBLES

Meaning and Examples

Intangibles, at least as the word is used in this study, are simply some of the consequences of the alternatives compared, but they are consequences of a special sort. Their distinguishing characteristic is that they cannot readily be translated into the common denominator that is being used. Thus if gains are measured in terms of dollars, those effects which cannot be so measured are intangibles. Conversely, if gains are measured in units of "balanced development," then gains which can only be expressed in terms of dollars are intangibles. It is not necessarily true that *nothing* about such effects can be measured. It may be possible to describe them in some sort of quantitative terms which are helpful, in varying degree, to the decision-maker. But intangibles, as defined here, cannot be expressed in terms of the principal or common unit, and hence must somehow be taken into account "on the side." Of course, if no single unit is used extensively enough to be regarded as a common denominator, there is no basis for distinguishing at all between tangible and intangible effects. This is often the case in consumers' research.

Intangibles are likely to mar the neatness of any analysis, whether it pertains to problems of business, the military, the government, or the individual. No matter how industriously the analyst works at devising a single quantitative test, considerations that must be measured in other units (if at all) will still be pertinent to the final decision. A good example from business experience is the evaluation of night openings at Bamberger's,[1] in which both gains and costs were measured in dollars. Intangibles, effects which the analyst did not feel could be given generally acceptable value or cost tags, included the goodwill of customers who worked during regular store hours, the dislike of night work by the store's employees, and the difficulties of scheduling night shifts. In connection with military problems, while the costs may be measured in dollars, the gains may be "fixed" as the achievement of a designated mission. There will almost certainly be intangibles, that is, consequences of the alternative policies, such as numbers of lives lost, which cannot be reflected *fully* in the cost of carrying out the mission.

The remainder of the discussion, however, will be directed toward and illustrated by the intangible effects of water-resource projects. As will be seen later, the major gains and costs of these projects are expressed in dollars, and hence any effects which cannot be translated into dollar terms are intangibles. A most important example is the effect of a water-resource project on the size of government. Does a decrease in the government's size have a positive value, and, if so, how much? Individual A may have one answer; individual B, another. There is no organized market for reductions in the size of government to provide a generally meaningful value for this "commodity." The value of changes in the size of government is of critical importance when comparing water-resource proposals with expenditures by the private sector of the economy. Indeed, that value may almost dominate decisions about government invasion of areas where private enterprise can function or about expansion of government activity instead of the private sector. For that reason, it does not necessarily follow that the government should embark on ventures even if it can produce some product at a lower cost than private industry. In all such cases, it is necessary to weigh the gains against the disadvantages of having a bigger government. It is because of this intangible, the value of reductions in the size of government, that cost-benefit analyses have more bearing on the allocation of a given budget among accepted governmental activities than on the choice between a government enterprise and a private investment. Cost-benefit estimates are

[1] Levinson, *op. cit.*, p. 226.

relevant to the second problem of choice, but the evidence that they provide is hardly conclusive.

Since "balanced" regional development can hardly be assigned a generally valid price tag, it too is an intangible. There is little doubt that regional implications play a large role in Congressional decisions and for reasons other than log-rolling. We need not, on the one hand, be as generous-minded as one Congressman, when he remarked to officers of the Corps of Engineers: "I thought it was a great compliment to the Corps of Engineers that was offered on the floor of the House yesterday when Member after Member rose to get his survey in the bill somehow, so that you could do some work in that particular Member's district. . . . I thought the eagerness that was shown on the part of the Members to have you come into their district and do work there showed that they had faith and confidence in you."[2] On the other hand, we should not be completely cynical about motives. Congressmen as well as numerous others are genuinely concerned about the development of certain localities, usually "underdog" regions, in which they have no constituents. Witness the appropriations and plans for Alaskan development.

But is the desirability of balanced development being accepted uncritically?[3] In order to encourage a more nearly balanced growth in various regions, it is necessary to eliminate, or compensate for, the natural disadvantages of some geographical areas. This is sometimes difficult to do. For instance, the Salt Lake City area was given an industrial boost when it got the Geneva steel plant, but the location had some disadvantages. When the plant was later sold to private enterprise, it brought a price about one-tenth its cost, and its operation has aggravated the water crisis throughout the area.[4] Representative Kirwan of Ohio expressed his feelings as follows: "How in the world did they build that $200 million steel plant out on the desert? Who recommended that?"[5] One must conclude that balanced development

---

[2] *Study of Civil Works,* Hearings before the Subcommittee to Study Civil Works of the Committee on Public Works, House of Representatives, 82nd Congress, 2nd Session (Washington, D.C.: U.S. Government Printing Office, 1952), Part 1, p. 81.

[3] For a provocative examination of this question, see Marcus Fleming, "External Economies and the Doctrine of Balanced Growth," *Economic Journal,* June, 1955, pp. 241–256.

[4] *Interior Department Appropriations for 1953,* Hearings before the Subcommittee of the Committee on Appropriations, House of Representatives, 82nd Congress, 2nd Session, Part 3, pp. 920–922.

[5] *Ibid.,* p. 921.

usually implies a sacrifice of natural advantages. Does it provide anything worthwhile in return, e.g., reduced vulnerability to attack, more wholesome democratic processes, the nursing of an "infant region" that promises to have comparative advantages in the future? Whatever the answers, it is counted here as an intangible whose worth cannot easily be priced.

Conservation, depending upon its definition, may be another intangible factor. If it means simply a particular type of measure (such as preservation of topsoil) *to increase future production,* the gains can be estimated and compared with those from alternative policies. However, conservation seems at times to mean the preservation of specific assets quite apart from the consequences for future production.[6] If preservation has value in itself, it probably must be treated as an intangible.

A good many other relevant factors may fall into this category in connection with specific projects—effects on scenic historic sites, municipal decentralization, the national defense, the distribution of income, the saving of lives, the degree and type of competition, democratic processes, the mobility of resources, the stability of families. Note that some of these effects may be gains and others may be costs. Note, too, that by definition there is no generally acceptable value tag for the intangible effects of water-resource measures. Assertions about their significance can be pondered but not checked against satisfying standards. However, intangibles ought to be described in a meaningful way before any weight is attached to them. If their effects are describable only in vague and elusive terms, they should count for little. The intangible factor mentioned by former Secretary of Agriculture Brannan, in his remarks to the Subcommittee to Study Civil Works, is a case in point:

> I say to you for a certainty that the cost of developing water for a specific acre of land, when it runs to $1,000 or in that area, cannot be borne by that land and be paid out except if you allocate it over four or five generations of people.
>
> Therefore you look at it and see there is a real public interest in putting more land into cultivation and therefore part of this money must just be charged off to the public interest, and that is all.[7]

Skeptical queries like the one raised about water-resource proposals by one Congressman in 1952 are definitely in order: "Mr. Furcolo.

---

[6] See *A Water Policy for the American People,* p. 2, and the section on "National Objectives," pp. 37–41.

[7] *Study of Civil Works,* Part 2, p. 224.

What I wanted to ask is this, Who says they are essential in the defense effort?"[8]

Possible Treatment

There are several ways of handling intangibles in quantitative analysis. One way is just to ignore them: if they cannot be put in terms of the common denominator, have nothing to do with them at all. This method is not recommended because the significance of the numbers in an analysis depends partly upon the importance of effects not encompassed by those numbers, and the recognition of this importance should not be left to chance. What effects are finally measured in terms of the common denominator must be made clear; what major effects are not so measured, though perhaps initially considered as candidates for inclusion, should surely be at least mentioned.

Can something beyond merely mentioning these consequences be done? Sometimes it is suggested that, if the analyst works hard enough, *everything* can be put in terms of the common unit; for example, that in cost-benefit analysis every effect can be given a meaningful price. For instance, the saving of a human life can be priced, it is said, by consulting (1) the implications of past decisions, (2) the cost of saving a life by the cheapest alternative method, (3) the average court award, or legal compensation, for accidental death. Now any of these devices may be useful, it is true, in particular problems, but their real meaning, in the absence of an organized market to which governments and individuals adjust their actions, is hard to unravel. The implied values attached to human life during World War II—the amounts that were in effect traded for lives—differed from one situation to the next, and were not necessarily the values that should have been, or ought now to be, assigned to lives. The costs of saving additional lives by alternative methods, such as stricter safety regulations, may suggest a maximum value in some circumstances, or they may suggest a reallocation of governmental effort among life-saving policies; but none of these figures need be a generally acceptable value for human beings. Likewise, the average court award need not reflect the "appropriate" value.

This is not to say that the attempt to "price" lives in *all* problems is unhelpful. Nor is it to say that it is hopeless to try to value other factors which appear at first glance to be "intangibles." In specific analyses, ingenuity can often go a long way toward the measurement

[8] *Interior Department Appropriations for 1953,* House of Representatives, Part 3, p. 789.

of such effects in terms of the common unit. But it must be conceded that, if a project's outputs cannot be freely bought and sold or cannot even be accurately defined, the derivation of values for them is at best not wholly satisfying, and is at worst subject to serious abuse. We cannot prescribe just where to draw the line between effects which should be measured in terms of the common denominator and those which should not. We can say, however, that insistence on the measurement of *all* effects in terms of a single common unit will not make for the most useful analysis.[9]

Even though analyses should neither ignore intangible effects of alternative policies nor try to convert them *all* to tangibles, useful information about these effects can be presented to the decision-makers. First, if both gains and costs are being expressed in dollars, as in cost-benefit analysis, it may be possible to show the minimum dollar value that one must attach to the intangibles if he prefers Project A over alternative investments. That is, suppose investment A costs $1,000,000 (all amounts in present values) and yields $2,000,000 plus the preservation of salmon-fishing in the watershed, while investment B costs $1,000,000 and yields $3,000,000. If one chooses A, he must be attaching a value of at least $1,000,000 to the salmon fishing. If this comes to $1,000 per salmon (and he sticks with Project A), then he must think rather highly of this sport.[10] This procedure ties no price tags to the intangible effects but brings out explicitly the minimum valuation that would be implicit in choosing the project.

Second, quantitative information about these intangibles in terms other than the common denominator may be helpful to decision-makers. Even if the intangibles are by definition not commensurable with the other costs and gains, clues to their impact can often be given. Indicators of the extent and quality of the salmon fishing can be presented even if it cannot be priced. Or suppose one policy involves

[9] This position appears to be consistent with that of the Green Book (*Proposed Practices for Economic Analysis . . .* , pp. 26–27) and with that of the House Committee to Study Civil Works, which concluded: "If Congress were to rely exclusively on a benefit-cost ratio as a measure of whether or not a project should be adopted, it would be abandoning its responsibilities. Some of the effort to place monetary values on indirect benefits is nothing short of ludicrous." (*Economic Evaluation of Federal Water Resource Development Projects,* p. 51.)

[10] However, if the alternative use of the resources also involves significant intangibles, not much can be said. The situation would then be like that in which the little boy valued his puppy at $50,000 and, according to his story, sold it for that amount. How? By accepting a couple of $25,000 cats as payment.

giving a subsidy to some group of persons. While a price tag (be it positive or negative) cannot easily be attached to this consequence, it makes a difference whether the subsidy amounts to $5,000 or $5,000,000,000, whether it goes to the very rich or the very poor. Such effects can be partially traced out, after the fashion of consumers' research, and presented in an exhibit that supplements the principal estimates.

UNCERTAINTY

Another consideration that cannot be priced is the degree of uncertainty about a project's cost and gain. In a sense, then, uncertainty also can be viewed as an intangible, but as an especially ubiquitous and significant one. The estimates of costs and benefits mentioned so far might be called average or expected outcomes. We know in advance that these amounts may be off the mark. For instance, benefits of irrigation projects depend upon such factors as technological innovations that affect relative prices, the occurrence of mountain slides and ice jams, and the actual fertility of the soil (which is estimated on the basis of a sample) ; and these things cannot be perfectly foreseen. As a consequence, Projects A and B may offer identical average outcomes, yet differ greatly with respect to other possible outcomes. These differences may be a matter of some moment if, say, A's possible results are nearly the same as the average, but B's range from fabulous success to utter disaster. Yet while such differences in the pattern of uncertainty—or, more precisely, in the "frequency distribution of outcomes"—are matters of great concern, it is ordinarily impossible to attach a value or price to them. A price, that is, which would have any *general* validity. In some situations and for some persons, to reduce the chance of a bad outcome is worth a great deal. In other situations or for other persons, even a slight chance of an extremely favorable outcome carries a high premium. Hence, the suggested method of treating uncertainty resembles the recommended way to handle other intangibles: to avoid concealment and to present some quantitative indicators.

Hedging in the Face of Uncertainty

It is essential for us to realize that the problems posed by uncertainty, like those posed by suboptimization and time streams, are not mere curiosities or conundrums which provide intellectual exercise. They are burdensome problems which confront men who "meet payrolls," people who deal in the commodity markets, men and women in any occupation.

A shoe manufacturer expects his operations to be profitable, on the average, but when he buys hides, he recognizes that prices may shift before he sells shoes. The result could be a nice increase in his profit, or it could be a disastrous loss. Often instead of taking a chance on such a loss (or profit), he will hedge, that is, sell hides for future delivery so that if prices sag later on, he gains roughly as much on the futures contract as he loses on his inventory.

To hedge against a bad outcome is a typical reaction to uncertainty by all sorts of decision-makers—businesses, households, military services, government agencies. A family plans an automobile trip, and finds that so far as average performance is concerned, the tires promise to be free of blowouts and flats. Is this average outcome the only relevant piece of information? Hardly. A hedge against the chance of fatal accident or even inconvenience may be worth the price of new tires. Other illustrations of hedging are abundant; any purchase of insurance is an example.

Of course, this is not the only sort of reaction that people have to uncertainty. They may prefer the chance of an exceedingly favorable outcome even if the average result is relatively unattractive or even if there is also a chance of catastrophe. The average return from uranium prospecting may have been comparatively uninviting, but the market for Geiger counters has been brisk. Whether we gamble or hedge, and whether the desire to do so is mild or intense, is irrelevant. The point here is that data about results other than the average outcome do properly influence one's decision.

Types of Uncertainty

It may help put this complication in proper perspective if we see how pervasive uncertainty is—if we see some of the reasons that results are seldom sure. Perhaps this process will also help show that uncertainty is inherent in the nature of things and is not necessarily evidence of lazy or careless estimation.

About Specified Gains and Costs. In setting up analyses, the objectives or gains to be achieved must be at least defined, and in many instances they are both defined and fixed as to amount. In the analysis of military problems, for instance, the gains may be fixed as the carrying out of a specified mission, or in the analysis of business problems the performance of a specified task. The criterion, it will be recalled, may then be the achievement of the specified gains at minimum cost, or maximum achievement of the defined gains for a specified cost. It is not certain, however, that this will be precisely the task or budget, as the case may be, which will apply after the "best" means are selected. If there is much uncertainty about the future task or budget, it is wrong to pretend that there is certainty when drawing conclusions from the analysis. If the same course of action is best for all plausible tasks or budgets, the correct choice is clear enough. If not, it may be advisable to hedge against the possibility of a bad outcome in case the task or budget should be different from the one specified, for example, by choosing a policy whose outcome is not so variable.

This procedure is especially important when the assumed task belongs to the distant future, and when the situation or the management is subject to considerable change. Thus in connection with the development of new gadgets, it may be undesirable to put all one's effort into those particular systems (such as carburetors, chassis, transmissions, *et al.*) which look best in terms of an overly specific job—namely, fitting into a precisely spelled-out larger system (say a *particular* dream car of the future).

ABOUT "GIVEN" PARTS OF THE SYSTEMS. As explained earlier, the systems that are being compared can be viewed as (a) the parts that are taken as given, plus (b) the parts that are being varied. In cost-benefit analysis, thus, the systems are (a) the rest of the watershed and of the situation, plus (b) Project A in one system, or B in another one, and so on. Now there is inevitably some uncertainty about the things that are taken as given. In one non-Federal project, undertaken in 1941, 100 acres of alligator weed in a reservoir was one of the factors given. With some chance that it would spread, it was possible for the outcome to range from fiasco to success. As it turned out, by 1948 thousands of acres were infested, the cost of removing the vegetation was prohibitive, and instead of the estimated benefits, an epidemic of malaria had been realized.[11]

As another example, it is difficult to predict exactly what will happen to river banks when powerful flows of water are released through spillways and penstocks over a long period of time. Expensive river-bank stabilization programs may later prove to be necessary.[12] Again, "because of the prohibitive cost of complete under-

[11] *A Water Policy for the American People,* pp. 402–403. Pages 404–407 describe other instances of uncertainty about the "given" parts of the system or environment.

[12] *Interior Department Appropriations, 1953,* House of Representatives, Part 3, pp. 927–929.

ground investigations it is impossible to forecast the exact needs for drainage before a project has been under irrigation for a number of years."[13] The point is also suggested by a question raised during a Congressional Hearing: "Mr. Jensen. . . . What was the name of that dam where we had to spend $10 million to pound cement into faults in the rock?"[14]

Naturally, the possible outcomes are not always worse than the average or expected result. Unexpected rates of growth have caused some measures to yield greater benefits than were anticipated. Even physical conditions are sometimes more favorable than those taken as given; in one instance, drainage from an irrigation project increased the local underground water supply more than had been counted on.[15]

ABOUT THE RESPONSES OF OTHER DECISION-MAKERS. One aspect of the systems being compared that is taken as "given" warrants being mentioned separately and given special emphasis. This is the reaction of other decision-makers to each of the policies that is being considered. It is sometimes called the "game" aspect of choosing one's course of action: we must anticipate that when we move, others will adjust their policies accordingly, which may affect the payoffs or costs of our move. What is being emphasized in this chapter is that there is inherent uncertainty about the adjustments that others will make.

This aspect is obviously relevant to the comparison of alternative military policies, where other nations adjust their actions, and of alternative business policies, where customers or rival firms adjust theirs. It is also relevant, however, to the comparison of alternatives in many other problems, such as the shaping of water-resource programs. If cost-benefit estimates are to be useful, the reaction of farmers, industrialists, laborers, and tourists to water-resource developments must be considered, and uncertainty about their reactions should be recognized.

ABOUT TECHNOLOGICAL CHANGE. Another uncertain feature of any system is technology. If a system includes some undeveloped gadget, what are the chances that it will not work at all? In any event, what might various innovations do to the gains or costs of the systems being compared? On this account too, a range of results, not a unique outcome, is associated with each of the alternative courses of action. It should go without saying that this applies to the analysis of water-resource measures as well as of alternative actions by firms, military services, or individuals.

[13] *Ibid.*, p. 1142.
[14] *Ibid.*, p. 794.
[15] *A Water Policy for the American People*, p. 406.

ABOUT THE CHANCE ELEMENT IN RECURRING EVENTS. In addition to doubts about the mission or budget, the "given" parts of the environment, the reactions of other decision-makers, and technological changes, there are elements of chance in even the most fully understood events. Data on rainfall from the beginning of time would not reveal precisely what storms will occur in any specific year. Identical floods in what appear to be identical circumstances would not do exactly the same damage. There are random elements, sometimes called statistical uncertainty, in the performance of any gadget or system. In addition there are uncertainties due to imperfect data and techniques of estimation, since it is not worthwhile to put unlimited resources into the preparation of estimates. As a consequence, the possible results of a course of action emerge as a frequency distribution, not as a single outcome.

Possible Treatment

When uncertainty is present, as it usually is, single-valued estimates of costs and gains by themselves may constitute insufficient analysis. The *expected* yield on United States savings bonds and Boston and Maine income bonds is not an adequate basis for choosing between the two securities. A prospective purchaser wants some clue to the potential variability of yield, or to the ranges of yield with which equal confidence can be associated. Similarly, in most cases of operations research or systems analysis, single-valued estimates provide insufficient information. To try to adjust such single-valued estimates to reflect uncertainty is not satisfactory; even if there existed allowances for risk which would make a single value expected with certainty the "equivalent" of a variable outcome,[16] such allowances could not be determined in practice. Hence, whether they are for the use of a recommender or a decision-maker, correct quantitative "results" should usually be multi-valued to show various "reasonable" outcomes, or supplemented with other clues to the uncertainty that is associated with the estimates.

In other words, uncertainty should be handled along the lines suggested for intangibles, as the term has been defined. It is not possible to measure the worth of different degrees of uncertainty. In cost-benefit analysis, for instance, it is out of the question to put a value

---

[16] J. R. Hicks, *Value and Capital* (Oxford: Clarendon Press, 1946), pp. 125–126 In any event, there is no "certainty-equivalent" in many problems. (See M. Friedman, "Discussion," *American Economic Review, Papers and Proceedings*, May, 1949, pp. 196–199.)

tag on the frequency distribution of results from each project and then to adjust each project's expected present value to arrive at its expected "utility." But it *is* often possible to use other quantitative indicators, such as the range of outcomes in different relevant circumstances, to describe uncertainty. Non-concealment and concise description are presumably better than nothing in aiding decision-makers.

What can be done, in more specific terms, to present such quantitative indicators? In connection with some of the uncertainties mentioned above, about all that can be done is to supplement the "most likely" outcome with other results that are rather definitely in the picture. That is, if the task or mission would be substantially altered by contingency X, a supplementary comparison of the alternative systems can be made in terms of that modified task. With respect to uncertainty about the "given" parts of the system, one can show how the alternative undertakings would shape up in case alligator weed should spread, or in the event that other decision-makers should adopt Response "1A" or "1B." If some technological innovation is on the horizon, one can indicate how this would affect the results. This does not mean that separate calculations must be made by the dozen, but they should be made whenever it is fairly clear that one of these contingencies is not too improbable and that it would seriously shift the outcome.

In connection with the chance element in recurring events, it may be desirable to show a probability distribution of outcomes, especially if the other kinds of uncertainty are relatively unimportant. Sometimes the probabilities that various outcomes would occur can be calculated analytically. Sometimes the sequence of events is so complicated that the probabilities cannot be so calculated. In the latter situations, a "Monte Carlo" technique may be useful. This technique consists of repeated calculations to learn the results when uncertain events are determined by drawing them from an appropriately rigged hat. Thus, if one of the uncertain events is annual rainfall and the probabilities of having 30 inches and 15 inches of rain are 0.2 and 0.8 respectively, the hat will contain two slips of paper labeled "30-inch rainfall" and eight slips labeled "15-inch rainfall." The hat can be replaced by other devices, such as a wheel of chance or a table of random numbers. Such calculations yield a series of different outcomes, not a unique answer, and will in some circumstances be a more helpful prediction than merely the average outcome.

Perhaps it should be noted, too, that this procedure may yield a more accurate average result than using the expected outcome of each event in the sequence. For instance, suppose that we wish to estimate expected flood damage. Suppose further that the tabulation shows how

Size of Storm (inches of rain)	Probability of Occurrence	Damage
4 inch	0.1	$1,000,000
2 inch	0.7	200,000
1 inch	0.2	0

damage varies with the size of the storm and what the chances are of having storms of various sizes. In this simple illustration, expected damage can be calculated analytically, and it amounts to $240,000 [(.1×$1,000,000) plus (.7×$200,000) plus (.2×$0)]. If it were a sufficiently complex case, however, the mean outcome would have to be approximated in some other way. One procedure might be to use damage from the expected *storm* as an approximation of expected damage. Damage from the expected storm, which is a 2-inch rain [(.1×4″) plus (.7×2″) plus (.2×1″)], is $200,000. A more accurate way, provided enough "plays" were carried out, might be to use the Monte Carlo method. The appropriately rigged hat would contain one slip of paper labeled "$1,000,000 damage," seven slips of paper labeled "$200,000 damage," and two slips of paper representing "zero damage." With numerous repetitions (in this case, merely the drawing of numerous slips), average damage would approach $240,000.

With respect to cost-benefit analyses, such procedures are used to some extent in calculating expected results, particularly in the estimation of flood damage. They might be used more extensively, and used to indicate the variability of results, but it would require a great deal of time and effort. On balance, the Monte Carlo method, and the probability distribution of outcomes that this technique produces, may not be worthwhile in cost-benefit analysis except in the exhaustive examination of very expensive proposals.

So far, this section has simply indicated some ways to derive a multiplicity of outcomes which are relevant to a final decision. Can these be used for a firm recommendation or formed into simpler exhibits? In many situations, the answer is Yes. First, if enough is known about the decision-maker's attitude toward uncertainty, sound recommendations can be based on multiple results. To use an extreme example, if it is known that the decision-maker wishes to minimize the worst that can happen, the analyst can point to the best course of action. Of course, to minimize the worst that can happen is an extremely conservative strategy, but other rules or the analyst's judgment may make it possible to draw up definite conclusions and recommendations.

Often, however, the analyst can help most by describing the patterns of uncertainty, leaving the evaluation to the decision-maker.[17] From a multiplicity of results, the analyst may be able to deduce ranges of results to which roughly the same confidence can be attached. Such a range, somewhat similar to a confidence interval, may be helpful even if it is derived subjectively (after pondering the calculations, of course). If this seems impossible, selected cases among the multiple outcomes may be presented. Finally, if none of these suggestions appears to be practicable, the major sources of uncertainty about expected results should at least be mentioned. For it may be misleading to invite attention only to the average result—to tell someone, for example, that if he flips a coin, he can expect a side that is half heads and half tails to turn up.

THE MEANING OF CRITERIA

Earlier it was convenient to discuss criteria as though the term referred to definitive tests of preferredness. These reflections on intangibles and uncertainty, however, make it clear that the word "criterion" must sometimes mean a partial test—one that is a significant rather than a nonsensical basis for the comparison of policies and yet not a basis that embraces all the relevant considerations. In many problems, the precise relationship between proximate criteria and the ultimate test will not be known, and hence the former must be incomplete tests.

Consider, for example, an attempt by the managers of a firm to apply the test of "maximum profits from available resources."[18] Let us assume that when the managers consider several alternative courses of action, they can predict expected profits, and also something about the variability of profits, under each alternative policy. In other

---

[17] In the end it comes to that, even if the analyst submits definite recommendations rather than just pertinent evidence. Few decision-makers accept a recommendation blindly; they want to know how the recommender reached his conclusions.

[18] See G. Tintner, "The Theory of Choice under Subjective Risk and Uncertainty," *Econometrica*, July–October, 1941, pp. 298–304; A. Alchian, "Uncertainty, Evolution, and Economic Theory," *The Journal of Political Economy*, June, 1950, pp. 211–221, or S. Enke, "On Maximizing Profits," *American Economic Review*, September, 1951, pp. 566–578.

words, they can say to themselves, "Under Policy 1, profits would be $1 million, plus or minus $200,000. Under Policy 2, expected profits would be $2 million, though there is a chance that they might run as high as $3 million or that losses of $1 million would be incurred." What *is* "maximum profit from available resources" in this situation? It may be defined as maximum *average* profit, but in any event, it will be an incomplete criterion, because its relationship to the ultimate test will not be fully traced out. The ultimate criterion is to maximize something—it can be labeled "utility"—which *depends upon* expected profits, upon the other possible profit figures, and upon the management's attitude toward risk and uncertainty. But the precise nature of this relationship is not ordinarily known. Hence to show which course of action yields maximum expected profit is to compare the policies in terms of one selected policy-consequence, that is, to apply a partial or incomplete criterion. To compare the policies with respect to other possible outcomes or to variability of outcome is to use other incomplete or partial criteria.

The fact that tests will usually be incomplete harasses the researcher and decision-maker in other comparisons intended to reveal the "best" stream of costs and benefits. If we use a little jargon from mathematics and economics, the general situation can be described with greater precision. Utility, the label for whatever should ultimately be maximized, depends upon a vast number of variables (some of which are aspirations and yield positive utility and some of which are aversions and yield negative utility). Since such functional relationships, and indeed many of the variables, are not fully known to us, the analyst cannot devise any perfect, complete criterion. What he can do is to specify a variable on which utility is believed to depend, say the level of real income, and then try to measure what would happen to that variable with alternative courses of action. Failing that, he can seek the best index (for example, maximum net profits, maximum performance of defined tasks at given cost) of what would happen, under each project, to that variable. If the analyst resorts to an index, he may in some cases be able to demonstrate that a certain relationship exists between this index and the specified variable, for example, between the maximization of net profits and the level of real income. In other cases, he may be able only to offer inconclusive evidence and make a rather weak probabilistic statement that rests largely on judgment. But he has at best a criterion *only in terms of that variable*. If there is widespread agreement or persuasive evidence that it is the most important variable, this criterion takes on added significance. If measurements in other units show what would happen to other variables (the so-called intangibles), the analysis becomes still more helpful. Nonetheless, this criterion is not a final test of preferredness, but is a partial test—a comparison in terms of selected consequences, knowledge of which would be helpful to the decision-makers.

For example, we have only fragmentary knowledge of the relevant utility function in connection with choosing water-resource projects. Let us assume, for the moment, that whatever we wish to maximize is a function of the nation's expected real income, the frequency distribution of results, the size of government, distribution of income, and the number of lives saved. We do not know how important some of these variables are in relation to others. Consequently we can devise no complete criterion which points to the correct set of investments; the determination of that set involves the judgments of the Executive Departments and of Congress. However, we can show what would happen under different water-resource investments to an index (the value of expected net-benefit streams) that is related to the nation's real income. If possible, we should show data related to some of the other variables (a frequency distribution of results, for instance). In any event, it is plain that maximum expected net-benefits for a given water-resources budget is an incomplete test, and it should be understood that the term "criterion" refers to such an incomplete test whenever it pertains to cost-benefit analysis.

Chapter 5

TIME STREAMS AND CRITERIA[1]

I**N ALL TYPES OF ANALYSIS,** time is a vital, and sometimes a neglected, aspect of criteria. The test of the best policy, it will be recalled, involves both those consequences that are called gains and those that are called costs. Gains are positive achievements which we like to increase, the carrying out of tasks which it is desirable to get done. Costs are negative effects which we like to decrease, values which must be given up in order to adopt a policy. That time is an essential element of both is plain to see, for one cannot fully spell out a task without saying when it is to be done or over what time period the achievement is to be maintained, and one cannot fully describe the costs of alternative actions without saying when they are to be incurred. Perhaps it should be noted, too, that the actions do not have to be durable investments in the usual sense. Almost any set of alternatives—industrial or military operations, methods of organization, sales policies, allocations of a budget among programs—will have significant effects on costs or gains in future periods. Without doubt, then, time is of the essence in comparing courses of action. But how should it be taken into account?

TIME HORIZON OR CUT-OFF POINT

First of all, how far into the future should one look? Presumably as far as one can see, but this usually means something short of

---

[1] Parts of this chapter—unavoidably, I believe—are more difficult to follow than the material in the earlier chapters. The general reader may wish to turn to Chapter 6 for a summary of the conclusions with respect to the treatment of time streams without attention to the technical argument in Chapter 5.

eternity so far as putting down cost and gain estimates is concerned. Suppose the purchase of some machine is contemplated. At the end of ten years, it is believed that the machine will be discarded and sold. If its subsequent costs and gains can be foreseen, its salvage value can be incorporated into the cost and gain streams. This procedure, depending upon the way in which salvage value is estimated, may be tantamount to peering into the indefinite future. If, however, nothing can really be foreseen beyond that date, salvage value, i.e., further costs and gains, may be ignored. This procedure is the equivalent of adopting a time horizon or cut-off date.

Such a time horizon would mean the length of time over which costs and gains were estimated, and beyond which one could not see well enough for estimates to be worthwhile. This device of using a cut-off date, like most simplifications that are adopted in dealing with uncertainty, is not wholly satisfying. It implies that, while uncertainty up to that point can be reflected by multiple estimates, beyond that point uncertainty suddenly becomes so overwhelming that any estimates can be discounted to the zero mark. Nonetheless, this device reflects the way people often have to think about their problems of choice, including military, business, household, and water-resource problems. Beyond *some* date, the gain from preparing hazy estimates is less than the cost. Unfortunately, not much can be said about the appropriate time horizon in general; it depends upon the problem and upon the policy-maker's attitude toward uncertainty. Later, in connection with the particular problem of selecting water-resource projects, more specific comments on these points will be made.

TREATMENT OF STREAMS MEASURED IN DOLLARS

Within the time span over which estimates seem to be worthwhile, how should costs and gains accruing at different dates be treated? Let us turn, for the present, to situations in which both gains and costs are measured in monetary units. Such situations do not often occur in the comparison of military systems, so the discussion is more likely to apply to analyses pertaining to other government activities and to business. Imagine that an electronics company is comparing several investments, new plants of various sizes and types. The natural criterion is the maximization of profits, that is, of gain minus cost.[2] But none of these investments would result in a single lump of cost and a

---

[2] In order to focus attention on the difficulties presented by time itself, uncertainty will be ignored in the remainder of the chapter.

single lump of gain. They would bring about streams of costs and gains through time, or, so to speak, many lumps that occur at different dates. What, then, is the meaning of gains minus costs? The meaning is surely not the simple sum of all gains minus the sum of all costs, because different significance must be attached to the same amounts if they occur at different times.

Counsel of Perfection: Maximizing Present Worth

One way to allow for this difference so as to compute gains minus costs is to discount future amounts and convert each stream to its present value. For example, if we discount future amounts at 5 per cent, the present value (the value today) of a dollar one year hence is about 95 cents. In many circumstances, the appropriate test for the best course of action is to maximize the present value of the gains minus the present value of the costs, with whatever constraints are applicable. For the sake of convenience, this test will be referred to as the maximization of "present worth," a term which is often used to mean the present value of gains minus the present value of costs. The circumstances in which maximum present worth is an appropriate test, and the discount rate that should be used to compute present worth, will be discussed at some length.

It will be helpful in this discussion if two concepts are clarified. The first is "investment cost," which is the value of the resources that must be put into a venture. Naturally this cost does not consist merely of the first year's construction outlays. Nor need it coincide precisely with total construction outlays. Investment occurs whenever more is being put into a project than is being received from it. Thus initial advertising expense may be a cost that must and should be provided for out of investment funds. As another illustration, if all operating costs are not at first covered by receipts, those outlays that are not covered must be regarded as part of the investment. Hence while investment cost will usually approximate construction outlays, it comprises, if we speak more precisely, the outlays which have to be covered from a source other than receipts. The second concept is a closely related one—"net receipts." These occur whenever more is being received from the venture than is being put into it, and they are available therefore for reinvestment (or for consumption, if total capital is gradually to be liquidated).

No "Capital Rationing." We shall turn first to situations in which the investment budget can be varied by borrowing money. These situations will be labeled as ones in which there is "no capital rationing." In these circumstances, the correct procedure is fairly clear, at least when we neglect uncertainty. If our electronics firm has investment opportunities, including chances to loan money, which yield more than the rate at which funds can be borrowed on the money market, it should invest in its projects until the next-best opportunity yields no more than that market rate. In this statement, the term "projects" must be understood correctly: it refers to increments in the size of an installation as well as to completely different installations. Also, in the same statement, the term "yield" must be understood. What does it mean to say that an opportunity "yields" no more than the market rate? The definition here is that the "yield" of a project is its "internal rate of return." This phrase is a technical term meaning the rate of discount which makes the present value of the project's receipt stream equal to the present value of its cost stream, or, in other words, the rate of discount which makes the present worth zero. For example, if a $100 investment provides $5 per year in perpetuity, its internal rate of return is 5 per cent; that is, with a discount rate of 5 per cent, the present value of the receipt stream would be the same ($100) as that of the cost stream.

Hence the rule just stated says that, when there is no capital rationing, one should invest until the internal rate of return from incremental investment is no higher than the market rate of interest. This is a fairly simple proposition, until the complications are introduced. It means, for instance, that if one can borrow at 2 per cent and buy bonds that yield 3 per cent, he should do so; but he should not do so if the market rate at which he can borrow is 4 per cent. Note that if a firm follows this rule, the market rate will be (approximately) equal to the firm's *marginal* internal rate of return, i.e., that from its marginal investment.

This rule has a rather serious shortcoming, however. It leaves the following important question unanswered: If several ventures are interdependent, which combination should be chosen? Interdependent ventures, it will be recalled, are projects whose costs or gains depend upon whether or not certain others are undertaken. To cite the extreme case, investments may be mutually exclusive sets of which only one can be carried out. That is, of some sets, such as separate plants or facilities, it is physically possible to have one or all of the alternatives; but of others, such as different ways of constructing a particular facility, it is physically possible to have only one.[3] If two such

---

[3] The term "mutually exclusive" is applied to such projects by Armen A. Alchian in "The Rate of Interest, Fisher's Rate of Return Over Costs and

mutually exclusive ventures are among those to be considered, the rule enunciated above may simply indicate that both would be profitable investments at the current market rate of interest. The rule does not reveal which is the better of the two.

Let us turn, therefore, to a more general rule, one which must be expressed in two parts. (1) The first part applies to "independent" projects, those whose costs or receipts do not depend upon whether or not any of the other ventures are undertaken. Of such investments, the firm should undertake those which have positive present worths when the streams are discounted at the market rate. Actually, this is equivalent to the rule stated previously: if a project has a higher yield than the market rate, its present worth will be positive when the project's cost-receipt streams are discounted at the market rate. If the project's yield is the same as that of the market, it will have a zero present worth when that rate is used for discounting. If the project's yield is less than the market rate, the investment will have a negative present worth when the latter rate is used to discount the streams. Hence, to invest until the next-best opportunities yield no more than the market rate is to undertake all projects which have positive present worths when discounted at that rate. Moreover, to do this is to maximize the firm's present worth with the given constraints, since it is impossible to increase present worth further by tacking on investments having zero or negative present worths. (2) The second part of this more general rule applies to interdependent projects, including those which are mutually exclusive. With respect to these ventures, the firm should choose those which have the highest (positive) present worths when the streams are discounted at the market rate.[4]

As mentioned above, in this situation the market rate is the marginal rate of return which could be earned on further investment, and this rate is also the marginal internal rate of return. So the rule that has been described is tantamount to the following: if money can be borrowed at the market rate of interest, undertake investments so as to maximize present worth when the streams are discounted at the marginal rate of return—which, since the two coincide, is both the market rate and the marginal internal rate of return.

Keynes' Internal Rate of Return," *American Economic Review,* December, 1955, p. 940. In case anyone wishes to pursue the technical implications, the existence of mutually exclusive projects presumably implies that the facility (e.g., a bridge or house) is not infinitely "divisible."

[4] These ventures will not necessarily be the ones with the highest internal rates of return.

But why should a firm want to maximize present worth with the streams discounted at this rate? What is so important about present worth at one particular discount rate? Consider the example in Table 2 in which the firm is trying to decide whether to undertake investment A, investment B, or both. Mere inspection of the streams does not reveal whether either or both should be undertaken. Nor

TABLE 2*

Alternative Projects	Investment to Beginning of Year 1	Net Receipts		Present Value of Receipt Streams	
		Year 1	Year 2	3%	7%
A	$100	0	$115	$108	$100
B	$100	$110	0	$107	$103

*Rate which must be paid, or sacrificed, is market rate of 7%.

does the computation of their present worths make the correct policy obvious: if the streams are discounted at the market rate of 7 per cent, B has a present worth of $3 ($103—$100), while A has a present worth of zero. But why not compute the present worths at some other discount rate, say 3 per cent? (In that case, both projects would have positive present worths, with A instead of B appearing to be the better of the two.)

The answers to these questions are that the firm can maximize its wealth—both at present and at later dates—by maximizing present worth with the market rate used for discounting. In other words, by following this rule, the firm can simply make more money than it can by following some other rule. For example, let us see what investments A and B would *really* do for the firm:

Suppose, first, that the firm resells the venture after construction. The investment costs (which may have accumulated over a lengthy construction period) are $100 for both A and B, but if the future receipt streams are then publicized and the ventures offered for sale, B will fetch $103, while A will bring only $100. Those are the values that the market will attach to the two projects once the facts about them are made public; because, to take B as an example, if each dollar can earn 7 per cent per year in the money market, $103 at the beginning of year 1 can become $110 at the end of year 1, and consequently $110 at the end of year 1 will be worth $103 at the beginning of the period. Potential buyers of investment B would be foolish to pay more than $103 but would be willing to pay up to that amount.

Suppose, second, that for one reason or another the firm has no interest in resale after construction. Consider the way events can unfold in this case. As the net receipts from any investment come in, they can be put to work at 7 per cent. Even if withdrawn for consumption purposes, the funds are valued at 7 per cent if equilibrium exists; for the stockholders of the firm adjust their consumption in accordance with the fact that extra savings can earn 7 per cent. That is, they stop saving when additional funds devoted to consumption are worth as much as the same funds are worth in the form of savings. Hence, the alternatives that should really be considered are A plus the use of net receipts and B plus the use of its net-receipt stream. Table 2A shows the results when the reinvestment possibilities are explicitly recognized.

TABLE 2A

Alternative Projects	Investment to Beginning of Year 1	Value Obtainable by Various Dates	
		End of Year 1	End of Year 2
A + investment of net receipts at 7%	$100	—	$115
B + investment of net receipts at 7%	$100	$110	$117.70

Investment B gives the firm more, in plain dollars and cents, at the end of each period. Put more generally, even if resale is not an admissible alternative, maximum present worth when the streams are discounted at the market rate gives the maximum value obtainable at the end of each year. If the net receipts are actually reinvested, this test leads to the maximum monetary return over the period under consideration. And as noted, if the net receipts are withdrawn and consumed instead, it can be assumed that they are being devoted to an equally valuable use.

Of course, as soon as resale is not an admissible alternative, the owners of the investments no longer have the option of liquidating fully at any moment they choose. In these circumstances, the criterion of maximum present worth at the market could conceivably be upset. In the example shown in Table 2A, it is difficult to see how one could prefer A to B[5] if he were concerned only with the positions at the end of each year. But suppose that the owner's time preferences were such that he wanted to maximize the cash obtainable as of May 15 in Year 2. In the absence of a perfect resale market for investments, it

---

[5] Unless he had an actual *aversion* to receipts at the end of Year 1, perhaps in connection with tax calculations.

is conceivable that A, or perhaps investment in the money market, would be preferred to B.

But these exceptions depend upon imperfections in the resale market *plus* time preferences which call for sudden shifts from investment to consumption; and they will merely be noted here. In general, with no capital rationing, the appropriate test for the correct set of investments is maximum present worth when the streams are discounted at the market rate (the marginal rate of return). All this is not to say that "the" market rate is an unchanging rate or an unambiguous concept. But it is to say that, in principle, if the size of the firm's investment budget can be nicely adjusted to conditions in the general investment market, then the discount rate should reflect those reinvestment opportunities.

PARTIAL CAPITAL RATIONING: RESALE POSSIBLE. If our electronics company (or perhaps a division of the firm) cannot borrow enough to undertake all the investments that would be profitable at the going market rate of interest, investment cannot be pushed to the point at which the additional gain would be matched by the additional cost. In other words, available capital is fixed, and, in this instance, it is "too small"; the next-best opportunity inside the firm would yield a net profit amounting to more than the market rate. If this is the case, then cash for the firm's investment, or subsequent receipts flowing from it, could be invested at that higher rate. If that higher rate is 8 per cent, $1.00 reinvested in 1956 is worth $1.47 in five years' time, and $1.00 that is anticipated in 1961 is equivalent to $0.68 in 1956. It appears, at first glance, that the firm would be well advised to discount all streams at 8 per cent to make sure that less lucrative investments are not undertaken. If one is to get the most out of his resources, he should always put them to their most productive uses.

But what if the firm is able to set up ventures (businesses, projects, investments) in 1956, resell them after construction, and set up some more, always keeping one eye on the possibility of resale? The firm may improve its position in this way, and in these circumstances its concern is with the market's evaluation of its assets. And in the market place, where other opportunities for investment *are* reflected by prevailing market rates, the streams will be discounted at those rates. Hence, when the firm compares alternative investments, even with this "partial rationing" of capital, it will often want to know how the market would value them, and therefore to use the market rate for discounting. This situation should be referred to as partial rationing of capital because the firm or division does manage to get additional capital, to some extent, through the intermittent sale of assets. It is neither a case of pure capital rationing nor a case of budget adjustment by borrowing.

CAPITAL RATIONING: RESALE VALUE IRRELEVANT. In this section we shall begin to talk about investment choice in government as well as in a business firm. With "capital rationing" and no concern about the market's evaluation of new investments, an investor would have no reason to use the market rate for discounting. The investment budget might either fall short of, or go beyond, the point where the marginal yield equaled the market rate of interest. The usual view is that, in this situation, the discount rate should be the marginal rate of return, that is, *the yield that could be earned in the next-best opportunities open to the investor.* The reasoning is that, if the cash initially available for A and B, and also the net receipts that accrued later, could be invested in C at 10 per cent per annum, then $0.68 today is worth $1.00 five years hence, and $1.00 five years from now is worth only $0.68 today. In this situation, the "yield" (10 per cent in the case of investment C) means the project's "internal rate of return," which, as indicated before, is the rate of discount that makes the present value of the gain stream equal to the present value of the cost stream. And the yield that could be earned in the next-best alternative project is the "marginal internal rate of return."

In order to clarify this matter, let us look at a numerical example. Table 2B shows the anticipated costs and returns associated with Projects A and B. Although this exhibit is almost identical with Table 2, it is the marginal internal rate of return this time which is

TABLE 2B

Alternative Projects	Initial Investment	Net Receipts		Internal Rate	Present Value of Receipt Stream	
		Year 1	Year 2		3%	7%
A	$100	0	$115	7%	$108	$100
B	$100	$110	0	9%	$107	$103
C	Alternative investments which yield 7%					

7 per cent, and the market rate is assumed to be 3 per cent. The budget is fixed at $100, which will permit only one project to be undertaken. Again, mere inspection of the time streams does not reveal what the best policy would be. If the streams are discounted at the market rate of 3 per cent, A is preferable to B. If the streams are discounted

at the marginal rate of return, which is 7 per cent, B is preferable to A. Which is really the better investment?

Resale is ruled out. Let us look at the outcomes on the assumption that the net receipts from each investment will be reinvested as they become available. As in the earlier case, then, the alternatives that are really being considered are A plus the reinvestment of net receipts and B plus the reinvestment of its net-receipt stream. Table 2C (a duplicate of Table 2A) portrays the outcomes when reinvestment at 7 per cent is explicitly taken into account.

TABLE 2C

Alternative Projects	Investment to Beginning of Year 1	Value Obtainable by Various Dates	
		End of Year 1	End of Year 2
A + investment of net receipts	$100	—	$115
B + investment of net receipts	$100	$110	$117.70

Again investment B gives the firm more, in dollars and cents, at the end of the two-year period. Are we justified in concluding that B is to be preferred? We are—unless we depart from the constraints that shape this problem of choice or from the assumption that net receipts will be put to work at 7 per cent. Naturally, if we alter the

TABLE 2D

Alternative Projects	Investment	After Construction*	End of Year 1	End of Year 2
A + resale + reinvestment	$100	$108	$115.56	$123.65
A + reinvestment of net receipts	$100	—	—	$115.00
B + resale + reinvestment	$100	$107	$114.49	$122.50
B + reinvestment of net receipts	$100	—	$110	$117.70

* Projects could be sold at these prices after completion, i.e., at the beginning of Year 1, if the data on the project were made public.

constraints, the problem and the answer are affected. For instance, if the budget is not fixed, both A and B should be undertaken with a 3 per cent market rate of interest. Or, if resale is possible, the picture changes as shown in Table 2D, where A becomes the preferred investment. Finally, if the list of admissible alternatives is altered—if the electronics firm decides to consider investing in Persian oil refineries, or if the Bureau of Reclamation is instructed to consider building steel mills—obviously the problem and the answer are altered.

If we alter the assumption that net receipts will earn 7 per cent, the answer is also affected. In this example receipts *can* earn that rate if reinvested. If they are consumed, however, it is not clear what they are worth, because the proprietors or stockholders may have adjusted their consumption to the fact that extra personal savings can earn the market rate of 3 per cent. Such maladjustment between time preferences in consumption and the marginal rate of return in production is possible whenever capital rationing exists. In such a state of disequilibrium, the proprietors or stockholders may attach a particularly high value to receipts in a particular year or block of years (for consumption purposes, not for reinvestment). Again, then, it is clearly possible to devise a set of time preferences which nullifies the test "maximization of present worth when the streams are discounted at the marginal rate of return."

Nonetheless the test is appropriate if the following assumption is accepted: that, in this situation, net receipts are to be reinvested, not consumed. An alternative way of expressing this is to say that, regardless of possible inconsistencies with stockholders' time preferences, the objective is to be maximum yield *over the planning period*, i.e., maximum growth of asset values through the period. Such an assumption seems warranted. Most firms do not undertake investments with the intention of eating up the capital or of maximizing receipts in a particular block of years. They have in mind the reinvestment of receipts at least to the extent necessary to maintain the stock of capital. Nor are government agencies instructed to disinvest, use their budget for consumption, or maximize net output for the nation as of a particular block of years. It is true that neither a firm's investment committee nor a government agency knows just what its budget will be in future years—just how much of the firm's or the nation's resources will be devoted to that investment budget and how much to "consumption." That means that there is uncertainty about what future reinvestment opportunities will actually be and about how valuable funds will be for consumption purposes. But neither the procedures recommended here nor any other procedure could eliminate this uncertainty.

The position taken in this study, then, is that the firm's investment committee or the government agency should assume that the capital invested is not to be liquidated, that net receipts are to be reinvested, and that maximum return over the period under consideration is to be sought. In these circumstances the test should be maximum present worth for the given investment budget *when the streams are discounted at the marginal rate of return.*

It may be worth emphasizing that the use of the marginal *internal* rate of return as the discount rate rests on the assumption that it *is* the marginal rate that can be earned. If net receipts can be reinvested at the marginal internal rate, its use as the discount rate gives the right answers. If net receipts cannot in fact be reinvested at that rate (because of, say, institutional restraints), then that "internal" rate is not the marginal rate of return, and is no more relevant than the internal rate of return on Saturn. Also, as has been indicated, this marginal rate of return may differ from the market rate. If investment is pushed until no additional projects yield more than the market rate of interest, then the latter is the marginal rate. But if the allotted budget does not permit that much investment, the rate that could be earned in alternative ventures will be higher than the market rate. And if the budget provides for more than that amount of investment, the marginal internal rate of return will actually be lower than the market rate. In other words, capital rationing may provide "too large" as well as "too little" a budget.

Before going any further, let us ask whether or not this capital rationing case is widely applicable. It is probably not, so far as private firms are concerned. The circumstances in which their investment choices are made are more nearly those of "no capital rationing" or "capital rationing with resale possible." Hence firms should usually compare the present worths of alternative investments when the projected streams are discounted at the market rate. But the capital-rationing case does appear to be applicable to government agencies. Their budgets are determined on the basis of a host of considerations, the final decisions being made by Congress. There are understandable reasons for imposing fixed budgets on government agencies instead of providing funds for all projects which appear on the basis of the agency's analysis to yield the market rate. The limited list of alternatives is also realistic: there are understandable reasons for confining certain agencies to "water-resource investments," barring them from devoting their budgets to consumption or to the construction of textile mills.

Let us also ask, before proceeding, whether or not it really matters much what discount rate is used. After all, the differences between the outcomes shown in Tables 2A, 2B, and 2C appear to be trivial.

But the reason the differences are trivial is that these examples pertain to a time span of only two years. The examples were designed so as to make the calculations relatively simple and easy to check. In actual investment proposals, the amounts are much larger, the pertinent time spans are longer, and the outcomes are highly sensitive to discount rates. The case studies in Chapters 11 and 12 will bring these facts out sharply with respect to potential water-resource investments.

So far it must appear that one has to know the preferred set of investments before he can determine the marginal internal rate. How in practice can the preferred set and/or the marginal internal rate be determined? One method is to discount the streams of net benefits at various rates and find the discount rate at which the budget is exhausted by projects with a positive present worth, i.e., with gain streams whose present values exceed those of their cost streams.[6] The lower the rate used for discounting, the larger the amount of investment which is "economically justified"—that is, which has a positive present worth. Hence, at *some* rate of discount, the amount of "economically justified" investment is equal to the budget. This rate is the marginal internal rate of return, the rate that makes the marginal project have a zero present worth. These projects with positive present worths that exhaust the budget constitute the correct set, the one that yields the maximum present worth with the given investment budget when the streams are discounted at the marginal internal rate of return. The present worth of the set of ventures cannot be increased by shifting from any investment with a positive present worth to one that has a negative present worth.

These steps amount to constructing what is sometimes called a "schedule of the marginal efficiency of capital." This schedule shows the best set of investment projects for various budgets, and therefore for various marginal rates of return. By entering the schedule at the size of budget which is given, one can find the set of investments that is correct. It is important to observe that this procedure would have to cope with interdependent investments, including those that are mutually exclusive. At different discount rates, different sets of such investments would be appropriate. For example, imagine that projects A and B in Table 2B are mutually exclusive; at 7 per cent B should be undertaken, but at 3 per cent A (*not* both, for that is impossible) should be chosen. As a consequence, the schedule of correct investments at various discount rates would have to reflect the results of

[6] This procedure is described by A. Alchian in *Economic Replacement Policy,* (RAND Corporation, R-227, April 12, 1952) pp. 48–49, footnote.

"side calculations." Various combinations of projects would be evaluated at each discount rate; and the final set presented in the schedule would include, from a group of interdependent projects, only the combination that had the largest present worth *at that discount rate.* Of two mutually exclusive investments, only the one that had the greater present worth *at that discount rate* would be included. Thus at lower rates, the set of investments having positive present worth would not merely become larger by the inclusion of more ventures; the composition of the set would change simultaneously.

Similarly, it is important to see that this procedure should not and need not ignore increments in the size of projects. As noted earlier, the alternatives that are considered should include different scales of each project (a special case of mutually exclusive courses of action). In fact, the whole problem could be rephrased to read, not "Pick the best set of ventures" but "Choose the best size, from zero on up, of the various projects." If alternative sizes are not considered, the procedure yields a set of investments that can perhaps be vastly improved upon by reducing the scale of some ventures and increasing the scale of others.

Thus the preparation of such a schedule requires a great deal of preliminary work—specifically, a host of calculations to determine the best project size, and the best combination of interdependent projects, for each discount rate.[7]

CAPITAL RATIONING: AT WHAT LEVEL AND IN WHAT PERIODS? Although the above procedure is thorough in many respects—indeed it is thought of here as a "counsel of perfection"—it should be understood that the difficulties of suboptimization are not escaped. For the next-best project and the marginal rate of return depend upon the portion of the over-all problem which is broken out to be analyzed, that is, upon the portion of the firm and also the block of time that is being examined. For one thing, just what is the next-best project and the marginal internal rate of return depends upon the level of optimization. If only ventures open to the firm's Latin-American division are to be counted as admissible alternatives, the next-best project will

───────────

[7] It may be argued that one cannot draw up such a schedule of correct investment-sets at various discount rates independently of the market rate of interest, since a shift in the market rate would realign all prices and affect the cost-benefit estimates. This is true, and it means that in this schedule, as in any other, many things must be predicted to the best of one's ability and then fixed—market prices, the market rate of interest, climatic conditions, and numerous other features. The schedule will give good results only to the extent that these projections are correct.

turn out to be one sort of investment. If ventures open to all the divisions are counted as part of the problem, the next-best project may be a very different undertaking with a different internal rate of return.

For another thing, the proper marginal rate of return depends upon the alternatives that will be admissible in the future and hence upon the way in which capital will be rationed in future years. Part of the investment or net cash outgo will occur in periods other than the first year. What will be the budget, how stringently will capital be rationed, in those years, and hence what will then be the yield on the marginal project? But let us look still further ahead. Net receipts may occur many years hence. How will capital be rationed then, and what will be the next-best opportunity in which these net receipts can be invested? One way to tackle such difficulties is to impose specific constraints on future budgets.[8] Another possible path is to forget all about capital rationing and use a market rate of interest for discounting. A host of assumptions are possible—no capital rationing, fixed investment budget in the first period and ignorance about future budgets, fixed present value of the budget for the next five years, specific budget in each of the next two years, or a fixed budget in the first period and the same degree of capital rationing (same marginal internal rate of return) thereafter. Whatever assumption is adopted, it is going to be an abstraction from the real world. The important question is: What is the "best" abstraction to adopt if we seek to give practical and helpful advice to decision-makers? There is no single answer for all problems; and for the moment, we shall simply raise these questions and leave it at that, though in connection with the selection of water-resource projects, a position will be taken.

A Practicable Procedure

In order to implement the steps described earlier, what kind of exhibit would the analyst prepare for each project? Ideally he would show the present value of the cost-gain streams at a host of different discount rates. He would have to do this for a host of project sizes and, when ventures were otherwise interrelated, for numerous combinations of projects. In practice, the chore would have to be restricted in scope, because the improvement in decisions, if any, attributable to such complex exhibits would probably not be worth the analytical effort. But present values for a *few* project sizes and for a *few* combinations of interrelated ventures might be computed at a *few*

[8] L. J. Savage and J. H. Lorie, "Three Problems in Rationing Capital," *Journal of Business,* October, 1955, pp. 229–239.

discount rates. From this information, the correct set of projects for various budgets could be approximated.

Another Procedure: Ranking by Internal Rate of Return

Suppose, however, that the policy-makers say, "This is still too complex. Give us a means of ranking the projects so that we can go down the list as far as the budget will go. It doesn't matter if small errors are entailed. This ranking is the kind of information that we can digest." Let us see if this can be done. One possibility is simply to rank the projects according to their internal rates of return and then proceed down the list until the budget is exhausted. At first blush, it appears that this would point to the right set of investments without further ado. The internal rate of the first project not covered by the budget would be the "marginal internal rate of return"; if the net-benefit streams from all projects in the list were then discounted at this rate, all those with higher internal rates would have positive present worths, and would obviously be preferred to those with lower internal rates, which would have negative present worths. For larger budgets, one would proceed further down the list and encounter a different marginal internal rate. If projects above (or below) the marginal project were ranked according to their present worths, the ranking would shift as the different rates were used for discounting. But the shift in ranking would not matter if *all* the projects above the marginal project were undertaken and *all* the projects below the marginal project were excluded. It looks as though the procedure would indeed pick the correct set. Moreover, it would have the merit of eliminating the repeated calculation of each project's present worth at various discount rates.

Unfortunately, it is not this simple. We have forgotten about investments that are interrelated. The extreme case of interrelationships, mutually exclusive ventures, will serve to illustrate the point. Consider projects A, B, and C, which are described in Table 3, and suppose that A and B are mutually exclusive. Assume in this instance that the budget permits us to undertake two projects. If we merely rank them according to the internal rates of return, B and C appear to be the best investments. However, the rate of return on the next-best investment, D, is 3 per cent, which is then the marginal internal rate of return. If the net-benefit streams are discounted at that rate, A is a better project than B, and the correct set of projects is A plus C. If A and B were not mutually exclusive, *both* could be undertaken, and A and B would constitute the best pair of investments. In that circum-

TABLE 3

Alternative Projects	Initial Investment	Net Benefits		Internal Rate	Present Value if Net Benefits Discounted at Marginal Internal Rate (3%)
		Year 1	Year 2		
A	$100	0	$115	7%	$108
B	$100	$110	0	9%	$107
C	$100	$104	0	4%	$101
D	Alternative investments that yield 3%				

stance, a simple ranking by internal rates of return would point to the correct set. With the two projects being mutually exclusive, however, the ranking according to internal rates of return points to the wrong set. Moreover, in the real world, mutually exclusive projects—alternative sites, alternative ways of constructing projects—will and should be on our list for comparison. Indeed, if the projects refer to successively larger sizes of each proposal, as they should, many of the projects will be mutually exclusive.

How can these interrelated projects be handled? In the construction of the schedule of best project-sets at various discount rates, side calculations were used to choose the best project-size and combination of interrelated ventures, but in the end a *different* best-set of investments was presented for each discount rate. In the construction of a ranking, side calculations can be used again, but a single ranked list is supposed to be the final exhibit. (If a different list, ranked by internal rates of return, were presented for each discount rate, it would amount to the schedule previously described plus some unnecessary information, namely the ranking itself and the inclusion on each list of those projects to be rejected as well as those to be accepted.) If a single ranked list is to be produced, we must be prepared to accept rough results. If we are so prepared, the analytical task can be split into two parts: (1) The best project size and the best mix of interrelated measures can be selected by the use of a particular discount rate, one that is believed to be "about right" (in other words, close to the marginal internal rate of return which will emerge). (2) The ventures that remain in the competition[9] can be ranked on the basis

[9] Actually, there is another class of projects which would have to be treated in this manner—namely, projects which have cost and gain streams such that there is more than one internal rate of return. Savage and Lorie (*op. cit.*) have pointed out that in some circumstances the concept of the internal rate of return is ambiguous, because present worth may be zero at two or more discount rates. In order for this to happen, costs must exceed outlays in the final time period

of their internal rates of return. The higher-ranking projects can then be accepted until the budget is exhausted. This procedure is admittedly rough—it is far from a counsel of perfection—for there is danger that the project sizes and the combinations of interrelated projects will be wrong in terms of the marginal internal rate of return which does come out of the final selection. But if a ranking is to be made, the internal rate is an acceptable basis provided that interrelationships *are* properly taken care of "on the side," and provided that net receipts *can* be reinvested at that rate.[10] It might be noted, inciden-

---

or in a block of final time periods; it cannot happen, for instance, if investment costs are incurred in the first years and are followed only by net receipts. Now, operating costs ought not to exceed receipts in any terminal group of years; if they do, the proper policy is not to operate. Hence the later periods should be ones in which gains exceed operating costs. However, the project may involve a *contract* to incur a heavy cost, e.g., to pay a sum of money, to raze or perhaps restore a structure, in the final time period. Or the project may involve the physical destruction of some asset at the outset. In that case the value of the replaced or destroyed item is a cost of the project. This value is the worth of the receipt stream from the destroyed asset. And while this stream is sacrificed, i.e., the cost is incurred, at the time the old asset is destroyed, the worth of the stream must be calculated by discounting it. In other words, the cost must be calculated as though it were spread over future years, and thus it is conceivable that costs would in effect outweigh gains in a final block of time periods. Such cases, as indicated at the beginning of the footnote, would have to be handled by means of side calculations.

Note that these cases, unless they comprise most of the investment alternatives, cause difficulty only if investments are to be ranked. They do not ordinarily cause difficulty if a schedule of economic investments at different discount rates is to be utilized. Of course, if *all* of the investment alternatives are such cases, there is no way to determine a marginal rate of return. Without knowledge of the marginal return, one cannot readily see how much is sacrificed by making any investment or how much could be earned by reinvesting net receipts.

There is another situation in which such cases (i.e., projects having more than one internal rate of return) could conceivably prove awkward. Over certain ranges of the discount rate, their present worths actually decrease as the discount rate falls. As a result, it is conceivable that *more than one* set of investments with positive present worths at some discount rate will just exhaust the budget. However, this sort of coincidence—like that in which one must choose between two projects that turn out to be equally attractive—is hardly a major source of concern.

A final note: in case any reader wishes to pursue the technical aspects of the matter, such cases can cause Irving Fisher's rate of return over cost, as well as the internal rate of return, to be ambiguous.

[10] Strictly speaking, the ranking of any two investments, or any two sets of projects, according to their internal rates of return implies, if the ranking is to be correct, that the net receipt streams can be reinvested *perpetually* at the

tally, that the criterion would not be to maximize this rate of return, a ratio, with the scale of the budget allowed to vary; the rate of return would be a ranking device, the real test being "maximum present worth for the given investment budget with the marginal rate of return as the discount rate."

Ranking by Other Rates of Return

Streams of cost and gain are often compared by transforming them into equivalent constant annual flows, allowing for depreciation of all facilities, and comparing the ratios of annual profit to investment. In fact, firms and investors often prefer to think in terms of annual profits and percentages of profit on investment rather than in terms of, say, internal rates of return. Often the former will be equally helpful and more convenient; indeed, it is possible to calculate these profits and percentages so that the latter are identical with internal rates of return. The trouble is that annual gains, costs, and rates of profit on investment can be calculated in numerous ways, and some of these ways would lead to foolish rankings. These terms, unlike "present value" or "internal rate of return," are equivocal in meaning. In order to appreciate this difficulty, let us consider the methods of treating receipt and cost streams shown in Table 4.

TABLE 4

PRESENT VALUES AND ANNUAL PROFIT ON INVESTMENT

Year at End of Which Benefit or Cost Occurs					Present Value of Stream	Various Conceptions of Annual Receipts, Costs		
						Annual Equivalents of Present Values	Straight-line Annual Averages	Average Receipts in Operating Years, Amortized Cost
1	2	3	4	5	(5%)			
Receipts	$0	$20	$40	$60	$60	$149.06	$34.43	$36.00	$45.00
Costs	110	10	10	10	10	138.53	31.99	30.00	29.91
Annual Net Profit							2.44	6.00	15.09
Annual Rate of Profit on Investment							2.2%	5.5%	13.7%

The present values of the streams are unambiguous. To calculate them, a discount rate of 5 per cent is used in this instance. The present value of the cost stream consists of the sum of $110 discounted for 1 year, $10 discounted for 2 years, $10 discounted for

---

marginal internal rate. See A. Alchian, "The Rate of Interest, Fisher's Rate of Return Over Costs and Keynes' Internal Rate of Return," *American Economic Review,* December, 1955, p. 941.

3 years, and so on. The same procedure applied to the benefit stream yields its present value. The concepts of annual receipts and costs, however, are fuzzy enough to give rise to several interpretations. The "annual equivalents" of the present values are simply the latter amortized (with interest at 5 per cent) over the 5-year period. In other words, with respect to receipts, they are the annual payments that one would receive in order to collect an amount equivalent to the present value of the receipt stream. With respect to costs, they are the annual disbursements that one would make in order to pay an amount equivalent to the present value of the cost stream. The "straight-line annual averages," in the next column of the table, are simply the totals for the period (undiscounted) divided by the number of years in the period. "Average receipts in operating years" is the simple sum of receipts divided this time by the number of years after completion of the investment, and "amortized cost" is the simple annual operating cost ($10) plus the annual payment that would amortize the initial investment over the period ($19.91).

Such variations—they become somewhat startling when converted into rates of profit on investment, as shown in the bottom row—are not far-fetched. Some of the variants are fairly common and the ever-present possibility of divergent interpretations makes for a good deal of confusion.[11]

TREATMENT OF STREAMS IF GAIN (OR COST) IS IN PHYSICAL UNITS

The preceding discussion pertains to the treatment of streams that are measured in monetary units. Often, however, and particularly in the case of military problems, the gains cannot be measured in monetary units. It is hard to say how many dollars an extra sortie, or "victory" in a peripheral war, is worth. It is hard to say how great is the deterrence value, in dollars, of a stronger Strategic Air Command. Therefore costs and gains cannot both be measured in terms of dollars or any other common denominator. That being true, the maximization of gains minus costs is ruled out as a criterion, and probably the most satisfactory procedure is to "fix" either the gain or the cost in each set of calculations, measuring the gains in some physical unit. As noted earlier, the gain can be fixed as the achievement of a specified

---

[11] In the analysis of one of the water-resource measures discussed later, this ambiguity about *annual* value led to one benefit-cost ratio of 1.5 to 1 and another of 1.7 to 1 (future benefits being discounted in the former case).

task, and the criterion can be to carry out that mission at minimum cost; or the cost can be fixed, and the criterion can be to achieve the most gain (the nature of the achievement being defined but not fixed as to amount) at the given cost.

With this sort of criterion, the time dimension is just as important as ever. For instance, suppose that alternative defense systems are to be compared. Consider the case in which the criterion is to maximize our capability of preventing damage for a fixed cost or budget. It is necessary to define the nature of this gain though it is not fixed as to amount. And one must immediately ask: capability *as of what dates?* Maximize capability *when?* These questions are crucial ones and must be faced. One possible procedure is to examine higher-level aims, try to decide the dates at which this capability would be appropriate, and specify the time path as a "requirement" in defining the nature of this gain. In some cases, it may be possible to adopt a better procedure; to allow the time path to vary instead of specifying it, and to compare the values of different time paths that could be obtained. The comparison might be made by discounting[12] physical capabilities (rather than dollars) at the more distant dates, or it might be made subjectively by policy-makers on the basis of the analyst's exhibits. In a few extreme cases, time might be the only variable; that is, the cost might be fixed, and the task might also be fixed in all particulars except for the date of achievement. If it is reasonable to impose all these constraints, the test then is to achieve the task with the specified budget at the earliest possible date.

Time also enters into the cost side of this criterion. Future outlays have to be discounted in figuring out what can be bought with a fixed budget. A system which entails a million-dollar expenditure (and only that expenditure) five years from now costs less than a system which entails a million-dollar outlay today. The million dollars of resources today, because they can be productive in the interim, are worth more than the same resources five years later.

Let us look at the other case in which the gain is fixed as the execution of a specified task, and the criterion is to minimize the cost of achieving it. Here not only is the nature of the gain defined, but also a particular amount or level of accomplishment is specified.[13] A hypothetical example from industry will show how time has to be taken

---

[12] In some circumstances, it might be possible to derive a reasonable discount rate from evidence as to the value of capabilities at different times.

[13] If uncertainty were introduced, some "probability" of carrying out a particular job would have to be specified.

into account. Suppose a petroleum company is interested in different methods of storing gasoline. Assume that the analyst feels unable to trace out the precise impact of each storage method on sales and revenues, yet has some feeling for the required physical characteristics that should be maintained. Of course, the belief that these requirements are sensible must rest on some notion of their influence on sales, costs, and profits. But assume for the moment that the task of achieving these requirements is given, the criterion then being to pick the least-cost method of carrying it out. The point here is that again the time path is an essential aspect of both gain (the specified task) and cost. For the required physical characteristics simply *have* to involve time, e.g., maximum gum content of the gasoline after three months' storage and after six months' storage. As for costs, if some of the methods entail future outlays, they must be discounted in order to find out which *is* the minimum-cost pattern of outlays.

Thus in the type of analysis in which gain and cost cannot be expressed in terms of a common unit, time must usually be taken into account as follows. Future costs should be discounted, unless it is the budget which is to be fixed *and* unless costs are also to be fixed in each year rather than just in total. The time path of the task or achievement must usually be specified. To require this time path rather than to compare explicitly the worth of different paths that can be achieved is not ideal, but it is the best that can be done in many cases. Sometimes, however, the time path of the gain or achievement can (or must) be varied, comparison being made by discounting physical achievements in periods when they are less valuable or simply by the exercise of judgment.

Chapter 6

WHAT CAN BE DONE:
A RECAPITULATION

T HE QUESTIONS that have been raised are somewhat forbidding. So far as answers to them are concerned, it is natural for us to be modest, because after all we have so much to be modest about. Yet the outlook for quantitative analysis is not as bleak as this succession of methodological problems may possibly suggest. First, it should be remembered that these problems stem from the obstructionist nature of the real world, not from the tools of operations research. These unruly difficulties are present when choices are to be made, whether the decisions are to be based upon systematic analysis or upon irrelevant assertions. Analysis is an attempt to grapple with these difficulties, but it does not generate them. Second, despite these troublesome questions, careful quantitative analysis does in many instances lead to larger profits, greater military capability at the same cost, and better decisions by consumers. Like Fulton's steamboat, it shows promise, even though the obstacles are great and even though there are frequent breakdowns. Third, a number of suggestions which appear to be useful do emerge from a close inspection of these methodological problems. Some are almost like exhortations to face the problems and keep doing better. In fact one can go further than that: they *are* exhortations. However, most people look upon recognition of the difficulties as being at least more constructive than disregard of them.[1] Besides, there are other suggestions that are not mere admonitions and whose application can be more easily perceived.

These suggestions as to what can be done have appeared in bits and pieces in the preceding chapters. Many, if not all, are pertinent to

---

[1] Provided that awareness of these "headaches" does not paralyze us or completely divert us from the improvement of practical aids to decision-making.

cost-benefit analysis. They are summed up here for purposes of convenient reference, and are presented as though they were answers to the question, "What can be done about these difficulties?"

GENERAL CRITERION–DIFFICULTIES

1. Guard against particularly treacherous tests. One ubiquitous and untrustworthy candidate is the maximization of the ratio of gain (i.e., effectiveness) to cost.

2. Use the generally suitable form of criterion, the maximization of gain *minus* cost,[2] if both can be expressed in the same unit. If they cannot be so expressed, generally suitable forms are maximum gain for a specified cost or minimum cost of achieving a specified gain. Of course, these will usually be partial tests if intangibles or appreciable uncertainties about the outcomes are present. Also, it should go without saying that the adoption of these general forms does not *insure* that the test will be an appropriate one.

3. Examine the criterion for consistency with higher-level criteria. Is the test the achievement at minimum cost of some traditional intuited "requirement"? Is the test the maximum achievement of a defined task for an uncritically chosen budget? Does the criterion ignore spillover effects? It will be necessary at least to ponder about higher-level tasks that might constitute the objectives in comparisons of larger systems.

4. Guard against tests which involve erroneous concepts of cost or gain, such as treatment of valuable inputs as though they were free goods, or the inclusion of historical costs.

THE APPROPRIATE ALTERNATIVES

1. Decide on the scope of the systems to be compared in conjunction with the selection of the criterion. Consciously weigh the apparent disadvantages and advantages of expanding the context.

2. Give careful attention to the devising of the alternative courses of action to be compared. Sound models and criteria will not result in picking out good policies if only poor ones are considered. In this connection, different sizes of each project and different mixes of policies or project features should not be overlooked.

3. Watch out for possible effects of adopting one policy upon the costs or gains from other policies, especially if they are to be ranked.

[2] Wherever the terms "gain" and "cost" appear, they refer to the extra or incremental amounts attributable to the course of action that is being considered.

INTANGIBLES

1. Explore the possibilities of measuring effects which seem at first glance to be intangibles—that is, of measuring those effects in the same units of gain or cost used for the principal estimates.

2. In some special cases, show the value of the intangibles that would be implied by preference for one course of action over another.

3. Try to devise indicators of the magnitude and nature of major intangibles, using units of measure other than those adopted for the principal estimates.

UNCERTAINTY

1. If practicable, show ranges of outcomes to which roughly the same degree of confidence can be attached. Explore this possibility even if these ranges must be subjective estimates.

2. If the above procedure is not practicable, present, as clues to the variability of outcomes, the results as they would be if the task or budget were altered or if certain relevant contingencies occurred.

3. If multiple results are not shown, at least describe and emphasize any major contingencies that are on the horizon and that would substantially affect the outcomes. Estimate the cost of insuring against the more important unfavorable contingencies.

4. Use Monte Carlo techniques to make repeated calculations which reflect the chance element in various events, if a comparatively detailed model seems advisable and if other types of uncertainty do not dominate the picture.

5. Look for "dominance"—that situation in which the same course of action is best in all "relevant" circumstances (i.e., with the occurrence of major contingencies or modification of the task or budget). This may not be a hopeless search if analysts redesign promising courses of action, as they often should, during the analysis.

TIME STREAMS

1. If gains and costs can both be measured in monetary units, discount the streams to their present values and choose the set of investments that yields maximum present worth for the investment budget. If there is no capital rationing or if resale value is relevant, the market rate of interest should be used for discounting. If there is

capital rationing and resale is out of the question, the marginal internal rate of return should be used. In practice, this rate and simultaneously the correct set of investments can be approximated by finding the best project sizes and the best combination of interrelated ventures at several discount rates; by finding, next, the sets of projects that yield positive present worths at those several discount rates; by determining, finally, the set that exhausts the given investment budget. That set is the preferred one, and that discount rate is the marginal internal rate of return.

A less ambitious approach, bound to give rough results, must be adopted if a single ranked list is to be exhibited. In this procedure, one step is to choose the best project size and best mix of interrelated investments by using a plausible discount rate, one that is expected to be close to the marginal internal rate of return. The second step is, with the interrelationships taken care of on the side, to rank the remaining ventures according to their internal rates of return. The correct set comprises those projects which the budget can accommodate, if one proceeds straight down the list. If the cost and gain streams are discounted at the internal rate of the next-best venture, the projects chosen will have positive present worths, and the ones rejected will have zero or negative present worths.

Ranking by means of other rates of return, such as annual profits as a percentage of investment, is generally to be avoided, because several of the ways in which annual rates of return may be defined can lead to an incorrect selection.

2. If gains and costs cannot be expressed in the same unit, the best that can be done usually is to specify the time path of the task as a "requirement" and to discount the cost stream. In some cases, it may be possible to discount physical achievements in time periods when they are less valuable, and thus compare the worth of different time paths. In other cases, it may be best to show what can be achieved in different time periods and leave the comparison to the judgment of recommenders or decision-makers.

INTERPRETATION

Consider the nature of the criterion and the limitations of piecemeal analysis when drawing conclusions from analyses. These considerations may influence the content of such conclusions or the confidence with which they are held. For instance, some studies have found a course of action to be "best" on the average, but have pointed out that, because it entailed an appreciable chance of utter failure, this course of action was probably the worst one; in other words, the limitations of the criterion, where uncertainty was a vital consideration, were explicitly taken into account in interpreting the results.

Part 3

Special Problems
in the Analysis
of Water-Resource Projects

Chapter 7

CRITERIA IN THE SELECTION OF WATER-RESOURCE PROJECTS

W<small>E SHALL TURN NOW</small> from the methodological difficulties that plague analysis in general to those which afflict the analysis of water-resource projects in particular. We will be concerned, not with the comparison of possible actions from the viewpoint of a firm, an individual, or a military service, but rather with the analysis of an investment choice from the standpoint of the nation. The first question to be taken up is: what is the appropriate criterion by means of which to select preferred water-resource projects, and, for that matter, to *help* select the water-resources budget? In attempting to answer this question we shall, following one of the precepts set forth earlier, inquire into the relationship between possible criteria and higher-level aims. This must be done not only in devising the form of the criterion (the way in which gains should be related to costs) but also in choosing the right concepts of gain and cost.

THE CONCEPTS OF COST AND GAIN IN VIEW OF HIGHER-LEVEL AIMS

By and large, so far as the private sector of the economy is concerned, market prices of outputs are accepted in this study as measures of the value of those outputs to the whole economy. Likewise, the market prices of inputs are accepted, for the most part, as the measure of their cost, that is, as a measure of the value of alternative products which those inputs could produce.

Acceptance of these prices as appropriate measures of value and cost to the economy as a whole is implicit in most of our institutional arrangements, in our approval of a competitive economy in which the preferences of all consumers help allocate resources among uses. We place the burden of proof upon those who support a different means of valuation. Moreover, there is a logical basis for identifying market prices of outputs with their value to the nation and market prices of inputs with their cost to the nation. Such prices, by guiding the choices of firms and individuals, do lead to "maximum production" or "efficiency" from the viewpoint of the whole economy, if certain conditions are fulfilled (for example, the existence of a high degree of competition). For those who wish to examine it, the rationale for using market prices is summarized in an Appendix to this chapter. As explained there, the foregoing terms refer to maximum production or efficiency *in a restricted sense,* namely, efficiency for a particular distribution of wealth.

Turning now to the government sector, we cannot feel as confident. In government activities, whether or not prices generated by the market mechanism should be used to value outputs and inputs is a more complicated question. The answer depends upon the ultimate aims which lead to government activity in each sphere. Why do "the people," through their government, intervene at all in such areas as flood control, irrigation, and water pollution? Perhaps the reason is that they would not, under any circumstances, want prices to regulate the output of flood-control or irrigation services, just as most people would not want free markets to regulate the output and nature of court decisions. If that is the situation—if they dislike the performance of the price mechanism in this sphere—it is hardly appropriate to simulate its results, even in part, by the use of market prices.

In exploring the aims underlying government action, we must expect only clues, not full revelation. There is always room for debate about ultimate values, even in the form of a list of aspirations.[1] As for individuals, who among us has not pondered over his "real" aims? To avoid any metaphysical discussion, though, consider a concrete incident which brings out the point. Some time ago, Parker Pen received an order from India for 3,000 pen tops. This may sound like a foolish sort of purchase. But if you get the Indians' slant on this

---

[1] It was stated earlier that a mere listing of goals or ultimate aims gives scant aid in choosing the best course of action. A list of aspirations tells us nothing about their relative values, about how much of one should be given up for some of another. However, when proximate criteria of the best action are selected, they should be consistent with higher-level criteria and finally with such a list of the things that it would be nice to have. We don't want lower-level tests to imply that some things are nice when in fact they are horrid. Or that some things are horrid when we really believe them to be nice.

matter, that is, see their real aims, it makes much more sense. "In that country, it's a mark of caste distinction to carry fountain pens. But natives who can't afford the full pen buy just the tops."[2]

Even the ultimate aims of business firms may be difficult to perceive. They may include large expected profits, expansion, jobs for relatives, being in a particular location, and possibly a confusing sort of catch-all, "contributing to community welfare." There is far greater confusion, however, about the ultimate aims of government. Consider a highly simplified picture of the governing process. Executive Departments propose programs, Congressmen propose bills, then Congressional Committees modify and accept or reject these proposals; next, the two houses of Congress modify and accept or reject the Committee's proposals; and periodically a majority of the voters accept or reject each legislator and official on the basis of his full campaign—his promises and/or performance as a whole. These actions do tell us something about ultimate aims but what do they tell, and whose aims are being revealed? Even within a small committee, it is not easy to discover the group's basic values. This is suggested, in a lighter vein, by one of Lichty's cartoons, in which a committee chaired by Senator Snort has been comparing alternative salary structures for the Senate. Says the Senator: "Granted that higher salaries would attract men of higher caliber, gentlemen . . . but do we want every Tom, Dick, and Harry running against us?"[3]

Nonetheless, though ultimate aims cannot be fully and clearly unveiled, we must at least examine several possible reasons for government intervention in water-resource development. One explanation is that we wish to encourage the "small" farmer, to increase the number of 160-acre farms. Originally it was intended that the benefits of irrigation projects should go to holders of such farms. In recent years, however, this aim has been relaxed.[4] Another fact which reduces the plausibility of this explanation is our attitude in other connections: we do little more than pay lip service to the "family-size farm" in general agricultural policy.

A second possible explanation is sheer megalomania, a desire to increase the scope of government activity, which is given at least tacit approval by the voters. To alter Professor Schumpeter's phrase

[2] *The Wall Street Journal,* December 9, 1954, p. 1. The purchase may still seem unwise if you probe further and question whether or not people *ought* to have such aims.

[3] "Grin and Bear It" by Lichty, *Los Angeles Times,* February 2, 1954, courtesy of George Lichty—Chicago Sun-Times Syndicate.

[4] See Chapter 12 on the Santa Maria Project.

slightly, perhaps we simply prefer government-baked bread even if it has mice in it. However, at some point in the growth of government, the preferences of the majority are surely the contrary, namely, that it would be nice to have smaller government, other things being the same. In fact, it seems likely that most persons do not like big government per se but accept it for the sake of other aims.

A third possible reason for government intervention in water-resource investment is that we wish to disperse agriculture and related activities. In support of this position, we note that dispersal for defense was recently stated as a reason for constructing the Upper Colorado River Basin Project. But in opposition, we see that flood-control measures seek to protect and encourage existing concentrations. Nonetheless, while there is no consistent effort to stimulate dispersal for purposes of defense, it is fairly clear that one aim is to influence the locational pattern in *some* way. The majority of most Congresses and apparently the majority of the people attach a positive value to something called "balanced development." As a legitimate aim, however, this is not altogether satisfying. Why should we struggle to be equitable in the treatment, not of different persons, but of different acreages and watersheds? Do we really wish to compensate for such "injustices" as the lack of heat in Alaska or of rain in Death Valley?

Although such explanations of the government's water-resource activities are no doubt partially correct, past history and Congressional hearings do not suggest that they constitute the whole reason for such undertakings. (Nor do they constitute "good" reason, in the opinion of many persons.) A final explanation, the one on which the case for cost-benefit rests, is that government gets into these ventures largely in order to affect the outputs of goods and services that can be priced. These outputs are not left to private enterprise mainly because a private firm would not feel the full cost or gain from a water-resource investment and therefore would not be moved to take appropriate action. For instance, if a farmer installed gully plugs to reduce soil erosion and flood dangers, much of the benefit would go to other persons, yet it might be impossible for the farmer to charge them for his service. If a firm built a dam for flood control, it would be difficult to identify the beneficiaries precisely enough to sell the flood protection to them even if all the legal complications could be solved. Of course, some discrepancy between gain to the firm that acts and the total gain results from *any* action, but in connection with water-resource measures, the discrepancy is deemed both serious and capable of being partly eliminated through government construction of such projects. (Public ownership and operation of such facilities is not, of course, the only possible form of government action, but it is the type of policy which has often evolved.)

Another reason for not leaving these ventures entirely to private enterprise is often mentioned. Under special circumstances, it is argued, the government may be able to produce a product cheaper than can a private firm. If it is going to build a dam for one purpose, say flood control, it may be able to add extra features and storage capacity cheaply and produce irrigation services or power at a lower cost than would otherwise be possible.[5] But this comes back to the previous justification of government projects; private firms could build multi-purpose dams also, if they could sell flood control to the beneficiaries. Sometimes, to cite another reason, it is said that government has to carry out these water-resource projects because private capital is not available in the necessary quantities. But this, too, comes back to the other point, because private capital has sometimes been collected in huge amounts when ventures have been sufficiently attractive.

In summary, the reasons for government intervention in water-resource development do *not* make cost-benefit estimates irrelevant to the selection of projects. The government is interested mainly in something akin to the market values of projects' outputs. Our concern in such projects is not chiefly with outputs like justice, which cannot be vended to individuals or valued at market prices. Hence, it is urged here that it does make sense to look at cost-benefit estimates in which prices that would apply in the private sector of the economy are extensively used.

THE FORM OF THE CRITERION: BENEFIT-COST RATIOS

As mentioned earlier, the traditional test of water-resource projects has been the ratio of benefits to costs. The rule is not to maximize the ratio, or even to rank projects according to benefit-cost ratios, but is simply to exclude projects with ratios that are less than unity. In practice, however, projects with the higher ratios are inevitably re-

[5] The economies of multi-purpose dams can easily be exaggerated, however, because the same storage capacity will not serve competing purposes: if the water is pumped into irrigable lands, it cannot be sent through the penstocks to generate power, and if it is stored for either irrigation or power, the space cannot be used for flood control.

garded as preferable to those with lower ratios (apart from intangible considerations).[6] The number of projects with relatively high ratios influences the size of the budget, and the ranking of projects according to the benefit-cost ratio helps determine the particular measures to be undertaken with a given budget. Some examples of benefit-cost ratios may help make it clear that they *are* computed and used. A 1.19 relationship was estimated for a proposal to improve the navigable portion of the Hackensack River. This compares with such ratios as 3.58 for channel improvement in Rice Creek, Florida, and 0.06 for stone dikes near the junction of Pantego Creek and Pungo River in North Carolina.[7]

Ratio of Annual Benefits to Annual Costs

In estimating these numbers, the preliminary steps are to spread the installation costs over time, converting them to "annual costs"; to add in average annual operating costs; and to estimate the value of the projects' average annual output (annual outputs multiplied by their "prices" per unit). The streams are often discounted so as to determine the present value of costs, the present value of benefits, and the "annual equivalents" of those present values. Whatever method is used for handling the time streams, the final step is to compute the ratio of annual benefits to annual costs. Details of sample analyses and possible improvements in estimating procedures will be taken up later. The question here is: what are the limitations on this *form* of criterion?

That something is wrong with this test can be shown most clearly by means of numerical illustrations. Let us consider two hypothetical projects, A and B. For the sake of convenience, the calculations will be greatly oversimplified. The facts to be assumed are presented in Table 5. Each project requires an investment of $10 million, to be written off in 10 years. Project A has operating costs of $4 million, annual depreciation of $1 million,[8] total annual costs of $5 million, and total annual benefits of $15 million. Hence the ratio of annual benefits to annual costs is 15 to 5, or 3 to 1. Project B has no operating costs,[9]

---

[6] For example, the particular reservoir recommended in the Santa Maria Project was the one with the highest benefit-cost ratio (see Chapter 12).

[7] *Economic Evaluation of Federal Water Resource Development Projects*, pp. 22–29.

[8] As mentioned already, the assumptions are extreme, and the calculations oversimplified, in order to make the point with a very simple example.

[9] See Footnote 8.

TABLE 5

CRITERION FOR RANKING TWO PROJECTS
(Amounts in millions of dollars)

		A	B
Investment		$10	$10
Annual Benefits		15	5
Annual Costs			
Operating	4		0
Depreciation	1		1
Total		5	1
Ratio of Benefit to Cost (Annual)		3/1	5/1

annual depreciation of $1 million, total annual costs therefore of $1 million, and total annual benefits of $5 million. Therefore the ratio is 5 to 1.

Suppose there is capital rationing, and only one project can be undertaken. According to current practice, B is presumably to be recommended because its ratio is higher. Yet its net "profit" over the period is less than that yielded by A as is shown in Table 6. (Or, to use a more precise concept, B's internal rate of return, about 49 per cent, is lower than A's, which is approximately 110 per cent.)[10]

TABLE 6

NET "PROFITS" FROM THE TWO PROJECTS

	A	B
Annual Benefits	$15	$ 5
Annual Costs	−5	−1
Net Profit Each Year	10	4
Net Profit Over Life of Project (10 Years)	100	40

Project A is clearly more profitable, and is surely the better investment. The benefit-cost ratio is simply the wrong test. What it shows is the relationship between *total* receipts and *total* outlays under each project. Let us assume for a moment that these are ventures under consideration by a businessman, in which case "benefits" would bear the label "receipts." If the businessman looked at the ratio of

[10] It is assumed for the moment that benefits are the same thing as cash receipts to the decision-making unit. The situation in which operating costs are matched by benefits to someone but not by receipts to the Treasury will be taken up later.

receipts to expenses, what would he conclude? Probably that anyone would be foolish to undertake Project A—say a venture in the grocery business, or in some sort of retail trade—because the annual turnover or volume of trade is comparatively high and the receipt-cost ratio, consequently, is comparatively low. It is fortunate that investors and businessmen do not think in this fashion too much of the time, for otherwise investment might flow largely into the "low-turnover" industries, which would be detrimental to the entrepreneurs and to the rest of us as well. What ultimately matters is not the ratio of gross sales to expenses or the rate of return on sales. If a venture promises annual sales of $102 million and annual expense of $100 million (2 per cent on sales), it may still be anything from a bonanza to a dud. What matters is the profit on investment or, more precisely, the prospective change in present worth.

Similarly, the most significant test in public investment, wherever measurable benefits and costs are important, is surely not the ratio of gross benefits to total costs.[11] The only thing revealed by that ratio is whether or not *some* net return can be expected. It provides little basis for doing what governmental agencies must usually do, that is, judge the relative merits of projects whose ratios are greater (or less) than

[11] For a different view, see the unpublished dissertation by Otto Eckstein, "Benefits and Costs, Studies in the Economics of Public Works Evaluation," Harvard University, Cambridge, Massachusetts, April, 1955, pp. 61–96. He reaches the conclusion that the benefit-cost ratio is an appropriate criterion ". . . for certain kinds of investment decisions"—that is, for choosing among projects that do not differ greatly in "capital intensity" or riskiness (*Ibid.*, p. 78). In that case, to use the terminology of the present study, the problem would be restricted to choosing among projects that have similar "turnover" and risks.

But this restriction raises two major questions: (1) How similar does turnover have to be in order for the benefit-cost ratio to be a good criterion? The only way to answer this query is to introduce a better criterion. Presumably turnover must be similar enough for the benefit-cost ratio to point to the same set of investments that would be indicated by a better criterion. (2) If one uses the benefit-cost ratio only in comparing projects with sufficiently similar turnover, it can point to the same projects that would be selected by applying the criterion recommended here. But the projects compared would be only a small fraction of the water-resource investments open to the agencies. How are the majority of the projects to be compared?

Thus, the use of cost-benefit measurements is considerably restricted if the benefit-cost ratio is the test. It can properly be applied only in the comparison of "similar" projects. As Dr. Eckstein recognizes, its validity is suspect when its use is extended beyond these cases. The position in the present study is that the ratio test is undesirable because its use might be so extended by the uncritical, and because cost-benefit measurements, while they can *never* serve as a definitive criterion, can often yield relevant information—if not expressed as a ratio—for the comparison of "dissimilar" investments.

unity. If the conventional benefit-cost ratio is used for this purpose, a project that has high gross returns and operating costs will be at a relative disadvantage, whatever its potential contribution to net worth. This may seem to be an elementary sort of error. It is stressed here because this is the error that is being made whenever ratios of sales to expenses (i.e., benefits to costs) are used as criteria by Congress, departments, or agencies within departments.

Ratio of Present Values

Perhaps it is felt that the foregoing example is too simple, that everything would turn out all right if the illustration were less extreme and if the time streams were properly discounted to their present values. In that case consider the more complicated calculations shown in Table 7.

TABLE 7
BENEFIT-COST RATIOS AS CRITERIA

	Project A		Project B	
Investment*		$100,000		$100,000
Each year's out-of-pocket expense†		50,000		5,000
Each year's benefit		70,000		20,000
Present value of 20-year cost stream—discounted at 5 per cent				
Initial investment	$100,000‡		$100,000‡	
Recurring costs	623,000	723,000	62,300	162,300
Present value of 20-year benefit stream—discounted at 5 per cent		872,200		249,200
Ratio of present value of benefits to present value of costs		1.21		1.54
Mean annual costs§				
[$100,000+(20×5,000)]÷[20]†		—		10,000
[$100,000+(20×50,000)]÷[20]		55,000		—
Mean annual benefits‡		70,000		20,000
Ratio of mean annual benefits to mean annual costs		1.27		2.00
Increase in present worth†				
(Present value of benefits minus present value of costs)		149,200		86,900

* Investment is assumed to be in plant. However, examples in which part of the investment is in working capital lead to the same kind of demonstration.

† Interest is taken care of by the use of present values.

‡ Both procedures "allow for depreciation" by counting initial investment in project cost.

§ This method of calculating "annual values" is not correct procedure, as it gives future benefits and costs the same weight as initial benefits and costs; the calculation is shown here because the method is often used.

In this illustration, each project requires an investment of $100,000. We must choose between them because our investment budget is only $100,000. Project A would call for recurring expenses of $50,000 per annum and would bring in benefits amounting to $70,000 each year. Project B would call for recurring expenses of $5,000 per annum and would yield annual benefits of $20,000. Let us calculate the benefit-cost ratio and also the absolute increment in present worth under each of the two projects.

Assume that the discount rate is 5 per cent and that the facilities wear out completely in 20 years. For Project A, the ratio of the present value turns out to be 1.21, while for Project B, it is 1.54. For purposes of camparison, the ratios of mean annual benefits to mean annual costs are also shown, and they give the impression that B has a still greater advantage over A. Yet Project A would increase our present worth nearly twice as much as Project B. (Or, as will be seen in Table 10, A's internal rate of return exceeds that of B.) The trouble here does not lie in the failure to discount the time streams properly; it lies in the fact that this ratio is comparable to sales as a percentage of expenses.[12]

Lack of Uniformity

If the reader is not convinced that the ratio of benefits to costs is inherently an incorrect criterion, it may be instructive to see how this type of ratio behaves when the benefit stream is not gross, but is net of varying amounts of the cost stream. Let us look at Project A, mentioned above. As before, the analysis may present gross benefits and costs in full ($70,000 and $50,000 per annum, respectively). This procedure leads to the modest benefit-cost ratios shown in the first column of Table 8. Alternatively, the analysis may be in terms of benefits that are partially net. For example, costs amounting to $47,500 may be deducted from the $70,000 figure, leaving benefits of only $22,500 and expenses of only $2,500. As shown in the Table, this procedure leads to benefit-cost ratios that are almost twice as large. And the ratio of mean annual benefits to mean annual costs rises from 1.27 to 3.00, the two ratios pertaining to precisely the same project.

Although few, if any, benefit estimates exhibit such extreme differences in the "degree of grossness," most of them do differ to a less

---

[12] A more technical discussion of this type of ratio as a criterion is presented by Friedrich and Vera Lutz, *The Theory of Investment of the Firm* (Princeton: Princeton University Press, 1951), pp. 16–24.

TABLE 8

BENEFIT-COST RATIOS AND "DEGREE OF GROSSNESS"*

	Project A (using gross benefits as in Table 7)		Project A (counting most benefits as net of expenses)	
Investment		$100,000		$100,000
Each year's out-of-pocket expense		50,000		2,500
Each year's benefits		70,000		22,500
Present value of 20-year cost stream				
Initial investment	$100,000		$100,000	
Recurring costs	623,000	723,000	31,150	131,150
Present value of 20-year benefit stream		872,200		280,350
Ratio of present value of benefits to present value of costs		1.21		2.14
Mean annual costs				
[$100,000+(20×50,000)]+[20]		55,000		
[$100,000+(20×2,500)]+[20]				7,500
Mean annual benefits		70,000		22,500
Ratio of mean annual benefits to mean annual costs		1.27		3.00
Increase in present worth (Present value of benefits minus present value of costs)		149,200		149,200

* Footnotes in Table 7 also apply to this Table.

extreme, yet significant, degree. (For an example of an estimate of benefits that is partly net, see the case study on the Green River Watershed in Chapter 11.) This lack of uniformity is not the result of a deliberate attempt to put some projects in a more (or less) favorable light than that in which they would otherwise appear. Indeed, in this situation, lack of uniformity is hardly something to be deplored or rectified. For what *is* the "fair" and correct way to arrive at an incorrect criterion?

WHAT COSTS ARE COVERED BY THE GIVEN BUDGET?

The Source of Error in the Benefit-Cost Ratio

If the benefit-cost ratio has little meaning, why is this so? We found earlier that ratios were treacherous, because they revealed nothing about the absolute scale of gains or costs. Could they not be used, however, to rank alternatives when the scale is fixed (via a given budget in the case of water-resource measures)? Thus if we have a budget of $200 to be allocated among A, B, and C, each costing $100, the maximization of the over-all gain-cost ratio should lead to the same result as the maximization of absolute gains from the fixed budget. Moreover, the maximum over-all gain-cost ratio can be achieved by devoting the budget to those projects with the highest individual gain-cost ratios.[13] If A returns $120, B $130, and C $140, we ought to buy C and B, which have the highest and next-highest ratios (1.4 to 1 and 1.3 to 1) and yield the biggest absolute gain that can be got for our $200.

In order for this to be true, however, *the denominators of the ratios must be those costs to which the given budget is to be devoted.* Note what happens in benefit-cost analysis. Presumably we think initially of the allocation of an investment budget. But the costs of individual projects may include not only investment costs that would be part of the specified budget but also future operating expenses. In that case, the denominators of the ratios are costs that have little relation to the specified budget. A "fixed scale of operations" becomes very elusive, and the ratios of benefit to cost lose their significance.

What Investment Budget Covering What Costs?

Should we turn to a total-cost budget embracing operating expenses for future periods? No, the problem, for either a government agency or a businessman, is not really the allocation of such a budget. The funds to be allocated need not cover operating expenses that are matched by receipts. The problem is rather the allocation of investment funds, that is, of resources which must be brought to these ventures from outside because the resources are not made available up to that time by income from the ventures themselves. But in government projects, since benefits are not always matched by cash income *to the agency,* when do the gains make the outgo available? Ought the investment budget refer to all funds which must be brought to these ventures by, say, the Bureau of Reclamation because they are not provided by receipts *to the Bureau?* Or to funds which must be brought to these projects initially because they are not covered by benefits to *anyone?* (Note that in neither case would the budget provide for *all* operating expenses, or a random portion of operating expenses, which are elements in the denominator of the conventional benefit-cost ratio.)

Suppose we say that the Bureau's budget is the one to be allocated

---

[13] Some reshuffling may be required when the "last" project more than exhausts the budget.

and the costs to be covered are its own outlays not matched by receipts to the Bureau itself. For this given budget, we choose projects that provide the greatest total national benefit. What kind of project does this test favor? It probably favors ventures that involve relatively large investments by other government agencies. This view of the investment budget is too narrow, leaving important segments of investment cost free to vary. Congress should surely take a broader view of water-resource development.

Perhaps officials should think of a Federal water-resources budget, the costs to be covered being total Federal outlays not matched by receipts to the Federal Treasury. In that case, the budget is essentially the combined water-resource budgets of the Bureau of Reclamation, Department of Agriculture, and the Corps of Engineers; the investment costs to be covered include only the Federal outlays. What kind of projects are favored by this criterion? It tends to favor undertakings that involve relatively large investments by State-local-private groups and relatively small investments by the Federal government.[14] This is a matter of some consequence, because the scale of the operation cannot be allowed to vary willy-nilly in the process of selecting the right set of projects. And in order to fix the scale (the budget, in this discussion), total investment costs of the right set should add up to the budgeted amount.

Again, it seems preferable to adopt a broader viewpoint. The position taken in this study is that we should think in terms of an over-all or national water-resources budget. The costs to be covered by such a budget are outgoes in excess of *benefits*, i.e., receipts to the nation, in any period. (These excesses turn out in most cases to be mainly the initial construction costs.) To repeat, the problem is considered here from a national point of view. The investment budget to be allocated embraces Federal-State-local-private investment in water-resource development. Benefits to whomsoever they may accrue are treated as receipts,[15] and the costs to be covered by this budget are outlays not matched by such receipts. As a consequence, when the present worths of projects are calculated at several discount rates

---

[14] As a corollary, it may favor projects whose benefits take the form of early receipts *to the Treasury,* reducing the required Federal investment in comparison with projects whose benefits accrue in some other way.

[15] It might be noted now that ranking projects by internal rates of return, which will be taken up later, appears to be relevant only if this is the budget being allocated. Or, with reference to private firms, ranking by internal rates of return seems useful only if the budget being allocated is supposed to cover the excesses (in various periods) of expenses over receipts.

in order to prepare a schedule of appropriate investments for different budgets, those present worths are based on cost and benefit streams in total.

The validity of this position rests on a fairly optimistic view of Congress's approach to the problem, namely, that Congress will deliberate about the allocation of an over-all water-resources budget. If Congress and other officials think only of allocating each agency's budget separately, then the costs to be covered should be each agency's outlays minus its receipts (which would be considerably more than construction outlays). With this "second-best" procedure, the test should be maximum "national benefits *minus other agencies' costs and all state-local-private costs"*—for each agency's budget. In the present study, however, the problem will be viewed as the allocation of an over-all water-resources budget.

One implication might be noted. Many of these benefits do not take the form of receipts to the government, since they are never collected from the beneficiaries of water-resource projects. These hypothetical receipts, therefore, are not necessarily available for reinvestment in water-resource programs. Are we plainly wrong in assuming net receipts to be reinvested at the marginal rate of return (as argued in Chapter 5)? No, the government will probably continue to collect taxes on the general public equal to (or greater than) these hypothetical receipts and invest them in water-resource programs. Each agency will depend on Congress instead of receipts for most of its budget. Consequently, the budgetary constraints, the degrees of capital rationing, that each agency faces in future periods may be less certain. The amounts that will be available for new projects and hence the marginal rates of return may be less certain. But the situation is not really altered much. Far too little is known anyway about future limitations to permit using specific budgetary constraints in each of several years. About the best that can be done is to assume that the degree of capital rationing and the outlook for investment opportunities will continue to be much the same in future years.

THE "RIGHT" CRITERION IN THE COMPARISON OF PROJECTS

In view of the preceding discussion, it becomes even more apparent that no single test can point clearly to the set of projects that is optimal. The relevance of intangibles and the case for showing more than one outcome in order to reflect uncertainty were indicated earlier. Now a further limitation on a single test has been elaborated: namely, that it is not clear just what and whose budget is really being allocated. In these circumstances, any criterion must be regarded as only a partial one. But one of the most significant partial tests—presented here as the "right" criterion of the economically efficient set of investments—is the maximization of present worth for a given investment budget, when the streams are discounted at the marginal internal rate of return.[16] The basic idea is to keep high-valued capital from being put to low-valued uses. Under the conditions of capital rationing that confront government agencies, the use of the above test can help accomplish this objective. The pertinent arguments have already been presented in Chapter 5.

It is sometimes said that we should use an artificially low discount

[16] Again for a different view, see that of Otto Eckstein in *Benefits and Costs* . . . , pp. 120–138. Given his conclusion that the benefit-cost ratio is a suitable test in certain circumstances (see footnote earlier in this chapter), it is not surprising that he differs from the present study in regard to the discount rate. Instead of discounting the streams at the marginal rate of return in order to weed out the less productive proposals, he uses the marginal benefit-cost ratio as a "cut-off," thus eliminating proposals with lower benefit-cost ratios. As for the discount rate, he feels on the one hand that it should be low in order to assure "high evaluation of future benefits and the design of installations of great durability" (*Ibid.*, p. 133). (As noted in the text, however, one can attach high prices to future benefits without disturbing the discount rate, and great durability of a *particular* form of capital is not necessarily an economic way to provide for posterity.) He suggests on the other hand that one might want the return from public investments to compare favorably with private rates of return—say 6 per cent. He then shows several combinations of discount rates and benefit-cost ratios that "approximate" a return of 6 per cent. For a particular example, he cites a cut-off ratio of 1.4 and a discount rate of 3 per cent as a combination that would result in the marginal project yielding "approximately" 6 per cent. The combination that would be equivalent to a 6 per cent rate of return, however, is sensitive to turnover, i.e., to capital intensity. Therefore, the cut-off ratio of 1.4 and discount rate of 3 per cent could still point to a different set of projects from the ones that would be chosen if one maximized present worth with the streams discounted at 6 per cent. While suggesting the use of the above combination, Dr. Eckstein concludes that "Others may prefer different value judgments; it should not be expected that their conclusions [about the particular discount to be used] will agree with those set forth here" (*Ibid.*, p. 138).

As indicated in Chapters 5 and 7, the position in the present study is quite different. The criterion that should be adopted does depend upon what budget is being considered, what costs are covered by that budget, and what aims are adopted when capital rationing wrenches apart the rate of return in production and the pattern of time preferences. But it is urged here that the discount rate is an integral part of the criterion (so far as economic efficiency is concerned) and should not usually be left up to individual judgments.

rate in order to favor durable investments and put aside more capital for posterity. The way to provide more wealth (or fewer hardships) for future generations is surely to choose investments with the highest rates of return and to increase the size of current and future investment budgets. To use a discount rate lower than the marginal rate of return in *comparing* projects does nothing to increase the volume of investment; it merely discriminates in favor of proposals whose benefits occur in the distant future and against projects (education? training?) whose benefits occur in the near future. The only circumstance in which it may preserve more for posterity is when we doubt our determination to reinvest the proceeds as they accrue from current investments.

The argument is similar for one's personal investment choices. If one wishes to save more for his children, should he analyze investments by discounting the streams at an artificially low discount rate? Perhaps so, if he does not trust his will power in the future and wishes to commit himself to "durable" capital in order to avoid the painful choice between investing and consuming the near-future proceeds. But, if he has the will power to reinvest periodically, he can do better for his children by choosing the most profitable investments at all times—that is, by maximizing present worth when the streams are discounted at the marginal rate of return.

Possible Discount Rates with Special Time Preferences

A case is sometimes made for having the government use a discount rate other than the marginal internal rate. One view that is sometimes defended is that the government should use a market rate of interest. The reasoning behind this view is probably not that the government is interested in selling out its water-resource projects. Ownership may be shifted occasionally, but governmental units do not get into such activities as flood-control and irrigation in order to build up a business and reap a capital gain. The reason might be, however, that a market rate would approximate the real marginal rate of return through future years better than would the internal rate of the marginal project. After all, it must be conceded that little can be known about internal investment opportunities a decade hence. (Similarly, though, not much can be known about general investment opportunities and market rates of return in the distant future.) Or the argument might run that the government in its water-resource activities *ought* to aim at simulating the efforts of private firms. In this case, market evaluation of the streams might be the relevant measure of a project's worth.

If it is argued that the market rate should be used, it may also be argued that the analyst should estimate the market value of water-resource measures directly without resorting to any roundabout discounting procedure. It is sometimes suggested that this can be done by observing the increases in the value of land and other capital assets that are produced by "similar projects." Now, to reach this value directly rather than indirectly would be fine, if it yielded equally good results with the expenditure of less time and effort. But this procedure raises questions that are just as hard as those raised by the customary procedure. What is a "similar" project or situation? What mixture of changes (e.g., construction of projects, shifts of population, changes in interest rates, technological advances) underlie observed increases in land values? What asset revaluations would reveal the worth of a feature like the improvement of navigation? "Direct assessment" for some water-resource proposals might be more satisfactory than discounting the cost-benefit streams. No doubt most private investors estimate the worth of assets that are regularly bought and sold, say a common stock or a plot of land, without employing any discounting process. But it would be difficult to follow this procedure, on the basis of either intuition or observation, for water-resource measures that are unique and complicated. It would be somewhat like estimating the incidence of a new tax on the basis of historical changes in prices from 1933 to the present. But, regardless of practicability, the market rate of interest, the use of which is implicit in directly assessing the market value of a project, is not necessarily the correct rate of discount for *comparing* public ventures.

Another possible view about the discount rate that should be applied to government projects will be mentioned in passing. It can be argued that a discount rate different from the marginal internal rate of return is sometimes appropriate because policy-makers may have time preferences or subjective rates of return that differ from the marginal internal rate of return. Suppose, for example, that they must choose between projects A and B, because the budget is $100 (that is, there is capital rationing). The internal rates are 4 and 3 per cent, respectively; but these decision-makers do not have the opportunity of adjusting the amount of government investment to their time preferences. Hence those rates of return, 4 and 3 per cent, may bear no close relationship to their personal attitudes toward the future. Perhaps this fact should affect their decisions. Assume that these policy-makers hold pessimistic views about long-run prospects, and attach great weight to output in the near future. While they cannot increase consumption and reduce the government's investment budget, they can discount the future at a high rate. For the sake of being specific, assume that they prefer a discount rate of 7 per cent. In this situation which should be chosen—A or B?

If we compare their present values (Table 9) when the streams are discounted at the marginal internal rate of return, A is the better of the two. However, if we compare their present values when the streams are discounted at 7 per cent, B is the better choice. There is an obvious objection: with any discount rate higher than the internal rates of return, neither project will have a present value that is as large as its costs. Surely neither project is warranted, so far as measurable gains and costs are concerned, if the discount rate is 7 per cent. That is true. May one conclude that neither project will be undertaken? Not necessarily; there is "too much" investment if the 7 per cent discount rate is used, but according to the assumptions in this example, the budget must be taken as given.

TABLE 9

PRESENT VALUES WITH SPECIAL TIME PREFERENCES

Alternative Projects	Initial Investment	Net Benefits Year 1	Year 2	Internal Rate	Present Values At 3%	At 7%
A	$100	0	$108	4%	$102	$94
B	100	$103	0	3%	100	96

Now one is often faced with the problem of finding the best course of action when decisions at other levels are non-optimal. In this instance, however, the higher-level decision about the size of the budget is not necessarily wrong. To these decision-makers, the budget seems to be too large because their personal discount rate (7 per cent) is relatively high. There is no persuasive evidence that would lead others to the same figure, no operational procedure for determining it. Moreover, there is something artificial about giving credence simultaneously to the higher subjective discount rate and to the prices and benefit streams which yield the lower internal rates. Therefore the use of such a personal time preference does not appear to be justified. As argued in Chapter 5, it seems far more reasonable to use a rate that is consistent with the degree of capital rationing imposed at higher levels, consistent with the attitude toward the future that is implied by higher-level decisions. This means using the marginal rate of return as the discount rate, and the test to which we return is the maximization of present worth for a given investment budget, when the streams are discounted at the marginal internal rate of return.

The Practicable Procedure

In order to apply this test, one could use the procedure described in Chapter 5, that is, prepare a schedule of the best proposals at various discount rates and then select the set that exhausts the budget. It would not be practicable, of course, to determine the best combination of projects at dozens of discount rates (3 per cent, $3\frac{1}{4}$ per cent, $3\frac{1}{2}$ per cent, and so on). But it would be practicable, and important, to try at least two rates, separated by a fairly wide interval.

To see how this would work in the selection of water-resource projects, consider four proposals: a high dam in location A, a low dam in location A, a large-scale reforestation project in location B, and a small-scale reforestation project in location B. Present worths would be calculated at say $2\frac{1}{2}$ and 8 per cent. The present worth of the project involving the dam might turn out to be very sensitive to the discount rate (for example, see the case study of the Santa Maria Project in Chapter 12). Assume that the low dam has a small positive present worth at 8 per cent and a much greater worth at $2\frac{1}{2}$ per cent, while the high dam has a positive present worth only at the $2\frac{1}{2}$ per cent rate, yielding a substantial loss at 8 per cent. The worth of the reforestation project might turn out to be relatively insensitive to the discount rate (for example, see the case study of the Green River Project in Chapter 11). Assume that each size of the latter project has a positive present worth at both discount rates.

Using this information, officials could reason along the following lines: at $2\frac{1}{2}$ per cent, the large-scale reforestation project and the high dam are profitable. At 8 per cent, the large-scale reforestation project is still economical, but the high dam is not. At still higher rates, even the low dam is probably uneconomic, since the worth of the project is sensitive to the discount rate. Hence if the budget is exhausted by the projects having positive present worths at $2\frac{1}{2}$ per cent, the large-scale reforestation project and the high dam are acceptable. If, however, the budget will cover (roughly) only projects having positive present worths at 8 per cent, the reforestation project and the low dam are justified. And if the budget is more than exhausted by the "8 per cent projects," the dam should be eliminated altogether.

Consideration of only two discount rates, like the examination of two sizes of each project, would not make possible hair-splitting refinements in choosing water-resource programs, but it would point to the more urgent improvements.

A Method of Ranking Projects

The foregoing procedure does not make use of any unique ranking of projects. The use of such a ranking, if it did not entail gross errors in the selection of water-resource investments, might seem preferable to many officials. If a single unique ranking could be devised, decision-makers could simply go down the list of projects as far as the budget would permit in order to select the "right" set of projects. (Of course, a little reshuffling might be necessary because this set of projects would rarely exhaust the budget right to the penny.)

It has been pointed out that projects should not be ranked according to conventional benefit-cost ratios, that is, ratios of gross benefit to total expense or of "partly net benefits" to "investment plus a random selection of operating expenses." These ratios make use of the wrong denominator. The correct denominator is the cost which the nation's water-resource budget is really supposed to cover; and this is essentially construction costs, or, more precisely, the excess of outgo over benefits during the early years of the project. Hence, those projects *that are not interrelated* might be ranked according to the ratio of present worth to investment cost with the streams discounted at the marginal internal rate of return.[17] Or, to use a simpler device, one that would point to the same set of investments, the projects could be ranked according to their internal rates of return.

It should be emphasized again, however, that interdependent projects cannot properly be ranked. With respect to such ventures, there is no ranking that is independent of the acceptance or rejection of related projects or independent, therefore, of the discount rate. Side calculations must be used to select the combination of interrelated measures that produces the greatest present worth at the anticipated marginal rate of return.

In practice, the side calculations might be made, on the basis of a predicted marginal rate of return, at "lower levels"—that is, in designing the best size of each project and in designing the best combination of interdependent measures. Then, if the list of projects for the consideration of Congressmen and higher-level administrators is narrowed down to a group of independent investments, these ventures can be ranked according to their internal rates of return. In the

---

[17] This rate could be determined (approximately) by seeing at what discount rate the projects having positive present worth would exhaust the budget.

example presented in Tables 7 and 8, this ranking would be correct, whether the benefit stream was considered on a gross or on a partly net basis (refer to Table 10).

TABLE 10

INTERNAL RATES OF RETURN

	Project A (using gross benefits)	Project A (counting most benefits as net of expenses)	Project B
Investment	$100,000	$100,000	$100,000
Each year's out-of-pocket expense	50,000	2,500	5,000
Each year's benefits	70,000	22,500	15,000
Internal rate of return	18%*	18%*	15%*

* Approximately. These figures were reached by calculating present worth at three discount rates, by free-hand interpolation to plot present worth as a function of the discount rate, and by observing the rate at which present worth appeared to be zero.

Exactly how this method operates can be seen by referring to the example of the dam and the reforestation project. If a unique ranking is to be produced, the task must be performed in two stages. First, the best combination of the interrelated projects must be decided upon. In this example, the interrelated projects are alternative sizes of the dam and the reforestation project. The officials responsible for choosing the design and scale of projects make a rough forecast of the marginal rate of return for the water-resource program. If the forecast is in the neighborhood of 8 per cent, these officials propose the low dam and the large-scale reforestation project. If the forecast is in the neighborhood of 2½ per cent, they propose the high dam and the large-scale reforestation project.

Second, once the design and size have been selected for each project, the two can then be ranked according to their internal rates of return. The use of such a ranking in allocating the water-resource budget would be far from an ideal procedure, yet it would tend to yield the correct selection.

Replacement Investments and Sequential Review

The whole discussion of criteria is also relevant to the comparison of alternative actions pertaining to old facilities. Existing projects need to be reviewed periodically just as new ventures need to be analyzed. In this process of sequential review, not only replacement but also repair, modification, or sale may be pertinent alternatives that are worth consideration. Also, outright abandonment of a project is sometimes the efficient course of action, even though the project is partially or fully constructed and even though the venture originally appeared to be economic.

There are some special points to be remembered in analyzing these courses of action: (1) In determining the cost of retention, modification, sale, or abandonment of existing facilities, one should not add in the historical cost of those facilities. Once they have been built, their cost is simply their worth in alternative uses, possibly in the scrappile. (2) To abandon, retain, sell, or replace existing facilities are interrelated courses of action—mutually exclusive ones, in fact—and they should be handled accordingly. Nonetheless, despite these special characteristics of policies pertaining to existing projects, the criterion indicated previously does apply to their comparison.

SUGGESTED EXHIBITS IN THE ANALYSIS OF EACH PROJECT

The raw materials for the comparison of numerous projects are exhibits pertaining to each individual project, and the preparation of such exhibits is the analyst's first, and for that matter his principal, task. What counsel pertaining to this task is provided by the discussion thus far?

Present Worths with at Least Two Discount Rates

The main exhibit concerning any one particular project should be the present worth of the venture (present value of the receipt stream minus the present value of the cost stream) calculated for a range of discount rates. The potential use of this exhibit has just been explained with reference to the example of the dams and the reforestation projects. To recapitulate, one can turn to this exhibit, in connection with interrelated proposals such as alternative sizes, and find out the present worth of each one at the two (or more) discount rates. Next, the size and mix of interdependent features that have the highest present worth at each rate can be selected, other sizes and mixes at each rate being eliminated from consideration. Then, as soon as the budget level is known, one can turn to these exhibits (there would be one for each project), determine the set of ventures which have positive present worths at various discount rates, and find out which set approximately fits the budget.

Even if not employed in precisely this fashion, the exhibit can help decision-makers by showing (1) the sensitivity of a project's outcome to the discount rate, and (2) the outcome for various rates in case it is decided that, say, a market rate of interest ought to be applied.

Another reason for using more than one rate is inherent in the nature of governmental processes. Suppose, for instance, that in everyone's view the net benefit streams should be discounted at the marginal internal rate of return. Analyses are prepared in say 1955, 1956, and 1957. The Executive Departments and Congress reach a tentative selection (in other words, certain projects are authorized) in 1958 on the basis of analyses available at that time. By the time a final selection is made and the funds are appropriated, say in 1960, new proposals have been analyzed, and the budget level that is relevant, which was unknown previously, is finally determined. What marginal internal rate of return should have been used in the analyses that were made in 1955 and 1956? As a practical matter, then, the exhibit should show present worths at more than one discount rate.

In the calculation of present worths at several discount rates, what should be done about the selection of a time horizon? There are several things that can be done, but they do not reveal the "correct" time span. We can look to various decisions by the voters and by Congressmen in an effort to gage the "nation's" attitude toward uncertainty. We can inquire into the character of the uncertainty that beclouds the future. But unless we have a great deal of other information, rarely obtainable, we cannot point to the "correct" time horizon. What this appears to suggest is, again, the presentation of multiple results that reflect more than one time horizon. If policy-makers could handle a further proliferation of results, perhaps more than one time horizon should be used. There is danger, however, especially after we have dealt with uncertainty, of overloading the analytical exhibits with multiple outcomes. Moreover, results that reflected two discount rates would already reflect a range of attitudes toward the future. It is better, at least in my judgment, to show the outcomes with at least two discount rates and to use a standard middle-of-the-road time horizon. Government Agencies in the past have estimated benefits and costs over future periods of from 40 to 100 years (with a salvage value sometimes thrown in at the end of even the larger period). In the case studies to be presented here, a 50-year period was used for the calculations. As it turns out, the longer time horizon does not matter as much as one might expect, if the discount rate is not a very low one. If a rate of 5 per cent is applied, the outcome is comparatively insensitive to events more than a half-century hence.

Time Streams

At best, however, present values do not exhaust the types of information that analysts should exhibit to the policy-makers. For the spacing of the "lumps" of cost and gain through time is important in ways which cannot be reflected by discounting the streams. Because of uncertainty about future budgetary restrictions, the time periods in which the absolute amounts of cost and benefit occur are relevant data. Even if there were widespread agreement as to useful time horizons and discount rates, it would often be important to know which projects yielded their benefits comparatively early, or which ones entailed higher costs in future years. ("Present equivalents" of future streams are not fully satisfactory in this situation, just as "certainty equivalents" of uncertain outcomes are not always adequate.) Congressmen want to know how outlays for big projects will be spread over future periods, for Congress is quite properly concerned about several matters that are not reflected in the present values, such as the relation of the time paths to future budgets' flexibility, to present and future tax management, to the risk of premature abandonment of projects. As an example, it is not enough to know that the Hell's Canyon project would involve annual costs of $18 million and annual benefits of $37 million (as estimated in the Bureau of Reclamation); it may be necessary to know also that the estimated time paths would be somewhat as follows:[18]

TABLE II

TIME STREAMS

(millions of dollars)

	Construction 1950–60	Ten Years 1961–70	Eighty Years 1971–2050	Ten Years 2051–2060
Costs	$469	$ 53	$ 424	$ 9
Benefits	—	370	2960	370

Internal Rate of Return

As has been said, projects that are not interrelated may be ranked by their internal rates of return. Hence, another exhibit for each project might well be its internal rate of return; but the exhibit should

[18] This is a crude illustrative approximation of the way the costs would be incurred, and the benefits reaped, through time—using the data presented in *Hell's Canyon Project Idaho-Oregon,* Bureau of Reclamation, Project Planning Report No. 1–5.75–0, Region 1, Boise, Idaho, April, 1948, pp. 69, 97–98.

be accompanied by a warning against the ranking of mutually exclusive or interrelated projects according to internal rates of return.

Supplementary Exhibits To Reflect Intangibles and Uncertainty

Finally, it has been implied in earlier chapters that separate exhibits are urgently needed to help decision-makers take uncertainty and intangibles into account. An indication of the variability of the outcome is extremely important. Also of significance are the effects of each project on the personal distribution of wealth (what group, if any, would be subsidized if the project was adopted, and how much would the subsidy be?) and possibly on the regional distribution of wealth (to what extent would one region be developed, and to what regions would resources otherwise have gone?). Clues to these impacts might well be presented along with the other data.

APPENDIX ON THE USE OF MARKET PRICES AND THE MEANING OF ECONOMIC EFFICIENCY

It is stated in the text that the price consumers pay for a good or a service is accepted as a measure of its value to the economy. Similarly, the cost of an item, the value that must be given up in order to use it, is the price that consumers would pay to have that item put to its next-best use. The rationale for these propositions rests on a rather lengthy chain of reasoning. This appendix presents, though still in a highly oversimplified fashion, this rationale.

It is assumed that, by and large, we want the preferences of individuals, mainly in their capacity as consumers, to guide the allocation of productive resources. Moreover, we approve of accomplishing this objective by means of buying and selling in competitive markets (possibly the only practicable way of having resources directed by those preferences). If in addition we approve in principle[19] of the distribution of purchasing power that emerges, as modified, of course, by such social influences as the tax system, we can define an efficient allocation of resources. Even if we refuse to pass judgment on the distribution of purchasing power, i.e., wealth, we can still define a set of allocations that are "efficient" in a restricted sense: that is, in the

[19] Most persons would like to have more personal wealth, of course, yet they may approve, on the whole, of a certain wealth distribution as affected by the competitive process.

sense that no reallocation could make anyone better off without making someone worse off.

A diagram may help clarify the matter, even though it necessitates shrinking our world to one in which there are only two commodities. In this world the amount of productive resources (labor, equipment, ideas, and so on) are given. The curve represents maximum produc-

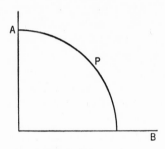

tion possibilities—various combinations of the two commodities, A and B—that can be produced with the given resources. If one of these combinations, say P, was produced and distributed among a group of individuals, these persons could no doubt do some trading that would be mutually advantageous. That is, by free exchange, the satisfaction of some could be increased without decreasing that of others. When no further exchanges would be mutually advantageous, the group would have made the most of the possibilities, given combination P and its initial distribution.

Combination P need not be taken as given, however, because A can be transformed into B or B into A. This possibility of converting one product into another by reallocating the resources which produce them opens the way to further trade that is mutually advantageous. Thus, suppose commodities A and B are apples and bread. Starting from combination P, people trade until nobody can improve his position by free exchange. One man ends up with a pound of apples which he would be willing to trade for a loaf of bread, but no one wants the apples at that rate of exchange. But what if the inputs that can be released by giving up one pound of apples can produce an extra loaf of bread? In that case, resources can be shifted, and the man who preferred bread to apples can be made better off without making anyone else worse off.

Now suppose that relative prices show how much people would pay, given the distribution of purchasing power, for additional amounts of various items, and that costs of production (other sets of prices) show what must be given up in order to produce extra quantities of these items. If resources are shifted to the production of those outputs whose prices exceed incremental costs,[20] the extra supplies drive down their prices. An equilibrium is reached in which prices equal incremental costs, and the only way to increase further the satisfaction of some is to reduce the satisfaction of others. Such a position of equilibrium is called an "efficient point." Of course, with an altered distribution of wealth, this position of equilibrium shifts; the pattern of consumers' demands is different, and accordingly the structure of relative prices and the allocation of resources that would exist at equilibrium are changed. In other words, there is a different "efficient point" for each distribution of wealth. We can imagine a new sort of boundary curve connecting these efficient points, a curve which may conveniently be called the "production boundary" or simply the "set of efficient points." This curve is not the production-possibility curve shown in the diagram. Nor does this boundary represent the positions of "maximum total satisfaction" for the group (whatever that might mean). It represents the resource allocations which, for each distribution of wealth, make each person as well off as he can be without having to make someone else worse off. In other words, at one of these efficient points it is impossible to make any adjustment which would give anyone greater satisfaction without impairing someone else's well-being.

Let us restate these propositions with respect to any particular point, to be referred to as "X," on this so-called production boundary. If the distribution of wealth that goes with point X is preferred to any other distribution, that point is optimal.[21] If we refuse to take any stand with respect to distribution, we can still say that at point X, no adjustment can make anyone better off without making someone worse off. There are, of course, other points on the production boundary, one for each possible distribution of wealth, about which this can be said. Moreover, there are other points short of the production boundary that some may nonetheless prefer to X because of the distributions of wealth which they imply. Indeed, we cannot even say that X is unequivocally preferred to *any* other point if the shift to X would not actually make some better off without making

[20] The term "incremental cost" is used to mean the extra total cost that results from the production of a unit increment in output.

[21] Some qualifications and additional considerations will be mentioned in later paragraphs.

others worse off. In other words, if those who are hurt by a shift to X are not in fact compensated, we cannot demonstrate that X is a better position. Nonetheless, it is an efficient point in the limited sense described, and to move to the production boundary maximizes the size of the pie, so to speak, *for that particular distribution of wealth*. The implications of each policy for efficiency in this sense constitute one item of information—and an extremely important one—which should be considered by policy-makers.

It is through comparisons of cost and gain, i.e., of the prices at which alternative outputs could be sold, that we can see how to move toward maximum production in the sense described. If the gain from producing more of a commodity exceeds the cost, people are doing without additional units that they value more than the other things which the inputs are now producing. If the gain is below incremental cost, people are consuming extra units that they value less than the other things which the inputs could produce. In either situation, someone's satisfaction *could* be increased without reducing anyone else's. Of course, the prices that must ordinarily be used are market prices, and there are several conditions that have to be fulfilled before production of items whose market prices exceed their costs would necessarily take us to the production boundary. The production of those items must not provide gains for which consumers do not bid, that is, provide gains which are not reflected in price. Also, the production of those items should not impair the physical productivity of resources in ways that are not paid for, causing sacrifices which are not reflected in the price structure. Moreover, if the efficiency argument is to be rigorous, individuals' utility functions must not be interdependent; there must be no keeping up with the Joneses. Furthermore, there should be "perfect competition" in both buying and selling throughout the economy so that an individual buyer or seller cannot by his own action noticeably affect prices. A full list of the conditions need not be presented here.[22] Those already mentioned will serve to bring out the main qualification: those conditions are not completely realized, and moving toward the achievement of *one* alone is not necessarily a step in the right direction.[23] However,

[22] They are contained in many source materials, including A. P. Lerner, *The Economics of Control* (New York: The Macmillan Company, 1944), pp. 72–77; T. Scitovsky, *Welfare and Competition* (London: George Allen and Unwin, 1952), pp. 148–188; and P. A. Samuelson, *Foundations of Economic Analysis* (Cambridge, Massachusetts: Harvard University Press, 1947), pp. 219–243.

[23] *Ibid.*, pp. 252–253. See also R. G. Lipsey and Kelvin Lancaster, "The General Theory of Second Best," *Review of Economic Studies*, 1956–1957, pp.

if a frequency distribution of the possibilities is imagined, it seems likely that increased production where price exceeds cost would usually be a step toward efficiency, even though the other conditions are only partially fulfilled. The conclusion here is that prices and costs do show how to "maximize production."

It should also be recognized that uncertainty is ignored whenever the conditions of being on the production boundary are discussed. Actually, it is not clear just what it means to expand output until incremental cost is (almost) equal to price when both appear to the decision-maker, not as unique numbers, but as frequency distributions. Again, the conclusions here rest on an assumption: namely, that measurements in terms of expected values, plus clues to the variability of outcomes, are helpful in reaching "better" decisions; although they cannot really reveal, in a world of uncertainty, how to reach a well-defined production boundary.

The argument so far has pertained to the adjustment of outputs when resources are "given," but it can be adapted to adjustments of output when innovations and investments are considered. In the latter circumstances, price is what people would be willing to pay for the investment's output stream, and incremental cost is the extra cost due to the venture. If an amount of investment sufficient to produce one extra unit of output is considered, the rule is essentially the same as before: expand each type of output until incremental cost is roughly equal to price. In other words, the rule is to keep selecting the most profitable investments, as they would be viewed by competitive firms.[24] We can still take resources as given with as much justification as existed in the previous case: if the ideas for the innovations and the budget for the investments are assumed to be in existence already, the discussion pertains once again to the conditions for being on the production boundary.

Hence, on the assumptions previously noted, plus the assumption that it is good[25] to maximize the size of the pie in this sense, price is

---

11–32. Despite the difficulties of finding a "second-best" solution, it is surely possible in many problems to distinguish better from worse courses of action.

[24] See A. P. Lerner, *op. cit.*, p. 248, and T. Scitovsky, *Welfare and Competition*, p. 430. The latter emphasizes some of the qualifications that may apply when one looks at possible effects on future innovations.

[25] There has to be, at bottom, an ethical basis for any statement about what ought to be done. When it is concluded that one measure is more "relevant" than another, some ethical assumptions are implied. The discussion in this Appendix has implied, for example, that to follow the dictates of consumers' sovereignty is good, that more of one commodity without loss of others is good,

an appropriate measure of the worth to the economy of another unit of some good or service. And cost-benefit measurements are pertinent to the selection of investments which lead to efficiency in this limited sense. Indeed, many persons might be willing to take an additional step and accept the distribution of wealth that would emerge as being the preferred one. In that case, these measurements would point unequivocally to the correct set of investments. This conclusion would also follow if one viewed the distribution of wealth after either investment as being essentially the same[26] or at least equally acceptable. Past experience probably supports this view. Initially, investments always provide windfalls for some men and distressing losses for others. Later, the processes of growth brings a higher level of income to nearly all. Imagine a frequency distribution of the number of investments that have resulted in different patterns of wealth redistribution. Surely the impacts of many alternative investments have been about equally acceptable (and, incidentally, a tolerable part of the price of growth.) Many persons would agree that the differential impact of alternative investments on the *distribution* of wealth is not a matter of great moment.

Still, it must be conceded that in some cases the effects on wealth distribution may not be equally desirable. Compensation to all those injured by the investments will not in fact be made. Projects (as they will actually be carried out) will provide gratuitous or deliberate subsidies—subsidies that do not always represent equal treatment of people in equal circumstances. Furthermore, while some projects will benefit a particular set of comparatively poor persons, others will subsidize a particular group of comparatively rich individuals. Strictly speaking, then, our partial criterion can only tell which projects are "efficient." By itself, this test cannot tell us which position is best in any ultimate sense. It is conceivable that we could formulate a rule about the relative "social worth" of wealth to different persons. Certainly someone has to do something of this sort in order for any decisions to be made. To refuse, in the end, to compare the worth to the economy of wealth in the hands of different persons is ". . . like

---

that increased satisfaction of one without loss of satisfaction by others is good. Ethical premises cannot be escaped. See Abram Bergson, "On the Concept of Social Welfare," *Quarterly Journal of Economics,* May, 1954, p. 249, and Samuelson, *op. cit.,* p. 249.

[26] See Scitovsky, *Welfare and Competition,* pp. 60–69, for a discussion of his "double criterion."

pouring out a glass of water and then refusing to drink."[27] However, the preparation of analyses to aid policy-makers is surely like pouring out the water for *them* to drink, which seems to be a reasonable procedure. Hence, it is deemed appropriate here to have the cost-benefit measurements shed light on efficiency in this limited sense, and to have further exhibits shed light on redistributional effects.[28]

[27] P. A. Samuelson, *op. cit.,* p. 249.

[28] For examples of such exhibits see the case studies in Chapters 12 and 13. The presentation of data about the redistributional effects corresponds to the recommended treatment of any "intangible."

KINDS OF BENEFIT AND COST:
SPILLOVER EFFECTS

L ET US TURN NOW to the measurement of benefits and costs. In this chapter, we shall discuss those special consequences of water-resource projects which have been called "spillover" effects. It will be helpful to review certain spillovers that occur in the private sector of the economy and to ask whether, from the standpoint of economic efficiency, they should be ignored or taken into account. Then the implications for cost-benefit measurements will be indicated, and later the case studies will show to some extent how this theory can be put into practice.

Spillover effects, it will be recalled, are impacts of actions by some decision-making units on the activities of others, impacts that are not directly felt by the first group. In economics, such spillovers are often labeled "external economies" and "external diseconomies." These terms sometimes refer to changes in the costs of a firm resulting from an expansion of the rest of *that industry*. In a more general sense, they refer to uncompensated effects on the costs or receipts of one group of firms caused by the actions of *any* other set of firms.[1] For example, an increase in sound track troubles and the cost of making movies because of the expansion of air traffic would be an external diseconomy. Such external effects have their counterparts within firms and within government, since Departments and Agencies often make decisions independently of each other. They also have their

---

[1] See, for instance, J. E. Meade, "External Economies and Diseconomies in a Competitive Situation," *Economic Journal*, March, 1952, pp. 54–67. External economies and diseconomies have to be *uncompensated* influences because if they are compensated, they are like any other output that is sold or input that is purchased.

counterparts in the consumer's world; that is, there may be uncompensated effects on individuals' costs or satisfactions traceable to the actions of other persons or of businesses. Thus, the cost of doing the family laundry is increased as smoke-producing factories expand their operations. As explained before, the term "spillover" is used here to embrace all of these types of external effects, whether they are economies or diseconomies, whether the cause is an industry's action or a government investment, whether the effect is on a branch of the government or an individual.

TREATMENT OF TECHNOLOGICAL SPILLOVERS

There is little doubt that "technological spillovers"—those which affect the physical outputs that other producers can get from their physical inputs—should be taken into account. The term "technological spillover" is used here to include also its counterpart in consumption, namely, uncompensated effects on the satisfaction that consumers can get from their inputs. Within practicable limits these, too, should be taken into consideration. For example, if a storage dam raises the water table so as to impair the productivity of surrounding acreage, the loss of production is a real cost to society, a genuine sacrifice from the standpoint of achieving maximum production in the economy.[2] Or, if a packing house pollutes the atmosphere for local residents, the result is a genuine cost, though it may be difficult to measure. Such spillovers result mostly from the use of a common pool of some resource, such as use of the atmosphere by the residents and the stockyards, of light waves by billboard advertisers and admirers of scenery, of oil-bearing sands by various oil producers.

Ideally, we would like firms to take these spillovers into account, and in practice at least some steps are taken to induce firms to do so. Ordinances are often passed to compel businesses to use higher-cost locations, more expensive fuels, or higher-cost methods in order to eliminate serious external effects. Those who are damaged can in some circumstances sue for compensation, and the threat of lawsuits may cause firms and individuals to take external impacts of their activities into account. In some instances, the pattern of ownership of the resources that are used in common, e.g., hunting or fishing areas, is altered in such a way that users must pay the costs inflicted on the economy; these costs, no longer uncompensated effects of the

---

[2] This means maximum production in a restricted sense, as indicated earlier and as described in the Appendix to Chapter 7.

users' actions, play their proper role. In various ways, then, the private sector of the economy is sometimes induced to measure these spillover costs and gains. Of course, it is not practicable or economical to trace out *all* such effects and adopt measures causing them to be reflected in firms' accounts. Many of them are too trivial or uncertain to consider. For instance, the increased use of bright colors in the painting of automobiles may be a source of pleasure (or pain) to traffic policemen—it may even affect workers' morale and hence influence firms' physical production possibilities. Yet few people would urge that the market be so arranged that General Motors' receipts would reflect such spillovers.

The implications for cost-benefit analysis are fairly clear. The measurements should allow for major external effects of the technological variety—that is, the variety which alters the physical production possibilities of other producers or the satisfactions that consumers can get from given resources. Indeed, much of the case for government intervention in water-resource activities rests on the belief that these spillovers should be allowed for, that private firms cannot take them into account, and that government can. Several examples of spillovers from water-resource projects were mentioned in the general discussion in Chapter 2. As further illustrations, a project that uses water upstream may reduce the production possibilities of power plants or irrigation facilities downstream. A reservoir may increase the amount of dredging and channel maintenance that is necessary to get the original output downstream. It may also increase the recreational services that can be obtained from other given inputs. If such impacts can be priced, their total values can be computed and added to the costs or benefits, whichever the case may be. Whether or not their values should be added in, if they affect production possibilities in a *potential* enterprise, depends upon whether or not (and when) the enterprise is really expected to materialize. Finally, a line must somehow be drawn between those external technological effects that are worth counting and those that are too trivial or nebulous to warrant any attention, just as such a line must be drawn in setting up rules for private industry.

TREATMENT OF PECUNIARY SPILLOVERS

There are other external consequences, however, which do not affect the units of output (or pleasure) that can be obtained from a firm's (or a consumer's) physical inputs. These will be called "pecuniary spillovers," for they are occasioned by shifts in prices.[3] Since these external impacts fall into groups which have somewhat different characteristics, they will be classified into four types.

Bidding Up Factor Rates of Hire

One case that has long been a subject of debate[4] occurs when an expansion by industry A raises the price of an input used by A. This naturally makes things harder for any other industry using that input. In other words, the action of industry A inflicts losses on other firms and may necessitate a reduction in their outputs. Are these losses a cost to society which industry A should somehow be induced to take into consideration?

Let us look at the sequence of events more closely. Firms in industry A find that consumers are willing to pay more for increased output than the firms would have to pay for the necessary inputs, allowing for the consequent rise in the price of input X. But this higher price of X causes the firms in industry B to incur losses. Presumably their best course of action is to employ less of input X at the new price. If all other inputs used in industry B are "specialized" so that they have no alternative employment, then they are earning "rents," i.e., payments greater than the amounts necessary to keep them at work in this use.[5] Their rates of hire, or in this case rents, will be reduced, but the inputs will continue to be employed in B, which in these circumstances is their best (their only) use. If other inputs are not specialized in this manner, they will be shifted to more lucrative employment as B's bid declines.

Similar repercussions will presumably occur in other industries. But note that two things are happening: resources are being reallocated to uses where they are more valuable, and rents are being transferred. The economy could keep the same old inputs at work in industry B, and get the same old output, if consumers voted by means of their purchases for this outcome. The only reason anything

[3] The distinction between "technological" and "pecuniary" effects has often been made in the literature of economics—e.g., in Jacob Viner, "Cost Curves and Supply Curves," *Zeitschrift für Nationalökonomie,* 1931, pp. 23–46, reprinted in *Readings in Price Theory,* American Economic Association, ed. K. E. Boulding and G. J. Stigler (Chicago: Richard D. Irwin, 1952), pp. 198–232.

[4] See the discussion and also the references in the article by Howard S. Ellis and William Fellner, "External Economies and Diseconomies," *American Economic Review,* September, 1943, pp. 493–511, reprinted in *Readings in Price Theory,* pp. 242–263.

[5] Henceforth the term "rents" will be used to mean such payments.

happens to the basket of outputs is that "consumers sovereignty" points to a better basket. So as far as the efficiency of the economy is concerned, the firms in industry A should not be induced to count B's losses as costs.

With respect to cost-benefit analysis, the same line of reasoning applies. The measurements should not reflect this type of pecuniary spillover in order to show the way to an efficient set of projects. It is true, of course, that somebody gets hurt in this process, by reductions of income in some cases and by painful changes in jobs or locations in other cases.[6] Moreover, there is little use in talking about compensation of everyone who is injured, because all such consequences could not possibly be ferreted out. Besides, an announced policy of compensation could eliminate a good deal of desirable readjustment. Hence neglect of this pecuniary spillover is claimed to be appropriate only in the estimation of cost-benefit streams and their present values, which are supposed to be partial tests—not in the preparation of other relevant exhibits.

Cutting Down Prices of Substitute Products

Suppose A, the expanding industry, is a new and thriving one, say the production of quick-frozen chop suey. The expansion seems sure to be profitable, but it will lower the price of the product by increasing the supply. This will bring lower profits or higher losses to firms which produce other close substitutes—say quick-frozen meat pies or canned spaghetti dinners. It may spread a little suffering rather thinly over the producers of a host of remote substitutes. At the same time, of course, these lower prices make certain consumers better off. Are such transfers real costs? Would their neglect keep the economy from achieving maximum production?

The similarity to the previous case is probably apparent. Again two things occur: inputs are shifted if there are better uses for them, and rents are reduced if there are not better uses. It should be noted that a decline in capital values is another name for a decline in rents, for the latter will be manifested by a reduction in the capitalized values of specialized resources. To speak of falling rents is somewhat more general because human beings may suffer reductions of rent on

---

[6] So far as *these* damages are concerned (i.e., with no gratuitous injuries or subsidies), many persons might find the income distributions after either of two investments equally acceptable. But acute distress may call for relief, and besides government investments often imply either gratuitous injuries or assistance.

their services, but not losses in the capital value of their services, since they are not bought and sold like buildings or equipment. Again, the only reason that the composition of output is changed is that, given the distribution of wealth that emerges, consumers want it that way. Maximum production can be reached by ignoring this spillover.

It might be noted that the monopolist's behavior differs from that of a competitive industry because this sort of spillover does enter his calculations. As the only producer of, say, frozen foods, he does, in estimating the gains and costs from a new plant, allow for the reduced profits (i.e., reduced rents on his specialized resources) from existing plants. As a consequence, he does not invest until what he pays for inputs to produce another unit (almost) equals the price that consumers will pay for another unit. His gain-cost measurements are not the appropriate ones, so far as the efficiency of the whole economy is concerned.

Similarly, suppose an irrigation project increases the supply of sugar beets, reducing the price received by existing producers of sugar beets or reducing the price received by producers of more remote substitutes. The resulting transfers should not be counted as costs (or reductions of benefit) of the project. The benefits are whatever the bidders[7] are willing to pay for the incremental output of the project; the costs are whatever must be paid to attract the extra inputs that go into the project. Thus the conclusion reached with respect to cost-gain estimates by firms also applies to the estimation of costs and benefits from water-resource projects.

Raising Prices of Complementary Products

Another possible external effect of industry A's expansion is to increase the demand for B's product and the profits of firms in industry B. Suppose A is engaged in baking delicious bread, which makes everyone's mouth water for bread-and-butter sandwiches. Butter-making becomes more profitable, and other undesignated industries become less profitable, since consumers will shift some expenditures away from other items. If the resources used in other industries are not specialized and can be used to expand butter production, their rates of hire will rise, drawing additional inputs to the butter industry. The process will continue until the cost of producing more butter (almost) equals the price that can be obtained for it. Some factors of

[7] Some qualifications are in order if one of the bidders is the government buying just in order to support the price, but the point made in this section is not affected.

production get increased rents, that is, payments greater than would be necessary to keep them in the butter industry. Other resources get reduced rents, since the shift of expenditures to butter must hurt some other industry and its specialized factors of production. Hence the process can be described in terms of the same two phenomena, a reshuffling of resources and a transfer of rents, that occurred in the other cases. Again, we would not want to include these transfers (B's new profits and other industries' losses, the reduced rents of some factors and the increased rents of others) among the gains from the investment in A.

Lowering the Price of the Output

An expansion in industry A may have another external effect. Suppose that its larger volume of output lowers the price of the item which is produced. This, it is often said, bestows benefits upon the original consumers of this item, and these benefits should by rights be counted in evaluating the new investment. Or it is urged that the lower price inflicts damages upon the original producers and that these damages should be counted in estimating the cost and gain from the investment.

This case is similar to the one in which the prices of substitute products are lowered. Suppose that, because of an expansion of output in industry A, the price of A's product drops by 1 per cent. This lower price applies to the new total output—that is, to the units corresponding to the earlier rate of production as well as to the incremental units. In order to estimate the worth of the expansion to the economy, the lower price should be multiplied by the incremental units. But the worth of the extra output should not be decreased so as to reflect the fact that consumers pay less than before for the "earlier" units. Nor should the worth be decreased to reflect the fact that producers receive less than before for those earlier units. The value of the incremental output, not the incremental value of the industry's total output, is what counts. To be sure, the lower price on the "earlier" units benefits those who had been consuming the item, hurts producers who had been selling at the higher price, hurts some factors of production that had been receiving rents, and benefits the producers of items on which consumers now spend more. But these transfers can be ignored in order to determine what investment gets the economy closer to maximum production. What people are willing to pay for the *incremental* output is still the measure of its worth, and what has to be paid to attract the inputs is still the measure of its cost. (However, if decreasing costs and indivisibilities exist, they pose a special problem, which will be taken up in Chapter 10.)

Repercussions on the Profitability of the Proposed Investment

This argument does not deny the fact of interdependency among investments on account of the reallocation of consumers' outlays. Because of interdependence, investment by A is almost certain to influence the profitability of other existing and potential ventures, leading to disinvestment in some industries and additional investment in others.[8] These transfers of rent, along with shifts of resources, are part of the process of reaching a new equilibrium at maximum production and should not be counted as costs or gains from A's investment.[9] However, there may be repercussions on A, affecting the cost or worth of the extra output. *These* impacts should be taken into account. We would want A, in estimating his gains and costs, to consider the action which B is expected to take; and B, in preparing his estimates, to consider the impact of A's action. That is, in the analysis of A's proposal, it is entirely proper to anticipate what B will do in response and to include any resulting change in A's gains and costs.

These repercussions on the profitability of A's proposal can be estimated, not by adding in part of the transfers, but by fitting A's proposed investment into the pertinent context. In other words, the systems to be analyzed (the investments plus their contexts) may have to be expanded in scope. Admittedly, if estimates are prepared by fitting the investments into inappropriate systems, by ignoring the investments and disinvestments that result from A and their effect upon A's profitability, an efficient position will not be reached. Hence, as pointed out in connection with problems of choice in general, the analyst may have to compare rather broad systems, embracing in this case numerous interdependent investments, although the estimates should not include miscellaneous changes in rents or capital values.

On the other hand, it should not be forgotten that there are pen-

---

[8] At the extreme, A's product and B's may be so closely related that they must in effect be treated as one article. They may be consumed in practically invariant proportions; imagine that A makes shoes for left feet and that B makes shoes for right feet. Or they may be produced in almost unchanging proportions; suppose A tries to produce egg yolks and B tries to produce egg whites. If the proportions cannot be varied, it only makes sense to consider investments for turning out the joint products—eggs or pairs of shoes.

[9] Incidentally, the shifts that could in practice be included would unavoidably be an incomplete (almost haphazard) selection, because these pecuniary effects would percolate throughout the economy.

alties for enlarging the scope of a system. If a firm looks at the whole economic system in gaging its profits from each investment, it may or may not improve the estimates; extra doubt and error as well as extra information are brought to bear. Similarly, when government compares alternative investments, it is not clear that each should be fitted into the broadest possible system. And if government undertook to direct *all* investment by means of gigantic cost-benefit analyses, one shudders to think of the results. Therefore, in spite of interdependence, statements such as the following may be misleading.

It is apparent from this list [of external economies and diseconomies] that vertical integration alone would not be enough and that complete integration of all industries would be necessary to eliminate all divergence between private profit and public benefit. . . . To put this conclusion differently, profits in a market economy are a bad guide to economic optimum as far as investment and industrial expansion are concerned; and they are worse, the more decentralized and differentiated the economy.[10]

This statement simply points out that profits are not a perfect guide to investment decisions; and, it could be added, neither are their counterparts, present-worth estimates, in cost-benefit analysis. Mistakes in estimating profits or present worth will certainly be made on account of interdependencies, and on account of other things as well. But the quoted statement should not be interpreted to mean that "complete integration," or the allocation of all investment by means of colossal cost-benefit analyses, would necessarily result in fewer mistakes and a better guide.

In fact, the repercussions on the projected profits of A (when evaluating A's proposal) do not cause much difficulty at all, from the standpoint of the economy's efficiency, unless the investments are to take place in large "indivisible" chunks. Even if A, in evaluating his proposal, ignores B's response at first, mutual adjustments will lead to economic efficiency as far as these alternative policies are concerned, provided both decision-makers proceed by small increments. If investment is to take place in great chunks, the chance of error is greater. That is, if two investments are interdependent, neither being profitable without the other, *and if they can be undertaken only in huge chunks,* both may be shelved for lack of assurance that the other will be undertaken.[11] But this possibility does not alter what has been said about

[10] Tibor Scitovsky, "Two Concepts of External Economies," *Journal of Political Economy,* April, 1954, pp. 149–150.

[11] Thus, in "underdeveloped" countries or wherever especially large lumps of investment are considered, it is sometimes urged that the "integration" mentioned

the way to measure costs and benefits. To reach equilibrium in these circumstances may require special intervention, it is true, but the trouble stems from indivisibilities, not just from spillovers. The difficulty may be that the profitable combination of investments is so large that institutional restraints prevent that combination from being undertaken. But to count transfers arising out of A's proposal as gains or costs of that proposal, and to count transfers attributable to B among the gains and costs of B's proposal, would not lead to the correct investment choice.

DOES THE DISTINCTION BREAK DOWN?

The position taken here is that the two general types of spillover—technological and pecuniary—are, in principle, distinguishable and mutually exclusive. The two can be confused, however, if one starts thinking in the following way. Pecuniary spillovers imply transfers of income, some of which can be, and are, translated into changes in capital values, that is, into revaluations of existing assets. But it is by no means true that any external effect which implies a change in capital values is a pecuniary spillover. For technological spillovers, such as an increased yield from A's orchard due to B's bees, also imply changes in capital values. The distinction really rests on the following basis: technological spillovers affect the physical outputs that can be obtained from other producers' physical inputs, while pecuniary spillovers do not.

The distinction also tends to become obscured because the same action is likely to involve both types of external effect, and it is sometimes difficult to unravel them. There may be complicated chains of events: the increased yield from A's orchard, a technological spillover from investment in the bee industry, cuts the price of apples and brings about some external pecuniary effects; these effects mean disinvestment in facilities for the production of substitutes (say pears) and investment in facilities for the production of complements (say, bread to go with apple-butter); but this disinvestment and investment may in turn have technological spillovers (the heat from baking the

---

in the preceding quotation would give better results than decentralized decisions on the basis of profit estimates. Or, in the terminology of this study, the analysis of broad systems would give better results than the comparison of narrow ones. For an exchange of views on this matter, see J. A. Stockfisch, "External Economies, Investment, and Foresight," and Tibor Scitovsky, "A Reply," in the *Journal of Political Economy,* October, 1955, pp. 446–451.

bread raises costs for an adjacent cold-storage locker business). In spite of the many possible sequences, however, the distinction between the two types of spillover still stands, and it is the technological spillover that should be counted.

Confusion may also result because the reshuffling of resources induced by pecuniary spillovers may alter the location of resources and produce technological spillovers. Location is often a significant physical attribute of an input or an output. If locational patterns are disrupted, a firm's production possibilities, its ability to produce the same physical output from given inputs, may be affected. If a reservoir floods out arable land, the effect on the land's possible output is obvious. But consider the plight of the local blacksmith shop that is not inundated. Its production potential may also be impaired. From the same old inputs, the shop can produce the same old outputs —except for one thing: the services are now in the wrong location. Alternatively, consider the operations of the mail order company that sends catalogs to farmers in the area. After the farmers have moved, the company can use the same address plates, equipment, and man-hours to address catalogs in the same old way. But the physical output is changed, because the catalogs no longer get to the right destinations.

These are technological spillovers. In most instances, such effects may be of little moment. The locational shifts may be slight or tend to offset each other, or the resources affected can be moved or replaced at little cost. But the distinction between "technological" and "pecuniary" spillovers can still be made, and must be made if we are to make efficient choices.

CONSISTENCY OF THIS POSITION WITH OTHERS

It will help keep the record straight if the views so far expressed are related to certain others.

The Position That National Income Should Be Maximized

One contention that is occasionally made and which sounds reasonable enough on first hearing is that the true test should be the "maximization of national income." This may be intended at times as a short-hand expression for efficiency in the restricted sense. Such usage would not be unnatural, for efficiency in this sense implies the biggest possible pie—of that particular kind. More specifically, it represents maximum production or maximum national income, given that particular distribution of wealth and, hence, that particular set of relative prices.

Alternatively, the criterion "maximum national income" may be intended to mean national income as it is measured. Such a test might still point to policies similar to those indicated by the test of present worth with pecuniary spillovers ignored. For national income is essentially the sum of wages, profits, rents, and other shares (minus a depreciation allowance), and therefore changes in national income reflect the cancellation of many transfers and pecuniary spillovers. In other words, to look at projected changes in real national income might point to the same set of investments as would the procedure suggested in this study. In practice, nonetheless, maximizing our measure of national income would not necessarily give the same results as maximizing the "value of *incremental* output minus its cost." Shifts of national income as it is measured mirror the combined influence of numerous events.[12] Instead of reflecting the change in terms of projected relative prices (the value and cost of the extra output in terms of a *particular* price structure), a shift in national income may reflect the changes from one price structure to another. For these reasons, the position taken here regarding pecuniary spillovers is not necessarily consistent with the position that maximum national income should be the test, and it is urged that attention be focused on the increments rather than on large aggregates which reflect offsetting pecuniary effects.

The Common-Sense Position Regarding Duplicate Facilities

Another view, one with which most people would agree intuitively, is that the building of duplicate facilities such as transmission lines is uneconomic. Does this view clash with the contention that pecuniary spillovers should be ignored? In order to avoid duplicate facilities, is it necessary to count as cost the fall in the rents of existing facilities (say transmission lines, sites, housing and all other specialized capital whose rent would be affected)? The answer is no. Estimates of the cost and value of the incremental output are still appropriate for the comparison of investment proposals. Of course, in making such estimates, the analyst must not be naive about the cost and value of the new output in competition with that of existing facilities. Consider a proposal to build duplicate transmission lines. Incremental cost to the existing producer, with his capital already sunk, may be low. If his

[12] For a classic discussion of these matters, see A. C. Pigou, *The Economics of Welfare,* 4th ed. (London: Macmillan and Co., 1948), pp. 31–42, 50–81.

prices are not already down to that point, he can cut them that far. Thus, the government could sell its new service only at a price that might be below its cost, which would have to include the construction of the proposed facilities. Of course, if the existing lines involved such poor service or such high costs that the government *could* sell at a price higher than cost, then the new transmission lines would be economical. To repeat, the analyst does have to recognize competition from other producers and from substitute products, just as he must always do, whether or not the facilities are suspected of being "duplicate," in estimating the value of the new output. That is, he should try to anticipate actual selling prices in the projected situation. But he does not have to count potential declines of rent as costs of the project.[13]

It may make this clearer if we recall that private firms do not count declines in their rivals' rents and capital values as costs. What keeps them from constantly building "duplicate" facilities? It is simply their realistic appraisal of the competition they face and the value of the contemplated output. Sometimes, of course, private entrepreneurs do make mistakes and construct "duplicate," i.e., uneconomic, facilities, but not because they should have counted somebody's capital loss as a cost of new ventures.

Official Positions

The position of government Agencies on this subject is not clear. In actual project evaluation, declines in the value of "displaced" facilities are not included as costs, nor are the corresponding gains included as such. Nonetheless, such losses and gains are sometimes referred to as though they ought to be counted. For example, the Green Book reports: "Displaced facilities are facilities whose present use is abandoned because project facilities provide essentially the same services . . . . It is recommended that the value of services that would have resulted from displaced facilities less their operation and maintenance costs should be subtracted from the total value of project services of the same kind to determine benefits attributable to the project."[14] Taken literally, this is a misleading way to look at the matter. It is true, of course, that the value of displaced facilities

---

[13] This is the way the analyst should view the matter in preparing cost-benefit estimates. In the shaping of final decisions, of course, both government and utility companies will probably have other motivations outside profit-and-loss statements and considerations of "efficiency."

[14] *Proposed Practices for Economic Analysis . . . ,* p. 31.

should be counted as a cost (or negative benefit) if the project makes it physically impossible to use the old facilities. This would be the situation whenever a project involved the replacement of existing machinery or structures, and it would be a technological spillover. However, if a project competes with some existing facility but does not impair its physical output, the decline in the value of the old facility should not be counted as a cost of the project from the standpoint of maximizing production of the whole economy.

The President's Water Resources Policy Commission seems to agree in part with the position taken here. In its report[15] it is suggested that a project might expand the output of some commodity so that the price would fall sufficiently to reduce the total value of the crop. The Commission viewed this as a paradox—greater output, greater welfare, yet lower "value." The Commission was properly suspicious of counting the change in income from an entire crop, industry, or nation as the project's benefits. But it did not conclude, as it should have, that the income from the *incremental* output should be attributed to the project, letting the chips fall where they may so far as rents of existing firms are concerned. The Commission might also have emphasized that the estimated income from the new output should be based on prices that could be expected with this kind of competition and not on prices that would prevail in some other situation.

Instead, the report of the Commission presented some highly confused comments on this matter and some startling conclusions. It stated that the benefits of water-resource projects should be measured in terms of "security values" rather than spurious "scarcity values," and piled error on confusion by stating that "this basic conflict between private values based on scarcity and public values based on plenty lies at the very heart of the conservation problem."[16] The statement is either meaningless or wrong. If values of goods and services are meant, the statement is clearly incorrect; such values, public and private alike, grow out of the fact that there are not enough goods and services to satisfy all wants. If value judgments or preferences are meant, the statement has little meaning; our values in this sense grow out of the whole of our environment and heritage, and it is meaningless to say that they are based on plenty or scarcity. Misled by this confusion, the Commission finally went so far as to recommend that benefits (presumably costs, also) be measured in physical units,

---

[15] *A Water Policy for the American People,* Vol. 1, 1950, pp. 55–56.
[16] *Ibid.*

like bushels of corn, tons of beef, and kilowatt hours! This might be interpreted as an attempt to confine the measurements to the incremental outputs and costs of a project—an admirable aim—but it would result in a chaotic exhibit for each project. Comparison on any relevant basis is not made easier by the knowledge that Project A would yield 10,000 bales of cotton and 50,000 bushels of sugar beets, and would cost 500,000 tons of concrete, while Project B would yield 1,000,000 kilowatt hours of power and cost 100,000 pounds of copper.

THE RANKING OF PROJECTS

The discussion thus far has pertained to the sorting of investments into two groups, those which are "efficient" and those which are not. If an investment would produce a unit of output whose price exceeded its extra cost,[17] it would be an efficient investment. If the price of the output would be less than its extra cost, the venture would be an inefficient investment. In such cases, there would be no need to rank the investments, for all the "efficient" ones would be undertaken, rates of interest making the volume of investment and the list of efficient projects consistent with each other.

However, the decision in which cost-benefit analysis figures is slightly different—namely, the selection of a preferred set of investments from a larger set of proposals, all of which may be efficient. In other words, the measurements are used not merely to sort projects into two groups but also to help compare one project with the other and to rank them. Moreover, this is the way things should be, for in the presence of uncertainty and intangibles, such estimates cannot be used to divide the proposals neatly into the acceptable and the unacceptable. Government Agencies do not compete freely with private industry for investment funds, but they must face assigned investment budgets. They may therefore have to compare the merits of one efficient (or inefficient) project with another.

The same measurements will help in this comparison. The necessity of choosing the better of two efficient projects is a constraint, one that is similar in nature, though not in origin, to a limitation on the stock of land or iron ore in the economy. The test, as described earlier, is maximum worth, given whatever constraints are applicable. Hence, if investments A and B cost the same amount, and the excess of output price over incremental cost is greater in the case of A, then

[17] Allowing, that is, for the technological spillovers, many of which would be left out of account in a private firm's evaluation of a water-resource project.

A is preferred. The earlier conclusions still hold. That is, technological spillovers should, and pecuniary spillovers should not, be taken into account in the *comparison* of projects, even if *all* are economic (or uneconomic).

SUMMARY AND CONCLUSIONS

If government builds a better mousetrap, other mousetrap producers—including owners, laborers, and managers—will be injured. Expenditures are bound to be rechanneled. Some resources will be reallocated to the uses that *now* pay best, whether to the production of old-style mousetraps or of Venetian blinds. Some resources that cannot be readily shifted to other uses will decline in value as their rents fall. Some resources will rise in value (for example, the site of the new plant) as their rates of hire go up. The process involves distress for some and good fortune for others.

But we are concerned with gains and costs from the standpoint of the whole economy. If we approve of consumers' sovereignty, then the measure of gains to the country is what people are willing to pay for the new mousetraps. The measure of cost—what the whole economy must give up—is what the new producer has to pay to attract the inputs away from alternative uses. These gains or costs should include the imputed value of spillover effects on *technological* production possibilities elsewhere. Needless to say, they should allow for any indirect repercussions upon what people are willing to pay for the new output and upon what must be paid to attract the inputs. But changes in *aggregate* capital values, wage bills, or crop values are beside the point. It once seemed paradoxical that more water, an item which is necessary to life, could not be sold for much money, while more diamonds, though clearly dispensable, could fetch a handsome sum. Then it was perceived (a long time ago) that the value of increasing any output is not measured by the worth of the *entire* output but rather by what we would pay for the *increment* alone. And what we sacrifice is not measured by the change in some aggregate such as the wage bills; it is the value of the inputs used to obtain the *increment* in production.

Thus if we take a national viewpoint in choosing among proposed investments, we should not, like a gigantic monopoly, try to maximize industry receipts minus industry costs, total crop values, the total value of manufacturing output, or aggregate profits. What we should attempt to do is to choose those investments to which people attach a value in excess of incremental cost. The ensuing redistribution of wealth and revaluation of assets are "intangible" considerations which are relevant to final decisions. But these pecuniary external effects should not be totaled and incorporated into cost-gain estimates whose purpose is to show which investments are most efficient given that distribution of wealth.

Finally, of two investments costing the same amount, the one which has the larger excess of benefit over cost would bring us closer to "economic efficiency." The conclusions immediately above are still applicable: even though cost-benefit measurements are used to compare the merits of individual projects rather than to sort projects into the economic and the uneconomic, technological but not pecuniary spillovers should be counted.

Chapter 9

KINDS OF BENEFIT:
OVER-COUNTING,
AND SECONDARY BENEFITS

DOUBLE COUNTING

FROM TIME TO TIME benefits have been defined hitherto as the amount that people would pay for the output of a project. In government Agencies' preparation of cost-benefit analyses, certain benefits that are called "direct" or "primary" have been defined similarly. The Agencies, too, have conceived of these so-called primary benefits as the value of the goods and services that stem from a project.[1] They have, however, measured these gains incorrectly at times.

Occasionally, for instance, these goods and services have been counted two or more times. Irrigation projects have sometimes been given credit not only for the imputed value of the water (that is, what the farmers would pay for it) but also for the value of the crops made possible by the water, the value of the livestock made possible by the crops, and the value of the milk products made possible by the livestock. In other words, the increase of farm income in a highly gross form has sometimes been attributed to a project, with the use of the intermediate products and the increase in farm expenses, for

---

[1] Secondary benefits will be discussed later in Chapter 9. The Green Book distinguishes between the two concepts as follows: "*Primary benefits* are the value of the immediate products or services resulting from the measures for which project costs and associated costs were incurred. In the irrigation project illustration, the primary benefits are the value of the wheat produced by the farmer" (p. 8). "*Secondary benefits* are the values added over and above the value of the immediate products or services of the project as a result of activities stemming from or induced by the project. In the cited example, the value of the bread over and above the value of its wheat content would be a secondary benefit" (p. 9).

example, the cost of the crops used to feed the livestock, neglected entirely. In private enterprise, a comparable error would occur if a corporation, in planning a new integrated steel works, counted as future receipts both the value of the ingots to be produced and the value of the sheets, bars, and tubes to be rolled.

In recent years, this error has rarely been made in formal cost-benefit analysis by agencies of the Federal government. Nevertheless, it appears occasionally in a less obvious fashion. In one analysis made a few years ago, the increase in gross farm income, though never *stated* to be the benefits with which the project's cost should be compared, was nevertheless the only figure on returns that was mentioned in the main part of the study. These gross returns to the farmers were again referred to in the "Summary of Benefits and Costs."[2] Recent Congressional hearings still point to the same danger —namely, that the growth of gross farm income will be regarded as benefits without allowing for the increase in farm expenses: data on gross crop values are sometimes presented along with the Federal costs of irrigation projects as though the two numbers should be compared.[3] An interesting result of such over-counting is that "benefits" per acre can easily come to much more than the beneficiaries can possibly afford to pay for the project. Occasionally this has aroused the curiosity of Congressmen and citizens: "But the individuals themselves who own the property will not pay the costs in view of the benefits. Why is that? . . . That is what makes me distrustful of some of these benefit figures to some extent."[4]

Over-counting of another sort occurs whenever both the value of the increased agricultural output and the increased value of the land are counted as a benefit. That this is duplication should go without saying. The increase in the land's valuation reflects the market's capitalization of the value of the new output stream, and both increases in value cannot be realized at the same time.

[2] "Payette Unit, Mountain Home Project, Idaho," U.S. Department of Interior, Bureau of Reclamation, Project Planning Report No. 1-5.5-5 (mimeographed), September, 1945, pp. 3–4, 16.

[3] See *Interior Department Appropriations for 1953*, Hearings . . . , House of Representatives, Part 3, pp. 1122–1124. The presentation of "Costs of and [Gross] Returns from Irrigation" is qualified with the following rather odd statement: "The importance of the products of western irrigation is measured more adequately in terms of the types and kinds of food and fiber produced rather than in the dollar value of the product." (*Ibid.*, p. 1124.)

[4] Statement of Mr. Dwight Payton in *Study of Civil Works*, Hearings before the Subcommittee to Study Civil Works (Robert E. Jones, Jr., Chairman), 82nd Congress, 2d. Session, Part 2, p. 370.

Costs, like benefits, can be counted in this way. For example, "the Blue River Study Association, with the assistance of the Chamber of Commerce, Manhattan, Kansas, made a study of costs to the community which would result from the construction of the proposed Tuttle Creek Reservoir."[5] In this study, the cost due to inundation apparently included both the value of the land lost to production and the value of its output stream.[6] The same sort of double-counting, in reverse, can exaggerate the benefits to be obtained from the prevention of inundation, that is, from protection against floods.

To show that some of these points are pertinent to Federal activities, we shall refer to the estimation procedure described in the "Bureau of Reclamation Manual" of March, 1952.[7]

1. Irrigation benefits are project effects comprising improvements in the general welfare and increases in values resulting from increases in production of goods and services or decreases in costs of production. They accrue initially from lands newly irrigated, from lands receiving supplemental water, or from rehabilitation of an existing project which improves the utilization of the existing water supply or decreases the costs of operation. Irrigation benefits include direct farm benefits and indirect, public, and intangible benefits.
2. Direct farm benefits comprise:

A. The increase in family living, which includes:
   (1) The increase in value of crops, livestock, and livestock products from the farm consumed by the farm family,
   (2) The increase in value of other perquisites, such as rent of the farm dwelling,
   (3) The increase in cash allowance for family living expenditures.

B. The increase in cash income remaining after (1) cash family living allowance (above) and (2) production expenses for farm investment and farm operation (excluding irrigation operation and maintenance cost of the project) have been deducted from the value of farm products sold. This item of benefits is identical with increase in payment capacity.

[5] *Economic Evaluation of Federal Water Resource Development Projects,* Report to the Committee on Public Works, House of Representatives, by Mr. Jones of Alabama from the Subcommittee to Study Civil Works, 82nd Congress, 2nd Session (Washington, D.C.: U.S. Government Printing Office, 1952), p. 42.

[6] *Ibid.,* pp. 42–44.

[7] "Bureau of Reclamation Manual," U.S. Department of Interior, Vol. XIII— Benefits and Costs (mimeographed), March, 1952, paragraph 2.2.1. This excerpt is a direct quotation. Since the estimation procedures used by government Agencies are steadily evolving, all of the statements made here may not apply to future procedures.

C. Allowance for accumulation of equity in the farm investment.

The procedure is aimed at the right sort of estimate: an approximation of the amount which the water would be worth to the farmer. It appears, however, to permit some multiple-counting. First, the rental value of the dwelling would go up because the value of the property would go up, presumably because of the increased value of the farm's output stream. The farmer cannot realize both at one time—the increased output stream and the increased property value—any more than he can spend a coin twice because it has two sides.

Second, the allowance for accumulation of equity in the farm investment also mirrors the increased value of the output stream. In a numerical example given in the "Manual," farm investment is assumed to be $400,000 without the project, $4,000,000 with the project. Of this increase ($3,600,000), 1 per cent is called interest on the increase in farm investment and is counted as an annual benefit.[8] As previously observed, the farmer cannot sell his property, reinvest and get this interest, and still have the output stream, just as he cannot spend the head of a coin and keep the tail.

SECONDARY BENEFITS

A related procedure is the inclusion of a "secondary benefit" in analyses prepared by the Bureau of Reclamation. This is the name applied to the increased incomes of various producers, from dry-cleaners to sugar-beet processors, that stem from water-resource projects. When we include secondary benefits, we go beyond counting both the value of the crops and the value of the cattle that eat the crops. For secondary benefits embrace the value of the meat-packing, for example, that springs up because of the cattle industry, and the value of the haircuts that the new barbers sell to the meat-packers.

Of course, since the incomes of such a variety of producers are counted, and since many of them sell to each other, it is palpably ridiculous to add up the increases in their *gross* incomes. Indeed, as pointed out above, the summing of gross incomes (without adding the extra private expenses to project costs) is seldom done any more in formal cost-benefit analysis even for the farming industry. Conse-

---

[8] Actually this is done because interest costs are said to be overstated. See John M. Clark, Eugene L. Grant, and Maurice M. Kelso, "Report of Panel of Consultants on Secondary or Indirect Benefits of Water-Use Projects," June 26, 1952 (mimeographed), pp. 39–40. But the argument above is no less pertinent.

quently, it is the sum of the increments to resources' net incomes which is usually included as a secondary benefit.

The procedure can be described in more specific terms in the case of irrigation if we turn once again to the "Bureau of Reclamation Manual."

4. Indirect irrigation benefits are project effects which comprise the *increase* in:

    A. Profits of local wholesalers and retailers from handling the increase in sales of farm products consumed locally off the project without processing.

    B. Profits of all other enterprises between the farm and the final consumer, from handling, processing, and marketing the increase in sales of farm products locally and elsewhere.

    C. Profits of all enterprises from supplying goods and services for the increase in farm purchases for family living and production expenses.

    D. Land value of local residential property.

5. Like direct farm benefits, indirect irrigation benefits shall be calculated from summaries of farm budget data representing future conditions with and without the project. Indirect benefit factors shall be applied to increases or decreases in the value of individual commodities listed in the budget summaries. The indirect benefit from the increase in land value of local residential property shall be calculated separately.

6. The following factors shall be used to derive net indirect irrigation benefits from summaries of farm budget data. Indirect costs were deducted in determining these factors.

Indirect Benefit A (Local Wholesale and Retail)   5 per cent
Indirect Benefit B (Processing, Marketing, etc.)

Cotton	83	per cent
Wool	78	" "
Grain (wheat, oats, corn, barley)	48	" "
Oil crops (flax, cottonseed, soybeans)	30	" "
Sugar beets	26	" "
Fruits and vegetables	24	" "
Dry beans	23	" "
Rice	13	" "
Livestock (meat)	11	" "
Seed crops	10	" "
Dairy products	7	" "
Poultry products	6	" "

Indirect Benefit C (farm purchases)   18 " "
Indirect Benefit D (higher grade land use)

A factor of 4 per cent will be applied to the increase in land value of local residential property to derive an annual value for Indirect Benefit D.[9]

The factors[10] listed under item 6 are supposed to be the net incomes of processors, marketers, and others whose incomes are affected by the new output, expressed as a percentage of the gross value of the product. For example, the secondary benefit from an increase in cotton production would include the value added (the net incomes generated) by ginning, transporting, and spinning the cotton; by making and transporting cloth; and finally by manufacturing and marketing the dresses. Hence, if the annual value of the extra cotton crop is $100,000, the secondary benefit, or the sum of these enlarged incomes, would be 83 per cent of that amount or $83,000 annually.

It should be observed that these terms are not always consistently used. For instance, "the Bureau of Reclamation considers as a direct benefit the increase in wages paid hired laborers and the increase in interest paid by farmers on borrowed capital."[11] Yet these increases seem to belong among secondary benefits, which are defined as increases in the net incomes of other producers due to the project.

The relationship of these "secondary" benefits to "spillovers" should also be noted. They are indubitably a species of spillover, though they do not fall squarely into any of the categories discussed in Chapter 8. As defined above, and as customarily measured, secondary benefits do not grow out of external technological effects, though the term has served at times as a sort of catchall and has no doubt occasionally encompassed technological spillovers. They are clearly not losses experienced by other producers as a result of the increase in factor rates of hire or of the decrease in the prices of substitute products. They are not gains experienced by other producers on account of an increase in the price of complementary products, or of a decrease in the price of the project's output. That they do not fall neatly into any of these categories is brought out by the example in the foregoing quotation. That example was an increase in wages paid to hired laborers. In connection with spillovers, such an increase in wages

[9] "Bureau of Reclamation Manual," paragraph 2.2.4. Again, this is a direct quotation.

[10] Perhaps it will help avoid confusion if the several uses of the word "factor" are recapitulated. It has been convenient and/or conventional to refer to "factors of production," meaning resources such as types of capital and labor; to "secondary-benefit factors," meaning numbers used as multipliers; and to "factoring out" suboptimizations, meaning the separation of subproblems of choice from a larger problem.

[11] *Missouri: Land and Water*, p. 90.

raised the question: should the bidding up of wages, since it inflicts losses on other producers, be counted as a cost of an investment? But in connection with secondary benefits, we find an interesting switch: should it be counted instead as a benefit?

As Gains to the Whole Economy

Whether or not these secondary benefits are gains to the whole economy has been a highly controversial question.[12] Moreover, the Agencies themselves have gone their separate ways in preparing cost-benefit analyses: the Bureau of Reclamation counts secondary benefits, while the Corps of Engineers and the Department of Agriculture do not.

There is no denying that the subject is confusing. Successive payments are undeniably gains to the recipients, and it is easy to slip into regarding them as net gains to the nation. But the result is a strange sort of multiple-counting. First to be counted are the values attached to the new output by those who purchase from the farmers. To these are added the incomes generated as the farmers take their receipts and pay them out to others. Also, as expenditures to build the project become incomes to laborers, cement producers, and steel fabricators, these incomes are included among the benefits. Finally, as the outputs of the project are processed, the resulting incomes to laborers, stockholders, and owners of equipment are also counted as benefits of the project. Right before our eyes, the farmers' costs, the project costs, and a good many other costs have suddenly turned into gains. That they add up to a large amount is not surprising. What *is* surprising is that these secondary-benefit factors are not still larger. Pushed to its logical conclusion, this concept of secondary benefits would surely lead to factors greater than such modest percentages as 78 or 83. One therefore suspects that they are arbitrary numbers.

In connection with secondary benefits, it may be enlightening to think briefly about the private sector of the economy. The same effects are present if a private investment is undertaken. If they are genuine gains to the economy, why is it that private firms are not encouraged to take them into account? Think what would happen to

[12] *Proposed Practices for Economic Analysis . . . ,* pp. 35–36; John M. Clark, Eugene L. Grant, Maurice M. Kelso, *op. cit.;* "Revised Statement on Secondary Benefits," Federal Inter-Agency River Basin Committee, Subcommittee on Benefits and Costs, January 8, 1952 (mimeographed); "Interior Minority Statement on Secondary Benefits," January 7, 1952 (mimeographed).

the worth of any private venture if the value of its output ought to be multiplied by a secondary-benefit factor.

WITH RESOURCES FULLY EMPLOYED. The answer is that private entrepreneurs are not encouraged to recognize such benefits because, from the standpoint of economic efficiency, they should not be recognized. Consider the following example of the way these alleged benefits are generated. Cotton is purchased by a processor, who buys until the worth of another bale to him is equal to what he has to pay for it. He hires other inputs, such as management, man-hours, floor space, and machine-hours, until the worth to him of another unit of each equals what must be paid for it. Some "factors of production," including the entrepreneur, may collect an increased rent, a rate of hire larger than would be necessary to retain the services of that factor, and the rents of some factors in other firms will decline. So far as economic efficiency is concerned, these transfers are irrelevant, though they are pertinent, naturally, to the distribution of wealth. The payments for additional inputs, which increase the firm's production, are relevant, but, since these resources are drawn from marginal uses, these payments represent what the resources would be worth in alternative uses. The only new value contributed by the project, to be compared with its cost, is the amount which the buyers of the new output would be willing to pay.

Consider further some examples that do not involve processing of the product. Suppose the local expansion attracts some new barbers to the community. If their incomes are included among the benefits of the project, the decline of haircutting in some other part of the economy is being ignored. Or suppose that farmers spend more in the local stores. If the stores cannot expand, somebody gets some more rent, with no increase in production. If they do expand, they draw inputs from other uses, causing a corresponding decline in output elsewhere. The conclusion is that when there is full employment, there really are no secondary benefits at all.

WITH SOME RESOURCES UNEMPLOYED. However, if some of these inputs, i.e., resources, would otherwise be unemployed or "underemployed," then part of the new net incomes represents an increase in production. If in the absence of the project, certain resources would be involuntarily unemployed[13] throughout the time period, usually as much as fifty years, then the incomes of these resources throughout the time period can be viewed as a gain due to the project. If those

---

[13] The difficulties of defining this state of involuntary unemployment are very real, but are not important to the position taken in this study.

resources would be unemployed over only part of the relevant period, then their incomes (that is, the value of their products) can be counted as a benefit over only that part.

The possibility of resources being "underemployed" may need a little explanation. Suppose that there are great lags in the reallocation of resources after capital growth, innovation, or changes in taste—lags that are due, say, to inertia, miscalculation, labor unions, monopoly, or lack of funds to effect the transition. In such circumstances, resources for the "expansion" generated by a project may be obtained from "submarginal" uses so that the value of their outputs is markedly higher in their new employment.[14] Many people believe, for example, that Southern agricultural labor was in a submarginal use in the thirties and that the Tennessee Valley Authority, by generating more productive alternative occupations which were close at hand, brought about a much-needed shift that would not otherwise have occurred.

Now it is safe to say that estimates of secondary benefits in the past have embraced more than the output of resources which would otherwise have been unemployed. Nonetheless, it is likely that the measurement of such output was often the primary intent. The following quotations, one pertaining to the extra work provided by the construction of a project and the other pertaining to the "make-work" aspect of a project's output, suggest this underlying concern for unemployment.

Benefits of the construction involved, although great at the site of the work, would be even greater elsewhere in the Nation. Estimates prepared by the United States Department of Labor indicate that for every man-hour spent on the site of a reclamation project, 1.6 man-hours must be spent off the site. Thus, for every five men employed at the project, eight men are required at widespread points in the Nation for production and assembly of the hundreds of materials and items which go into the construction of dams, power plants, turbines, generators, power transmission facilities, canals, and other project works. Such benefits . . . , particularly when brought into being during periods of lower employment in private industry, clearly have great national significance.[15]

. . . On the average, out of 594,000 kilowatts of prime power, about one-third would be utilized in diversified manufacturing, one-third in electro-process industries, such as production of metals and phosphorous, and one-

[14] Of course, it is extremely difficult to tell whether or not this happens; if the failure to shift location or occupation without the project were a result of locational preference, differential risk of unemployment, and so on, then the new higher-paying job may not really be more productive.

[15] *The Columbia River,* Bureau of Reclamation, Vol. 1, February, 1950, House Document 473, 81st Congress, 2d. Session, p. 76.

third in residential, farm, and commercial establishments. Such a usage would support an estimated 35,000 jobs in manufacturing, with an annual earning power of $140,000,000 in salaries and wages. Service industries would employ at least another 35,000 workers and add at least another $100,000,000 in annual salaries, wages, and other income. The estimated manufactured product produced would be an annual average of about $700,000,000 of industrial commodities of various sorts. This electric power would also stimulate estimated sales of residential, agricultural, and commercial electric appliances and equipment having an aggregate value of about $1,000,000,000.[16]

In effect these comments point out that the building of the project, and probably the processing of its output, would cause an increase in aggregate demand. Such an increase would be of no particular advantage during a period of prosperity and stable price levels, and it would be a real disadvantage during a time of inflation. It would be beneficial, as the first comment hints, *if* (not "particularly when") the increase in demand occurred during deflation and unemployment.

IMPLICATIONS FOR COST-BENEFIT MEASUREMENTS. This matter has been carefully considered by the Federal Inter-Agency River Basin Committee and its Subcommittee on Benefits and Costs. The recommendation of the majority of the Committee[17] was essentially that the extent of unemployment and underemployment be projected and that the secondary benefit be calculated as the net incomes of productive factors *with* the project minus their net incomes *without* the project. Thus, if any productive factors are pulled into full use from idleness or submarginal employment, the increased value of the product would be counted.

Now this is a logical position to take, and it represents a tremendous step forward. Nonetheless, a different position is taken in the present study, a position which might be inferior if there were certainty but which is believed to be better under actual conditions.

To begin with, let us examine some of the hazards of predicting the effects of a project on employment. First, it is difficult to predict the unemployment which would exist without the project. In this connection, it should be noted that the forecast we speak of pertains to a long time period. If a few of the resources are assumed to be unemployed for only a couple of years, the benefits under discussion will be trivial in comparison with the value of the project's output over the whole period. The only circumstances in which this benefit figure

---

[16] *Congressional Record,* Vol. 98, Part 6, 83rd Congress, 2nd Session, June 24, 1952, pp. 7931–7932.

[17] "Revised Statement on Secondary Benefits"; an opposing minority view was presented in "Interior Minority Statement on Secondary Benefits."

is worth much consideration is that of *prolonged* and *widespread* unemployment (or underemployment). And when we try to peer forty or fifty years into the future, it seems a little hazardous to predict how much of which resources in what regions will be unemployed for how long.

Second, it also requires some boldness to predict the effects of a project upon unemployment when we have no foreknowledge of the rest of the Federal Budget. It seems to be an empty sort of suboptimization to compare the increases in employment that can be attributed to several tiny portions of the Budget. In the writer's judgment, this subproblem should not be "factored out." How would the expenditure be financed? What would be happening to the total water-resources budget, to aggregate Federal outlays and taxes, to the money stock? *What would have happened to taxes and total expenditures in the absence of the project?*

It should be recalled that small variations in projects—small increments and different combinations of component measures—ought to be compared. But surely adjustments in tax rates, in total government expenditures, and in the money supply affect employment so greatly that it is impossible to assess the effect of a particular small outlay while ignoring these other adjustments. In these circumstances, to ask which project would increase employment more is like asking which of two grains of salt would improve one's scrambled egg more, when each grain must be administered along with the contents of a gallon jug that may be filled with more salt, with just the right amount of pepper, or with nothing at all. Also, the egg may have been salted already.

Third, the uncertainties are aggravated slightly by the fact that analyses are prepared well in advance of the final decision and the commencement of construction. They are used primarily to help compare projects prior to authorization, which may precede final commitments by several years. This is a minor point, though, for the projections of unemployment, like any of the other projections, could be revised prior to final decisions in the light of the latest information.

As a consequence of the first two difficulties, it is suggested here that the measurements might better rest on the assumption that resources will be fully employed. The reason is not that difficulties are an excuse for doing nothing. The reason is that uncertainty would be as great as ever, and in fact would be concealed by a specific forecast of unemployment.

A sounder way to factor out the problem of choosing water-resource projects would be to *compare* them in the context of a given level of employment, and to compare other alternative policies, whose effects would be more certain and powerful, for combating inflation and deflation. That is, to help determine the composition of water-resource budgets (the selection of individual water-resource measures), benefit measurements should be confined to the values of the incremental outputs. In determining the magnitude of *aggregate expenditures and taxes,* and possibly of the water-resource budget, the effects on employment could be more reliably estimated, and should be considered.

As Measures of Regional Development

In the preceding paragraphs it has been argued that secondary benefits are gains to the whole economy, and should be included in the estimate of benefits, only if unemployment would otherwise exist. In a separate exhibit, however, data similar to secondary benefits would be relevant. Most of the increases in income that constitute secondary benefits occur in the region in which the project is located. So far as this region is concerned, a project does ordinarily give rise to a net expansion. Indeed, the fact that the growth is concentrated in one region while the inputs are released through a long chain of adjustments and from widely dispersed operations is what makes the expansion appear to be a net gain to the nation.

As indicated earlier, one of the aims of many Congressmen, one which is evidently shared by a large number of voters, is to make some regions grow relative to others—to approach a more "balanced" development. The belief that such development, however ill-defined, is desirable comes up again and again in debates about water-resource programs.[18] Often, of course, the argument is motivated by the natural self-interest of persons in the region to be improved. Sometimes, however, the argument for regional development proceeds from the desire for a more equitable income distribution plus the assumption that people in the low-income area cannot, or will not, move to better-paying jobs in other areas. This may be a desire not to be "fair" to geographical areas as such, but to raise the income of individuals, given their geographical immobility, to some minimum level. At other times the advocacy of a region's development appears to

[18] For instance, see the testimony concerning the development of Alaska in *Interior Department Appropriations for 1953,* Hearings . . . , House of Representatives, Part 4, pp. 1217–1236; and statements concerning the reclamation program, *Ibid.,* Part 3, pp. 1210–1214.

spring from a genial desire to do good, regardless of the consequences. Consider the following statement (made by a Congressman from the Midwest, not by one from the project area): "I have in mind, gentlemen, the Estancia Valley in New Mexico, a beautiful valley. All it needs is water, and you can raise anything . . . . It is a big valley, a beautiful valley. If we could afford it, that valley should have water on it by all means."[19]

There is little need for us to assess the merits of the arguments for regional development. It is enough if we recognize that some Congressmen and voters favor steps to develop particular regions and that others oppose such steps. This much alone tells the analyst that the implications of various projects for the growth of some regions at the expense of others are important to final decisions. That being the case, a *description* of the local expansion due to each project, and if possible of the contractions which must occur elsewhere, is relevant information.

Hence, though estimates of secondary benefits as measured at present do not give an accurate picture of the local expansions, they might with some modification become helpful exhibits. Such an exhibit should only describe the local expansion. It should not attempt to price the regional expansion so as to derive an amount which could be added to the value of the incremental output. The cost-benefit analyst cannot determine a price having *general* validity that can be attached to the development of one area instead of another.

TREATMENT OF TAXES

Another age-old controversy pertains to the inclusion of local and Federal taxes in the calculations, either as reductions of project benefits or as additions to project costs. On the one hand, many persons agree with the Engineers Joint Council: "In computing the annual costs of Federal water developments, for determining economic justification or for any other purpose, there should be included amounts equivalent to the taxes which would have to be paid were the lands, physical improvements and business, if any, not exempt from taxation, whether Federal, State or local."[20] On the other hand, there are those who hold the opposite view. For example, the position of advocates of the Hell's Canyon "high dam," a Federal proposal, has been described as follows:

[19] *Ibid.,* Part 3, p. 1121.
[20] *Principles of a Sound National Water Policy,* p. 192.

Their fundamental objection is that, in calculating whether the high dam's extra power would be economic, the commission put the costs of the two schemes on an equal footing [privately built dams being the second scheme]. But the whole point of publicly-generated electricity, say its supporters, is that it does not have to bear the same costs as private power because, being an activity of the Federal government, no taxes are paid on the facilities and money for them can be borrowed at the cheapest rate.[21]

Which position is correct? Cost-benefit estimates, it should be recalled, are supposed to be guides to the set of efficient projects, and should therefore reflect all tangible costs and benefits to the economy. Do tax payments, or equivalent bookkeeping charges, represent genuine additions to cost (or, alternatively, reductions in benefit) to the nation? Presumably some of these payments reflect real costs of a project, for example, the use of extra resources in the local fire and police departments. On the whole, however, tax payments are probably not closely correlated with the costs to the economy that can be attributed to a particular investment. Many tax payments represent instead a transfer from one group to another.

Does this mean that allowance for taxes should not be made? Not necessarily. If government proposals are to be compared only *with each other* in order to select the best set of projects for a given budget, any property and income taxes that do not reflect real project costs may be ignored.[22] That is, costs and gains will be properly reflected, and, moreover, various government projects will be on a comparable basis, if transfers are not included in the benefit and cost streams. However, cost-benefit estimates may also contribute, albeit less conclusively, to the comparison of government proposals with private investment, for instance, to the determination of the size of the water-resources budget. Indeed, whether it is intended or not, these estimates, if they are presented at all, may influence the decision about the size of the budget.

Whenever cost-benefit estimates figure in the comparison of public with private investment, the two types of investment should be placed on a comparable footing. In the case of private investment as well as public proposals, only part of the anticipated tax represents addi-

---

[21] "Hot as Hell's Canyon," *The Economist*, August 20, 1955, p. 616.

[22] We could not leave out the excise taxes on inputs, e.g., on transportation of construction materials, or the impacts of the whole tax structure on the prices paid for inputs and on the prices at which the project's output is to be valued. It would not be feasible to segregate these impacts in order to leave them out of account; and it would not be correct to do so if prices, as affected by the tax structure, are accepted as measures of value.

tional cost to the economy, because a large share of the tax payment is just a transfer. Nonetheless such payments must be entered in the accounts of private ventures as cost items that reduce net profits. Thus net profit after taxes is too low as a measure of net benefit to the economy from a private investment. That being the case, what can be done to put the two types of investment on a comparable basis? We can hardly keep two sets of books on all private investments, one for the purpose of comparing private ventures with each other and the other for the purpose of comparing private investment with public projects. It is possible, however, to make a comparable reduction of the benefit stream from each public project by charging each with the estimated Federal, State, and local taxes which would be levied if there were no exemptions. The propriety of making such an allowance seems to be clear-cut when the comparison is between public and private facilities, as in the example of Hell's Canyon.

To sum up the conclusions, real costs imposed upon the community, such as extra usage of municipal services, should definitely be included in the calculations, whatever the comparison that is being made. If taxes that are transfers rather than payments for services are not allowed for, cost-benefit estimates should not be used in any comparison of public ventures with private investment. If such taxes are deducted from the public project's stream of benefits, the estimates should be relevant to, though by no means decisive in, the comparison of government proposals with private investment.

MISCELLANEOUS OVER-COUNTING

Naturally, the number of possible mistakes that one can make in the estimation of benefits and costs is huge, and no attempt has been made to prepare a catalog of the possible errors. Attention has been focused instead on those that are of major significance. A few important possibilities of over-counting remain to be considered.[23]

One potential source of error is the average quality of performance that is assumed in the use of new water-resource developments. Should optimal performance by farmers be postulated, or should some sort of

---

[23] There are also possibilities of under-counting. However, slips in proofreading appear to account for the most modest claims: "In addition, 700 thousand acres now irrigated by ancient methods and yielding but one crop a year could be brought to yield two crops in three years.—*Washington Post & Times Herald*," quoted in the *New Yorker*, January 14, 1956, p. 55.

operational degradation be allowed for? This type of question arises in the comparison of alternative operations or systems of any kind. What should be assumed about human behavior and the performance of other parts of the system in collaboration with innovations? What would performance be *under actual conditions?* In some analyses, a priori reasoning and previous experience have been drawn upon in order to make allowance for "degradation" of performance under field conditions. This procedure might well be copied in the analysis of water-resource measures.

The significance of this point may become clearer when the case studies in Chapters 11 and 12 are examined. In the official analysis of the Green River watershed program, it was estimated that the project would lead to dramatic increases in crop yield, increases of more than 50 per cent for the majority of crops. Such figures must be based on an assumption of almost 100 per cent efficiency on the part of the farmers, with little allowance for deterioration of performance "in the field." Actually, of course, it is unlikely that farmers would suddenly become much more efficient upon completion of the project. Degradation of their potential performance to allow for some slips 'twixt cup and lip would make for improved evaluation of such projects.

A somewhat related source of error is the average quality of the land, forest, or product that is assumed. Large acreages affected by the water-resource measures have to be treated as though they were homogeneous. This being necessary, one has to be careful to use a reasonable *average* fertility in estimating total output, and not assume that the entire acreage is uniformly of the best quality. It is easy to make a mistake here—to project results for the best forest lands and apply them to the whole forest acreage, or to estimate production per acre from the highest-quality soils and to apply this factor to all the lands that a particular project would irrigate. A similar mistake is to use factors based on harvesting the best quality of timber, neglecting the fact that in many years second-rate timber must be cut. It is essential, thus, when dealing with aggregates, to be on guard against biased average multipliers.

Still another possible error which leads to over-counting output is failure to allow for the farm-entrepreneur's alternative product. In a sample "Derivation of Direct Farm Benefits" presented by the Bureau of Reclamation, production expenses and "family living allowances" are deducted from gross farm income to calculate direct benefits.[24] The family living allowance, without irrigation, is set at $1,000 (presumably in 1952 dollars) per farm family. It is evidently assumed that the new farmers could have earned this amount in their next best use. If this is an inadequate estimate of the cost of their services, and it seems that it is, the net benefits are overstated.

[24] "Bureau of Reclamation Manual," paragraph 2.2.3. The relevant numbers, in case anyone wishes to examine them, are as follows: with irrigation, the 100 farms have additional gross income of $1,320,000, additional production expenses of $840,000. The family living allowances without irrigation for the 90 new farmers are $90,000. Benefits are $1,320,000 minus the sum of $840,000 and $90,000, or $390,000. This benefit figure is broken down into types A and B, amounting to $112,500 and $277,500, respectively.

Chapter 10

VALUATION OF BENEFITS

T HE TWO PRECEDING CHAPTERS have taken up certain *kinds* of effects
which should be included and certain others which should be
excluded from our measurements. We turn now to some of the questions that come up when we try to put a valuation or price tag on the
outputs which are to be included.

VALUATION IF INDIVISIBILITIES ARE PRESENT[1]

So long as investment proceeds by small increments, the value of
the output attributable to the investment is simply the price of an
extra unit (or that price multiplied by a small number of units). This
amount satisfactorily measures what people would be willing to pay
for the additional product. Suppose, however, that the investment can
be provided only in a "large lump," such as a big reservoir or canal.
We shall not worry for the moment about whether or not canals do
in fact have a minimum size, whether or not lumpiness does occur
frequently. We shall examine the implications of lumpiness first, and
indicate its applicability later.

If a factor of production—in this instance, the capital equipment—
comes in indivisible chunks, an extra amount just sufficient to increase
output by one unit cannot be added. The lump that has to be considered may increase production by so many units that the price per
unit of the product falls noticeably when the new output is marketed.
Would the additional output multiplied by this lower price correctly
measure the value which consumers attach to it? The answer is surely

---

[1] This section is based largely on Chapters 15 and 16 in Lerner, *op. cit.*,
pp. 174–199.

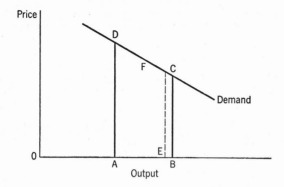

Figure 1. Valuation of benefits when indivisibilities exist.

no. The extra output contributed by the lumpy investment should really be multiplied by an average price in between the amount for which the first extra units could be sold and the price for which the last units could be sold.[2] The product of this multiplication approximates the amount that consumers would be willing to pay for the additional output.

A diagram may help make this clear. The line CD is a special sort of demand curve. It does not connect the prices at which various quantities of the output would be bought. Rather it connects the maximum prices that consumers would pay for various units[3] of the product when buying output OB. Thus if OB was bought, some units would be worth more to users than price BC, and, if the application of the indivisible lump of capital increased output from OA to OB, the worth of the increment to consumers would be measured by the area ABCD. Output OB times an average price in between AD and BC yields an area roughly equal to ABCD.

Note that if the increase in output was from OE to OB, and if it did not noticeably depress the price, then its value would be closely approximated by the number of units multiplied by that price, represented by the small area BCFE. In that case, the indivisibility would simply be too trivial to be of any consequence. Also, if the investment

---

[2] This procedure is described in Lerner, *op. cit.*, p. 197. Strictly speaking, one should multiply each of the extra units by the maximum price that would be paid for it, and sum the resulting amounts. H. Hotelling, "The General Welfare in Relation to Problems of Taxation and of Railway and Utility Rates," *Econometrica*, July, 1938, pp. 242–269.

[3] These units would ordinarily be rates of output per time period.

was perfectly divisible, it could be small enough to add just one unit of output, and then the price per se would correctly measure the value attached to the extra output by consumers.

Although this chapter pertains primarily to the valuation of benefits, the relevance of the present discussion to costs should be noted. If the indivisibility is of any consequence, so far as costs are concerned, it will raise the prices of the inputs used to build the chunk of equipment. Would the extra units of input multiplied by this higher price correctly measure their cost, i.e., the value of the alternative products which must be given up? Again the answer is no. These inputs should really be valued at a price in between the amount that would have to be bid for the first extra inputs and the price that would have to be paid for the last ones.[4]

The general rule, then, is as follows: with respect to the smallest increment in investment that can be considered, the benefit is the maximum amount that could be collected for the extra output, and the cost is the minimum amount that would secure the inputs' services. The cost to the economy of the additional inputs and the value of the extra outputs might be found by using "price discrimination,"[5] that is, by costing each unit of input at the lowest price that would attract it, and by valuing each unit of output at the highest amount that would be paid for it. But these magnitudes can be estimated with sufficient accuracy by using a single average price for the incremental outputs and a single average price for the new inputs. In appraising lumps of investment, these are the measurements of gain and cost that are relevant—from the standpoint of efficiency in the economy as a whole. If the benefit, measured in this way, exceeds the cost, also measured in this way, the investment should be made (so far as this test alone is concerned).

Implications for Measurement

Sometimes this method of measuring gain and cost would not affect the investment decision. Suppose we consider the addition of a lump of equipment, say a single-track railroad, when subsequent operation would be in a range of rising unit costs. For example, if the equipment was installed, we might anticipate cost and demand conditions like those shown in Figure 2. (Notice that output can be varied continuously within the limits shown; it is the input, the

---

[4] Inputs would be pulled from marginal uses, so that these amounts would reflect the sacrifice entailed by using them on the lumpy investment.

[5] Hotelling, *op. cit.*, pp. 242–269.

equipment in this illustration, which must be in the form of a lump.)
In the graph, the cost of the equipment is included, of course, in unit
costs. With this cost-and-demand picture, the proper policy (so far
as the economy is concerned) is to make the investment and produce
OA at price AB, which would more than cover unit cost AC. If output
was less than OA, additional units would be worth more than they
would cost; beyond OA, extra units would cost more than they would
be worth. Thus the addition of the lumpy input is shown to be a
step in the right direction[6] by applying to all of output OA the price
and cost of the "last" unit. In those circumstances, and provided that
all profitable investments are to be undertaken, it is unnecessary
to find out the maximum amount that consumers would be willing
to pay for the new output or the minimum amount that would attract
the inputs.

Suppose, however, that subsequent operation would be in a range
of declining unit costs. Figure 3 shows a second set of cost and
demand conditions that might exist, once the rail line was installed.
According to this cost-and-demand picture, outputs greater than OA
do not need to be considered, for additional output would clearly
cost more than it would be worth to any consumer. Furthermore,
outputs less than OA would not be efficient, because consumers would
be willing to pay more for additional units of output than the inputs
would cost (i.e., than they would pay for the alternative products

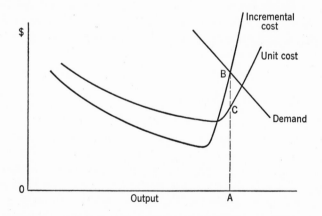

Figure 2. Rising unit costs after an indivisible investment.

[6] Our concern here is with this particular investment choice, not with further
adjustments that may be in order, given still more time.

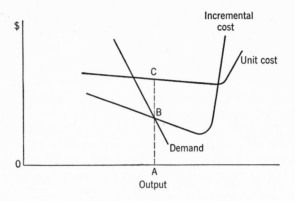

Figure 3. Declining unit costs after an indivisible investment.

of these inputs). Hence, if the plant is to be constructed at all, OA is the proper output for us to consider. But should the facility be constructed at all? At output OA, the price that could be charged per unit (AB) is less than the unit cost (AC). So the venture would have to be run at a loss if a uniform price was to be charged for the product. Nonetheless, consumers might be willing to pay more for the output AB than it would cost. It would not be sufficient in this case to use the price and cost of the incremental unit of output in appraising the worth of the lumpy investment. It would be necessary to turn to the special kind of demand curve described earlier, and then to value each unit of output at the highest price that would be paid for it, and to cost each unit of input at the lowest price that would attract it.

An illustration may help clarify what has been said so far. Suppose we were considering the construction of the Panama Canal. For the sake of simplicity, let us telescope the whole time sequence into a single period. The incremental cost of the first unit of output, passage of a ship through the canal, would be millions of dollars. But suppose that the incremental cost—the cost of the extra facilities and other inputs—of the ten-thousandth passage would be $100. Next, assume that the demand curve passed through this point, so that only ten thousand passages would be bought at a price of $100. In other words, a price of $100 would ration the use of the canal to those shippers to whom passage would be worth at least this much. Now assume that average total cost at that output would be $1,000. If price equaled incremental cost, the venture would clearly be unprofitable.

Should we abandon the whole idea? Not necessarily. *Some* users would be willing to pay much more than $100 per trip, perhaps enough more in all to cover total costs. Should output simply be restricted and a uniform price, high enough to recover costs, be charged? It would hardly be optimal, from the standpoint of the economy's efficiency, to do so. If the price was set at $1,000, for example, many shippers would go all the way around South America at a cost of, say, $500, using up more resources than those that could be used to send the ships through the canal. Thus, if a uniform price higher than $100 was charged, more than the necessary inputs would be used up to accomplish the transportation task. In accordance with the argument above, the investment should be regarded as an all-or-none proposition, and the benefits should be the sum of the maximum amounts that users would be willing to pay—*discriminatory* amounts. Similarly, the costs should be the sum of the minimum payments necessary to attract the inputs. To repeat the earlier conclusions, if the benefit, measured in this way, exceeds the cost, also measured in this way, it is efficient in our limited sense to build the canal.

So much for efficiency. What about another important consideration, the distributional implications? What about the financial loss that might be incurred under actual pricing practices? In the private sector of the economy, where an investment that yielded a financial loss would not be undertaken, two things might happen: (1) If monopoly was permitted, but with a uniform price to all customers, it might prove profitable to sell some smaller output than OA at a higher price than AB. (Incremental cost would be lower than price.) (2) If price discrimination was both possible and allowable, i.e., sale of the product at different prices to different persons, a larger output than that of the monopolist might prove profitable.

In the public sector of the economy, one possible policy would be to restrict output until it could be sold at a price equal to average cost. But while this policy would eliminate financial loss, output would be "too low," according to the foregoing argument, and the estimate of benefits would be wrong. One way out would be for the government to charge a uniform price equal to incremental cost but to get voluntary contributions from those users who were willing to pay more in order to have the canal. It would be very surprising, however, if this procedure was consistently successful in getting worthwhile ventures carried out. Another way would be to set a uniform price equal to incremental cost but to levy a special assessment on those persons to whom the project would be worth an extra amount.

With this method, sometimes used in connection with municipal improvements, it is difficult to be sure that the worth of the project to the taxpayer really is as much as the compulsory tax. Another possibility would be to pay discriminatory rates of hire to inputs and charge discriminatory prices to users. Although used to some extent, this method is administratively difficult and generally unpalatable. In many cases, the loss would probably be accepted by government and be financed from the general revenues—that is, by means of a compulsory tax on the population at large.

This sort of alteration in the distribution of wealth, just like the failure to compensate those who are injured, may as well be recognized as a concomitant circumstance when "decreasing cost investments" are undertaken. As stated earlier, therefore, it may not be possible to say that the maximum production reached by economic investments of this sort is *definitely* better than some other point.[7] But analysis can help nonetheless by providing the following data: (1) exhibits showing which investments yield the most benefit for a given budget, with valuations made as described, and (2) exhibits showing what distributional consequences are implied. Both pieces of information are important to proper decision-making.

Implications for Cost-Benefit Measurements under Actual Conditions

The decision to which such cost-gain measurements are directly relevant is whether or not an investment is economic. However, as was indicated in Chapter 8 on spillovers, cost-benefit measurements are used, not to divide projects into efficient and inefficient categories, but to compare individual projects. Even if all of the ventures are profitable, or unprofitable, they have to be compared because there is capital rationing. The measurements described in the preceding section can be used for the comparison of projects if we accept the proposition that the bigger the excess of benefit over cost, the better the investment because it puts us "closer" to efficiency.

Moreover, if individual projects are to be compared, the method of estimation that is appropriate when unit costs are decreasing should be used even if unit costs are increasing. That is, if lumps of investment are to be compared one with the other, one cannot merely

---

[7] If the investment budget is *given*—if the taxes are already scheduled—the problem is one of choosing the investments without regard for the means of financing. Even in that case, however, the project itself will have some uncompensated effects on wealth distribution.

separate the profitable investments from the unprofitable, even for projects whose unit costs are increasing. And one should not compare and rank projects on the basis of estimates that are prepared in two different ways, namely, with the benefits from some projects being the maximum that would be paid for their output while the benefits from other projects are the "post-project" price multiplied by the output.

Projects that involve no indivisibilities from a technical standpoint are often considered in large chunks anyway, partly because of the expense of analyzing numerous alternatives. In fact, when cost-benefit analyses are submitted to higher administrative officials or to Congress, the scale of the projects has already been decided upon in many instances, and the projects are submitted as though they were completely indivisible. At this stage, the numbers pertain to Project A, Project B, and so on, not to small increments in each investment. In principle, it is incorrect to calculate the value of these lumps by using the price of the marginal unit of output. To be sure, the list of projects to be considered should in principle comprise numerous project sizes differing by small increments. But, to repeat, so far as evaluation is concerned, the general principle is the following: with respect to the smallest increment in size that is considered, the benefit is the maximum amount that would be paid for the extra output, and the cost is the minimum amount that would secure the services of the inputs.

Should present procedure be modified? This question can be answered fully only in connection with the analysis of particular projects or, more accurately, particular water-resource systems. Nonetheless, a few observations can be made about present measurements in general. It is doubtful that the lumpiness of investments is a major source of error in the valuation of benefits and costs. Along this line, two things might be pointed out in connection with the products that are attributed to water-resource projects. First, the agencies usually do use prices that are suitable in the consideration of lumps of investment. They do not estimate the value of water, bucket by bucket, to each purchaser. But the agencies do apply to the new output a price that is probably *in between* the amount for which the first extra units could be sold and the amount for which the last units could be sold. It seems unlikely that they underprice the extra output that would be provided by the proposed investments. Second, particularly with respect to agricultural output, the indivisibilities of the investments are not as significant as they may appear to be at first blush. Even without price supports, a single project of the size that is customarily analyzed would not markedly depress the price of its product (or increase the price of its major inputs). In other words, these lumps, whether imposed by technology or by failure to consider smaller increments, are probably not serious indivisibilities so far as the principal products and inputs are concerned.

If we turn our attention to flood-control benefit, this, too, turns out to be largely the saving of agricultural output, and the preceding remarks are applicable. In any event, the reduction of flood damage is not a homogeneous output that can be sold at a uniform price; and the calculations are an attempt to determine the maximum amount which the farmers and townspeople, taken all together, would pay for the protection. With respect to prevention of damage to highways or reductions in the cost of purifying urban water supplies, estimates here, too, comprise the full amount that these services would be worth to the governmental units.

Thus, it seems likely that current estimation procedures already make adequate use of the principles of valuation that apply when investments are indivisible.[8] That is, the current procedures avoid the kind of error that might be made if a large lump of output were valued at the price of the marginal unit. Moreover, there are some disadvantages to increasing the emphasis, in practice, upon those principles of valuation. First, attempts to make more exhaustive use of discriminatory valuation might encourage us all to think in terms of indivisible chunks of investment when this is unnecessary. The crying need is to increase the frequency with which increments to projects are analyzed. Second, the presentation of refined discriminatory valuations might have the effect of concealing the uncertainty that attaches to cost-benefit estimates. The use of a whole series of product prices, one for each of several blocks of output, might give a false impression of great precision.[9] Another crying need, it should be recalled, is to reveal, rather than conceal, uncertainty so that it will not be ignored by policy-makers.

For these reasons, it is concluded here that, by and large, new efforts could better be used to improve other aspects of present procedures. This is not to say that the pricing of project outputs can be neglected. It deserves plenty of attention. But this should be mainly

---

[8] Analyses of power installations have not been studied by the writer, but it is likely that the prices used to value power output are sufficiently high.

[9] Intensive application of these principles of discriminatory valuation might also open the door to flagrant abuse of those principles, for there might be no common-sense restraints if a "new product" was contemplated.

an effort to get these prices "in the right ball-park," not to introduce subtle variations on account of indivisibilities. Consequently, although attention is given to the pricing of project outputs in the case studies of Chapters 11 and 12, these do not illustrate any dramatic adjustments designed to make use of the principles of valuation that apply when indivisibilities are present.

VALUATION IF ACTUAL CHARGES WILL DIFFER FROM INCREMENTAL COST

In the preceding discussions, it has been assumed that the outputs are to be put to their best uses, and that the actual pricing procedure will not prevent this. It may be, however, that the analyst can look ahead and see rather clearly that actual prices charged will differ from incremental cost. Should this affect the procedure for valuing costs and benefits?

If "Capacity" Is Reached

If incremental cost declines until suddenly the expansion of output hits a stone wall, the price should be adjusted so as to ration that output among the most valuable uses. In this case, price differs from incremental cost in the sense that such cost is indeterminate if output cannot be expanded. (Price would still equal incremental cost, not in the sense of the alternative value that would be sacrificed if another unit were *produced*, but in the broader sense of the alternative value that would be sacrificed if a unit were *put to some other use*.) The same situation would exist if output were stopped for any other reason before the cost of producing another unit equaled the amount that would be paid for it. Again price should ration the available units to their most valuable uses.

Such situations, if foreseen, are naturally pertinent to the estimation of the quantity and value of output, but the basic procedure— valuing output at the maximum amount that users would pay for it —is not altered.

If Deliberate Under-Pricing Is Expected

Nor should the deliberate setting of price below incremental cost, if foreseen, change that basic procedure. It would, however, alter the composition of the group which would use the product and the amount that it would be worth to them. For instance, in order to estimate the gains from an irrigation project, it is necessary to impute a value to the water. This value clearly depends upon the way the water is expected to be used. And the way one can expect it to be used depends partly upon the way the farmers are to be charged. If they are not to be charged by the unit, and can have additional units of water at little or no extra cost, farmers will use water "wastefully"— that is, many of their uses of water will not be as valuable as other uses would be. In these circumstances, whatever the true value of the water, they will grow what might be called "water-intensive" crops. (It may be interesting to note, in this connection, that one of the principal crops in some of our irrigated desert lands is watermelon.)

If the price is sure to be set too low to ration the water to its best uses, the value attached to water for purposes of the analysis should be a conservative one, for the water may not be devoted to the acreage where it would be most productive. In other words, the benefits should not be estimated on the assumption that the output will be used in one way, when prices will be set so that it will be used in some other way.

This is a nice example of one of the difficulties posed by suboptimization. In trying to reach the correct decision about one thing, what higher-level and lower-level decisions by others should be taken as given? In the estimation of benefits from alternative projects, should one assume that the outputs will be correctly priced by the government, or should one assume some inferior procedure? Should the analysis relate to a bigger chunk of the water-resource problem, in which one attempts to "optimize" simultaneously with respect to more aspects of it? So far as the present study is concerned, it was decided that the aim should be to help compare projects on the assumption that current pricing policies, which are often wrong, will continue. That is why possible improvements in the pricing of water, flood protection, and so on are neglected here. That other studies of alternative pricing policies, and consequent improvements in pricing practices, are important surely needs no elaboration.

ALTERNATIVE JUSTIFIABLE EXPENDITURE AS A PRICE

Sometimes, when an output is particularly hard to value, benefits are assumed to be equal to the cost of the cheapest alternative means of producing the same service. For example, a larger flow of water from a reservoir dilutes and aerates the impurities in a stream: "The benefit from such stored water released for pollution abatement is usually measured as at least equal to the cost of equivalent abatement by alternative means such as standard water treatment."[10] As another example, "the Corps calculates benefits from hydroplants on the basis of cost of power from privately financed steam electric plants."[11]

In some circumstances, this sort of procedure is fairly satisfactory. Suppose that some task is in fact being performed or is scheduled to be performed. Assume next that a new device for carrying out this task is discovered. How much is the new device worth? A way to answer this question is to find out how much it would save in performing the task. It would save the cost of the present method, which would be eliminated, minus the cost of the new device. In other words, the gain attributed to it would be the cost of the cheapest alternative means of doing the job.

There is considerable danger of going astray, however, when we shift to a task which is not definitely scheduled. The door is then open to counting as gain the cost of the cheapest alternative way of performing an unjustifiable task. Consider, for example, a project that supplies water to soils so poor that they can yield little or nothing even with irrigation. (Roughly speaking, this has been the fate of a few irrigation projects, so the example is not farfetched.) If we estimate benefits to be the minimum cost of supplying an equivalent amount of water to these lands by some other means, benefits may appear to be great, yet the whole operation may be practically worthless.

The estimation of navigation benefits provides a similar example. A convenient summary of the estimation procedure has been provided by the Engineers Joint Council.

. . . The benefits are computed by comparing costs of transportation by water with rail rates for similar hauls . . . .

To determine the probable tonnage that would move on a waterway, comparisons are made between the cost incurred by the water-carrier (including reasonable profit) and the rates charged by railroads for the same movement. When the water-carrier's cost of any movement, as thus computed, is substantially less than the rail freight rate for the same movement, and other conditions are favorable to movement by water, it is assumed that this movement will occur by water rather than by rail, since I.C.C. regulations will not permit a railroad to reduce rates in anticipation of waterway competition. In addition to diverted traffic, there is considered also any probable new traffic that will be generated by the new transportation facility. If the aggregate of annual savings is greater than the annual cost, computed as described above, the project is recommended . . . .[12]

[10] *Annual Report of the Chief of Engineers, U.S. Army, 1951,* Part 1, Vol. 3, p. 78.

[11] *Missouri: Land and Water,* p. 100.

[12] *Principles of a Sound National Water Policy,* p. 77.

In brief, the projected traffic (with railways not allowed to compete by cutting prices to short-run incremental cost) is valued not at what the shippers are willing to pay but at the "savings," that is, at the alternative cost to the shippers minus the project costs. This procedure is not quite the same as using alternative cost as the value of the services because project costs are deducted, but it raises the same questions. If a large volume of shipping can be attracted *by means of* comparatively low charges, should this volume be valued at a price higher than those charges? (Note that this would be a price which the newly generated traffic was evidently unwilling to pay.) Pushed to the extreme, this method would sanction charging a zero price for apples and then valuing the total quantity sold at the cost that buyers would have incurred had they bought at the Apple Commission price.

It is a different procedure, however, that is usually advocated in connection with alternative expenditures—namely, the use of the rule that estimated benefits should not *exceed* the cost of the cheapest alternative way of carrying out a task.[13] Yet this rule, too, seems to have some drawbacks. First, it is not a very good safeguard, for it may serve as an invitation to make benefits as high as the cost of the alternative method. That is, it may function as a floor as often as it operates as a ceiling. Second, it is not necessarily correct. If there are alternative candidates for the same job, they should be explicitly considered, and the costs of carrying out the task in the various ways should be compared. In case the alternative methods do not accomplish precisely the same task, the safer procedure is to estimate the amount that consumers would pay to have that task performed.

VALUATION AND MOVEMENTS OF THE GENERAL PRICE LEVEL

Most persons feel instinctively that movements of the *general* price level are irrelevant in the comparison of projects and should be kept out of the calculations. Moreover, cost-benefit analyses today are usually made in terms of a constant price level. The subject is mentioned here only because it was officially recommended not so long ago that future fluctuations of the general price level be taken into account. For example, the Green Book urged that changes of the price level be projected and that costs and benefits be calculated in terms of

[13] *Principles of a Sound National Water Policy*, p. 191.

the resulting *undeflated* prices. Thus, if gradual inflation was anticipated by the analysts, the benefits would be blown up relative to costs
because the bulk of the benefits would be realized *after* most of the
costs had been incurred.

Still another treatment of price levels would entail accepting prices current at the time of the investigation as a guide to prices pertinent over the
project life, modified only to the extent of allowing for anticipated changes
in relative prices of specified goods and services. In comparison with the
other alternatives already discussed, this method has the virtue of proceeding
from a prevailing basis of values, and of approaching the objective of expressing benefits and costs in terms of relative values which are independent of
changes in the general price level. An objection to this approach is that the
resulting estimates of benefits would be in constant dollar values that would
in most cases differ widely from the actual dollar values of benefits at the
time such benefits accrue. This basis might be inadequate for the purpose
of demonstrating the usefulness of the project to beneficiaries in terms recognized by them and would lead to difficulties in utilizing such benefit estimates in establishing repayment obligations, a purpose which benefit-cost
analysis should serve if practicable. Therefore, this approach also is not
recommended.

All things considered, the most satisfactory approach would result from
using prices estimated as they are expected to be at the time when costs are
incurred and benefits received. . . . Benefits and other costs [other than
investment costs] would be expressed in terms of a price level expected to
prevail at the time when these benefits and costs would be expected to occur.
This procedure is recommended as the best available alternative.[14]

Surely this is one point at which the government ought not seek to
copy the measurements used by private enterprise. Our position all
along has been that cost-benefit estimates should help us to see which
choices would take us nearer to maximum production. (Other exhibits
should throw light on the implications of each project for wealth distribution and regional expansion.) So far as efficiency in this sense
is concerned, movements of the general price level are beside the
point; if the price level rises from 100 to 300 by the time the benefits
occur, it is simply incorrect—and grossly misleading—to say that
benefits are trebled.[15]

There is good reason for permitting private individuals who make
good forecasts to gain at the expense of those who make poor forecasts.
Intervention by government to prevent or offset such gains, except for
actions to damp fluctuations, would have too many undesirable effects

[14] *Proposed Practices for Economic Analysis . . . ,* p. 17.

[15] It may be advisable to predict movements of the general price level in
order to foresee what groups will gain and how much they can be taxed or
charged—but not in order to gage the worth of projects to the whole economy.

on progress, efficiency, and freedom from coercion. But there seems to be no good reason for having the government bet on inflation in connection with water-resource projects, since a bet on inflation, even if it seems likely to be a good wager, makes projects spuriously attractive to the nation. Furthermore, it is a bet by government on its own failure to win in its struggle for stability—a type of wagering that is frowned upon in most contests.

Part 4

The Problems
as Illustrated
by Specific Analyses

Chapter 11

CASE STUDY I:
THE GREEN RIVER WATERSHED[1]

W E TURN NOW to analyses of water-resource projects that have
been prepared by the Department of Agriculture, the Corps of
Engineers, and the Bureau of Reclamation. There is a definition
that goes, "Agriculture is like farming, only farming is doing it";
similarly, the role of these case studies in relation to the methodological
materials is "doing it." However, the aim in looking at these cases is
not to make definitive calculations that would support revised recommendations concerning these projects. Nor is it to present systematic
appraisals of the analytical work done by these government agencies.
The intention is simply to draw upon analyses of specific water-
resource projects in order to make the methodological suggestions
clear and realistic.

The first water-resource proposal to be examined is the program
for treating the Green River Watershed that was recommended in
1951 by the Department of Agriculture.[1] This watershed covers about
9,000 square miles in Kentucky and Tennessee, the former state con-
taining 96 per cent of the area. The main objectives of the program
were supposed to be the alleviation of flood-water and sediment damages, although actually most of the benefits, as estimated by the
Agency, were not reductions of such damages but were increases of
output due to "conservation" measures. The program can be summarized as follows:

---

[1] Most of the information presented in this chapter comes from *Green River
Watershed, Kentucky and Tennessee,* House Document No. 261, 82nd Congress,
1st Session (Washington, D.C.: U.S. Government Printing Office, 1951). Page
references to this document will be given only in connection with a few statements which I think readers may particularly wish to check.

RECOMMENDED PROGRAM

Measure	Estimated No. of Units
Subwatershed waterways	3,500 miles
Farm waterways	12,300 acres
Terraces	110,600 miles
Structures to divert flows (slopes too steep for terracing)	5,400 miles
Gully stabilization and sediment control	4,400 miles
Road and railroad bank stabilization	6,600 miles
Perennial vegetation (e.g. Kudzu)	87,100 acres
Pasture development	685,000 acres
Farm ponds	22,600 ponds
Wildlife area development	14,100 acres
Adequate fire control	2,151,500 acres
Forest planting	728,000 acres
Acquisition and special management of lands	438,000 acres
Channel improvement and stream-bank stabilization	2,700 miles

Subwatershed waterways are the secondary channels that collect the runoff from numerous individual farms and carry it to the "tributary streams." The treatment of these waterways includes such steps as grading, removal of brush, and in some cases the construction of new channels. Farm waterways are simply the watercourses that dispose of runoff on individual farms. The general nature of the other measures is probably made sufficiently clear by their names.

The measures listed would be carried out over a twenty-year period. (In addition to this program, the conservation activities already going on are assumed to continue at the 1949 level.) It should be noted that the Federal government would not itself undertake all of the construction or much of the annually recurring activity. In general, the Federal government would provide only educational assistance, technical services, and subsidies of one sort or another to induce farmers to carry out this program. Thus, of the total installation cost, $87 million, the Federal government would contribute $56 million, non-Federal public agencies $1 million, and private operators $29 million.[2] For annual operation and maintenance, the Federal government would spend on the average less than $1/2 million, non-Federal agencies a little more than that amount, and private interests $20 million.

The benefits of the project—if we take for granted the physical effects that were estimated by the Agency—are fairly handsome.

---

[2] The sum of the parts falls short of the total because of "rounding."

According to the official projections, the venture would yield a present worth of $151 million at a discount rate of 8 per cent and $310 million at 5 per cent; and the internal rate of return would be about 55 per cent. Let us examine some of the details, for the preparation and use of these estimates raise many important issues. We shall first discuss the "models" or relationships that describe the program's physical and economic effects. Next, we shall comment on the cost estimates. Finally, we shall offer suggestions for the analysis of this type of water-resource project, including the form in which the exhibits might be presented.

MODELS THAT DESCRIBE PHYSICAL AND ECONOMIC BENEFITS

The "model" used to estimate benefits can be broken into six parts showing the effects of: channel improvement on peak stages of floods; channel improvement on flood damage; land treatment on peak stages of floods; land treatment on flood damage; land treatment on sedimentation and sedimentation damage; land treatment on crop yields and farm income. We shall take these parts up in that order.

Effects of Channel Improvement on Peak Stages of Floods

The aim in this part of the analysis was to estimate, for two sample tributaries, the peak stage of each flood during the period of record—as it was *without* the program and as it would have been *with* the program. (The next section will describe how these peak stages were translated into estimates of flood damage.) The two tributaries were the Barren River, used to represent the streams in one part of the watershed called the Pennyroyal, and the Pond River, used to represent the streams in the other part called the Western Coal Field.

The final exhibits were lists of peak stages,[3] under present conditions and after channel improvement, for floods from 1936 to 1949 (Pond River) and 1940 to 1949 (Barren River). These peak stages can be read from curves relating inches of precipitation and peak stages if one knows the precipitation that occurred in each flood storm. The curve that pertained to present conditions was prepared from data about observed storms. A second curve that pertained to conditions under channel improvement was prepared by adjusting the first curve to allow for smoother flow. This adjustment was made according to standard formulae for the calculation of the relationship between

---

[3] Above specified gages on these two streams.

discharge (cubic feet per second) and gage height.[4] This relationship depends in part upon a "coefficient of roughness." In the "after-channel-improvement" formula, this coefficient was based on "before-and-after" investigations of similar streams and on judgments about the nature of the proposed channel improvements.

Effects of Channel Improvement on Flood Damage

In order to convert the peak stages of past floods (under actual and hypothetical conditions) into estimates of damage, it was necessary to relate damage to peak stage. This was done in the following ingenious and rather intricate way.

A table was developed showing the average value per acre that was at risk as of the middle of each month. This was done for each sample tributary. The amount at risk referred to the values of damageable crops in open flood plain land, the numbers used being based usually on interviews with farmers in the region.[5] At first, the value per acre at risk was calculated for each important crop, including pasture. Then the value-at-risk, by months, was calculated for a composite acre, the crops being weighted by the proportion of open flood plain currently occupied by each crop.

The next step was to estimate the percentage of these values-at-risk that would be destroyed by different depths of inundation. These percentages multiplied by the corresponding values-at-risk yielded the expected damage per acre of open flood plain by months and by depths of inundation. Next, it was decided to put the data on a per-stream-mile instead of on a per-acre basis. This adjustment was made by taking four steps. The first was to estimate the number of acres that would be inundated to various depths at each different peak stage.[6] The second was to divide the number of acres inundated to each depth by the number of stream miles in the sample tributary in order to arrive at the number of acres *per stream mile*. The third step was to multiply these results (that is, acres per stream mile that would be flooded to each depth) by the estimates of damage per acre at each depth and in each month. The fourth was to sum up the total

---

[4] The method is described in somewhat greater detail on pp. 70–72 of *Green River Watershed . . . ;* the curves mentioned are Figures C-4, C-5, C-8, and C-9 on pp. 80–81, 84–85.

[5] For other sources, see *Green River Watershed . . . ,* pp. 92–94.

[6] These acreages were determined "from valley cross sections, taken at appropriate intervals, elevations of the flood line for two floods of record varying widely in stage, and planimeter work on aerial photographs of the sample tributary stream" (*ibid.,* p. 94).

damages that would be expected at each peak stage in each month. The results were put in the form of a table showing the expected monetary damage per stream mile *by months*[7] *and by peak stages*.

The next part of the procedure was to enter the table at the appropriate months and peak stages to estimate damage (per stream mile) for floods during the period of record. Actual months and peak stages were used to estimate damage under existing conditions. Actual months but hypothetical peak stages were used to calculate damage after channel improvement. Total damage during the period of record was divided by the number of years in the period to arrive at average annual flood damages per stream mile. In this way, the calculations were based on an average pattern of storms. Finally, these damages per stream mile in the two sample tributaries were multiplied by the number of stream miles in the two parts of the watershed. Thus, average annual flood damages, with and without channel improvement, were estimated. The reduction in average annual damages with channel improvement constituted its tangible benefits; they were assumed to occur in the years after completion of the channel modifications.

The major methodological problems raised by these models will be considered toward the end of this chapter. However, a few comments will be presented earlier in connection with particular aspects of the models. With respect to the model under discussion, showing the effects of channel improvement on flood damage, it seems advisable to emphasize three points.

First, the methods of calculating values-at-risk result in estimates that seem rather high. Values-at-risk on a composite acre of open flood plain land in the Pennyroyal were estimated to be $43.28 in July, $47.33 in August, $43.56 in September, and smaller amounts in other months (all in 1948 prices).[8] According to census data, the value of crops harvested in the entire year of 1948 was about $28 per acre of cropland in the Green River Watershed.[9] This amount includes some value added *after* removal of the crops from the risky area. Also, in any *one* month, the values-at-risk would presumably be less

---

[7] Damage to fixed improvements were also included at this point but were assumed to be the same regardless of the time of year.

[8] Of course, "sequent floods"—those following the first flood in any given season of the year—were assumed to do "proportionately less damage to the acreage previously inundated" than preceding floods. Once destroyed, crops were not assumed to be at risk again.

[9] Source of data: U.S. Bureau of the Census, *County and City Data Book, 1952* (Washington, D.C.: U.S. Government Printing Office, 1953).

than the whole year's harvest per acre, since different crops would mature in different months. Of course, flood damage, say, $5 per acre,[10] would have to be added back to the $28 in order to indicate values-at-risk.

One may object that the flood plain lands would be more productive than the acres to which the census data pertained. Actually this is doubtful, since the tobacco acreages, with harvests of from $200 to $500 per acre, are almost entirely outside the flood plain.[11] In other words, the areas accounting for the highest values per acre *were* included in the census data and *not* in the open flood plain data. Thus, some evidence suggests that the values-at-risk in the sample tributaries may have been too high to represent the flood plain in the whole basin. If true, this would overstate flood damages both with and without the program, but since a certain percentage of value-at-risk would be saved by the program, the net result would be to overstate the damage reduction attributable to the proposal. In other words, if the program saved 25 per cent of the values-at-risk which would otherwise be destroyed, damage prevented would go up with any increase in the estimated value-at-risk. It seems fair to say, at least, that the estimates of values-at-risk should be subjected to rough tests of the sort just described, and should be written down if they appear to be overstated. Or, cruder methods of preparing the estimates might be used. Results might be almost equally dependable, and the uncertainties might be less difficult to perceive.

Second, in the procedure used, the values-at-risk are held constant with and without the program. This may be substantially correct if we consider channel improvement alone, but the program as a whole, as will be seen later, is supposed to affect land use and yields so as to increase markedly the values-at-risk. Thus the "post-program" flood damage would be higher than estimated; and the reductions in damage, or benefits in this particular category, would be smaller than estimated. (This statement applies also to the effects of land treatment on flood damage.) This possible source of error could be eliminated by estimating and explicitly introducing the post-program values-at-risk. However, the procedure used in the survey report was at least superior to one that has sometimes been employed: estimates of damage reduction have occasionally counted all of the assets attracted to the flood

---

[10] Flood damage, as estimated in *Green River Watershed . . . ,* for the Western Coal Field Area, divided by acres of bottom land in that area.

[11] *Ibid.,* pp. 55–56.

plain by a project, not as values-at-risk, but rather as values-saved-from-floods by the project!

Third, average damage per stream mile multiplied by the number of stream miles is bound to give rather rough results. Annual damage per stream mile is assumed to be the same, on the average, throughout each of the two land units in the Green River watershed. Yet it is easy to see that the acres of flood plain, let alone the damage, per stream mile might vary a good deal, depending upon stream-size, meandering, position in the water basin, channel condition, and so on. For instance, the Western Pennyroyal has stream miles all right, but practically no flood plain.[12] It is easy to see also that damage per stream mile could vary greatly. For instance, along the sample tributary in the Pennyroyal, damage per stream mile was estimated to be $1,050, but along the sample tributary in the Western Coal Field area, it was supposed to be $1,633. Of course, these two samples were expected to differ; they were used *because* the two areas were known to have different characteristics. Nonetheless, they help show the variability of damage per stream mile.

The main question, of course, is whether or not a better procedure can be devised. Several changes might be considered. For example, the analyst might make the following inquiry: does the product of stream miles multiplied by damage per stream mile imply a larger flood plain acreage (given the average annual damage per acre in each sample) than in fact exists?[13] If so, this product should probably be deflated accordingly. Then, it might be worthwhile to work up additional samples in other parts of the watershed, although this would be expensive. Also, if the evidence of additional samples, past experience, or other analyses indicated that the results were not especially reliable, then it might be just as well to use a cruder model whose imperfections would be apparent without painstaking examination. Finally, the variability of damages per stream mile and hence of damage reduction might be explicitly mentioned.

Effects of Land Treatment on Peak Stages of Floods

Again the aim in designing the model was to estimate peak stages of recorded storms, with and without the program. As before, the

---

[12] *Ibid.*

[13] This check, even though not mentioned, may have been made in connection with the analysis of the Green River Watershed. Published materials do not give enough information for such a check.

peak stages for storms of record could be read from curves that relate inches of precipitation and peak stages. One curve pertained to present conditions, and another pertained to the situation that would exist after both channel improvement and land treatment. The second curve was prepared by allowing for a higher rate of infiltration of water into the land, and hence a lower runoff, after land treatment.[14]

This allowance was figured as follows: on the basis of infiltration data pertaining to the whole United States, formulae were developed to relate infiltration indexes to "cover conditions," soil types, and special correction factors for each watershed. In the formulae, a different coefficient corresponded to each cover condition, such as row crops, medium pasture, good woods, and good Kudzu, and to each soil type. Thus the cover condition, soil classification, and watershed that pertained to any acreage determined its infiltration index. In addition, curves were prepared relating these infiltration indexes and actual runoffs for various "design storms"—storms having rainfall of various intensities (inches per hour) and amounts. By means of those relationships the analysts estimated the runoff from the acreage in each land class in each storm.[15] Total runoff was simply the sum of these estimates for the various land classes within the Green River Watershed. Since the relationships were based upon past observations, the estimates were bound to be very close to actual runoffs in storms of record.

When the land treatment program was considered, the hydrologic relationships were held constant, but the acreage in each land class was varied. Thus it was assumed that much more of the land than at present would be conducive to a high infiltration rate.[16] Therefore, predicted runoff was smaller with the program than without it.

[14] This curve reflected the effects of *both* channel improvement, as described in the previous section, and land treatment.

[15] The model is fairly complex; calculations could be reconstructed in detail only with the aid of materials on file at the Soil Conservation Service regional office.

[16] Major changes in land use—e.g., from row-crops and idle lands to deep-rooted perennials and pasture—are indicated later. Some of the most significant projections were those pertaining to the amount and hydrologic condition of woodland. It was assumed that the fire-control measures would keep the acreage of woodland that was in "poor" hydrologic condition (due to burning) down to 5 per cent. The amount that was in "medium" condition (due chiefly to logging operations) at any time would be 15 per cent. The remainder would all be in "good" hydrologic condition. The present situation is considerably different, with 90 per cent of the woodland in "poor" condition, 10 per cent in "medium" condition, and none in "good" shape. As a consequence of these assumptions

At this point, it was possible to prepare the curves, mentioned at the beginning of this section, relating total runoff to total storm precipitation. Runoff, in turn, could be related to peak stages above particular gages in the two sample tributaries. The end result was a table similar to that described in connection with the channel improvement: lists of peak stages, under present conditions and after the full program (land treatment plus channel improvement), for recorded floods.

Effects of Land Treatment on Flood Damage

The peak stages were converted into estimates of damage and thence into estimates of benefits in the same way that was described earlier in the section on "Effects of Channel Improvement on Flood Damage." The same comments that were made before are applicable here, though some additional points need mentioning. The land treatment measures that were to produce these benefits included not only the recommended program but also the continuation of the going program. The annual costs of the recommended program amounted to 52 per cent of the combined annual costs of *all* the land-treatment measures; so 52 per cent of the aggregate benefits were attributed to the proposed program. The implication is that the inputs are perfectly divisible and the output can be obtained at constant unit costs. Actually the money would probably be spent on the "best" measures first, so that there would be decreasing returns, i.e., increasing costs, as more resources were devoted to land treatment in this watershed. If so, less than 52 per cent of the benefits should be attributed to the additional steps contained in the new proposal. However, without information on the effect of successive increments to the program, we cannot offer a better procedure than the use of this percentage.

In principle, analyses of successive increments should be presented in any event, rather than merely all-or-none analyses. However, formal analysis of numerous possibilities is not costless. Decisions

---

and of future planting and management, the projected acreage is as follows:

	Hydrologic Condition Class			
Situation	Good	Medium	Poor	Total
Without program (present)	0	199,000	1,787,000	1,986,000
With program (future)	1,721,000	323,000	108,000	2,152,000

about the alternative project-sizes to be examined must be governed by evidence concerning each case and by *ad hoc* judgments.

A reduction of the damage to roads and railroads was also counted as a tangible gain from the land treatment program. Estimates of annual damages, as of the present, were obtained from the State Highway departments and from officials of the Illinois Central Railway Company. A flat 20 per cent reduction, unexplained in published materials, was attributed to the going program plus the recommended measures. No suggestions concerning this procedure will be offered here. The gain in this case was an insignificant portion of estimated total benefits, and it is likely to be so in similar projects.

Effects of Land Treatment on Sedimentation and Sedimentation Damage

The only effects of the program on sedimentation that seemed to be worth taking into account were those on public water supplies. The cost of water treatment is the result, to a considerable extent, of "turbidity," the suspension of fine particles that results largely from soil erosion. The reduction of this cost would not be great, since turbidities are relatively low anyway; but it was estimated that the land treatment measures would lower filtration costs by 5 per cent. The estimated annual benefits amounted only to $4,700,[17] insignificant in comparison with total annual gains of $53,355,000 (1948 prices).

Other sedimentation damages, reduction of which would apparently be even less important, included damages to navigation, channel maintenance, drainage systems, reservoir capacities, fertility of flood plains, aquatic life, forage crops, and health. In most cases, losses caused by sedimentation are negligible even without the land treatment program.[18]

Effects of Land Treatment on Crop Yields and Farm Income

In point of fact, none of the benefits discussed thus far is very important in comparison with the estimated increases in agricultural output. The table showing average annual benefits indicates their relative magnitudes, as estimated by the Department of Agriculture. Of the total benefits attributed to the program, 97 per cent stems from the increased output that is projected.

The published appendices to the analysis do not include any of

---

[17] That is, 52 per cent of the $9,000 benefit attributed to *all* land treatment programs.

[18] *Green River Watershed* . . . , pp. 96–101.

AVERAGE ANNUAL BENEFITS ATTRIBUTED TO RECOMMENDED PROGRAM[19]

Channel improvement	$ 801,000
Reduction in agricultural flood damage	664,000
Reduction in flood damage to roads and railroads	40,000
Reduction in sedimentation damage to public water supplies	5,000
Increased output of farms	47,844,000
Increased output of woodlands	3,888,000
Decreased maintenance of roads and railroads	113,000
	$53,355,000

the relationships by means of which the yields were forecast. In any event, it would not be possible here to make many suggestions about this part of the model. This would require the services of agronomists and soil engineers. It is appropriate, however, to point out the sensitivity of this type of analysis to projected yields, and to urge that they always be "double checked." The increases used in this analysis are sufficiently dramatic to warrant a full presentation of them, given in Table 12. It should be remembered that these increases are supposed to be attributable solely to the soil-conserving practices that comprise the program (going plus recommended). Any increase resulting from direct fertilization of row crops, the use of hybrids, or new methods that would be adopted anyway are supposed to be excluded.

The woodland, too, was assumed to experience a considerable increase in yield. Annual growth of 300 board feet per acre was predicted for all acreage in "good" hydrologic condition; growth of 150 and 75 board feet per acre was foreseen for areas in "medium" and "poor" condition, respectively. These growth rates were multiplied by the acreages in each hydrologic condition class. The projected total annual growth, with and without the program, can then be divided by the acreage to show *average* yield per acre. Without the program, this average yield was approximately 80 board feet per acre (per year). With the program, it was about 265 board feet per acre—an increase of 230 per cent.

In addition to altered yields, the program would lead to altered land use. The major changes assumed in the survey report are the elimination of *all* "idle" land (623,000 acres); a 30 per cent increase in pasture (451,000 acres); an 8 per cent increase in woodland (166,000 acres); a 280 per cent increase in deep-rooted perennials (147,000 acres); and a 35 per cent decrease in lands devoted to the row-crop

[19] These amounts are in 1948 prices, unadjusted for projected changes in relative prices and costs.

TABLE 12

EFFECT OF LAND TREATMENT PROGRAM ON YIELDS PER ACRE,
GREEN RIVER WATERSHED*

| | | Percentage Increase in Yield | | | |
| | | Pennyroyal | | Western Coal Field | |
Crop	Unit	Eastern	Western	Sandstone-shale	Loess
Burley tobacco	Lbs. per acre	35%	35%	35%	35%
Dark air-cured tobacco	Lbs. per acre	35	35	35	35
Dark fired tobacco	Lbs. per acre	—	35	35	—
Corn	Bushels per acre	48	47	54	40
Truck and vegetables	Bushels per acre	38	54	43	40
Soybeans for beans	Bushels per acre	—	—	57	50
Oats for grain	Bushels per acre	74	59	48	64
Barley for grain	Bushels per acre	60	64	68	44
Wheat for grain	Bushels per acre	67	67	43	47
Small-grain hay	Tons per acre	100	80	78	43
Soybean and cow pea hay	Tons per acre	67	69	57	57
Lespedeza hay	Tons per acre	78	64	50	54
Clover and timothy hay	Tons per acre	64	67	67	60
Other tame and wild hay	Tons per acre	125	122	100	118
Alfalfa-grass hay	Tons per acre	58	55	55	46
Lespedeza seed	Lbs. per acre	50	50	62	29
Pasture	Animal unit-months per acre	150	120	140	140

* *Green River Watershed* . . ., Table D-14, p. 116. The published figures pertaining to pasture were evidently in error and have been revised.

corn (275,000 acres). These changes imply a much greater role, under the new program, for livestock. In order to evaluate the productivity of pasture, it was assumed that it could be used to raise "beef cows producing commercial fat calves"; and it was estimated that "carrying capacity" would increase from 521 to 906 thousand brood cows, that is, by almost 75 per cent.

These shifts in land use and in yield were responsible for the increases in gross farm income that were counted as benefits. Prices were in effect assumed to remain at 1948 levels in this part of the computation.[20]

Before we turn to costs and then to major methodological suggestions, the dependence of the projections of farm income upon certain parts of the model is worth reviewing. These projections rest to a great extent upon the assumptions about livestock production. Of the $92 million total rise in annual agricultural income, slightly more than one-third was attributed to increased livestock output. Moreover, this approximate one-third, or $33 million, was really "net income," for in connection with this particular item, the costs of production were deducted from gross income instead of being counted as costs of the program. Had they been handled as the other costs were, both costs and benefits of the watershed program would have been higher—and the percentage of benefits attributable to livestock would have been still greater.

In this connection, some investment outside the program, 100 per cent participation by farmers, and uniformly efficient techniques in livestock production were taken for granted in preparing the benefit estimates. Total benefits thus depend to a considerable extent on the shift to a "cattle economy," and the shift as projected does not appear to allow much for "slippage" in performance by some of the farmers.

The same comment is pertinent in connection with other crops. The projections of crop yield, of changes in the productivity of woodlands, and of land utilization appear to depend upon relatively efficient, indeed almost optimal, performances by *all* the farmers. In connection with this possible source of over-optimism,[21] it might well be desirable to allow for less than perfect adjustment to the new situation. Such "degradation allowances" might be derived from a com-

---

[20] Gross income per acre was estimated to be higher with the program than without it (*ibid.*, Table D-21, p. 123), but the increase was due to the projected rise in yields. After the estimates of aggregate costs and benefits were prepared in terms of 1948 prices, these aggregates were adjusted to reflect projected changes in relative prices. This adjustment will be described later.

[21] The methods used may also have yielded optimistic estimates of the watershed's gross farm income without the program. For gross income from *crops* according to the analysis (*ibid.*, Table D-22, p. 124) was about $80 million "at present" (i.e., 1948–1949), but the value of all *crops* sold in 1949 (estimated from materials in the *County and City Data Book, 1952*) was about $50 million. One would expect the census figure to be somewhat lower because of home consumption, under-reporting, and lower prices in 1949, but perhaps not that much lower. Even if estimates are too high both with and without the program, the difference (or benefits) will also be overstated.

parison of present output with estimated potential output, given existing resources and no "human frailties." These factors might be applied to the projected increments in *aggregate* gross income; it is doubtful that better results would be obtained by "degrading" each component.

COST MODELS

A breakdown of the total cost of the recommended program is shown in Table 13. The estimates appear to have been prepared in a

TABLE 13

COSTS OF RECOMMENDED PROGRAM, BY PARTICIPANTS
(Millions of 1948 dollars)

	Total	Federal	Non-Federal Public	Non-Federal Private
Installation costs	$86.6	$56.3	$1.3	$29.0
Annual operation and maintenance	20.9*	0.4	0.6	19.9*

* This is the estimated annual operating cost after installations are complete, including $14.4 million as the estimated increase in annual costs of farm operation, and excluding amortization of installation costs.

straightforward manner. Records of past experience with similar activities presumably offer the best basis that is available for the estimation of costs. From the records of the Department of Agriculture, costs per unit of each measure, e.g., $200 per mile of gulley stabilization, were estimated. Per-unit cost was then multiplied by the number of units planned for the program. Initial outlays for technical services, educational assistance, investigation, design, and inspection were added to give total installation costs. Yearly maintenance outlays per unit and recurring expenditures for technical services were used to estimate annual maintenance costs.

Total annual costs also included an allowance for increased costs of farm operation, since the larger crops that were projected would require more labor and equipment, e.g., for harvesting. This allowance was calculated in the following way. The annual cost of producing crops in various parts of the watershed was estimated, with and without the *entire* Agricultural Conservation Program for the watershed. The net increase, $29 million per year, was then apportioned between the going and the proposed portions of that program according to their average annual costs. The share of the latter was **49** per cent, or about $14 million per annum.[22]

The methods described appear to be aimed at the right mark: the incremental costs of the proposed program. But two observations are in order. First, the treatment of increased farm costs illustrates one of the dangers of looking at conventional benefit-cost *ratios* in order to rank projects. As mentioned earlier, one portion of the increased costs of farm operation, the increased cost of cattle production, was deducted from gross receipts instead of being included among the costs of the program. As a result, the benefit-cost ratio was higher than it would have been if all amounts had been presented on a gross basis, lower than it would have been if all had been on a net basis. In other words, the benefit-cost ratio shown in the Report is subject to the erratic and irrelevant influence of "annual turnover" that was described in Chapter 7. This influence is eliminated if one uses the criterion urged in this study. Whether the extra crop values are gross or net is a matter of indifference in the calculation of present worth.

Second, although the subject is never mentioned explicitly, the interest on investment that is counted as a cost seems rather inadequate. Thus the annual equivalent of the Federal installation cost is simply 2½ per cent of that initial investment.[23] This must cover interest on the investment and amortization of the principal. If the time period is taken to be 50 years, an interest rate only a little over 1 per cent is implied. Even if the time period is 100 years, interest on the investment is slightly less than 2 per cent. This is hardly enough to allow for the productivity of the capital if put to other uses, whether the admissible uses are internal or external to the Department. The trouble would be corrected if both benefit and cost streams were properly discounted to their present values at the appropriate rate, but annual costs and benefits are used, and in these undiscounted estimates—the only ones presented in the section on "Recommendations"[24]—the interest component of cost is probably too low.

[22] This percentage was derived through the use of a less inclusive definition of program costs than the definition used in calculating the figure (52 per cent) shown in footnote 17.

[23] *Green River Watershed . . .* , pp. 105, 107. I have not presented the annual equivalents of installation costs in this case study.

[24] *Ibid.*, pp. 17–19. The effect of discounting deferred benefits is taken up briefly on pp. 109–110. Also the letter from the Budget Bureau advising the Secretary of Agriculture about the relationship of the proposal to the President's program mentions the benefit-cost ratio that would result from discounting the benefit stream.

ADJUSTMENTS FOR RELATIVE PRICE CHANGES

The estimates of benefits and costs, as described up to this point, were in terms of 1948 prices. On the basis of projections prepared by the Bureau of Agricultural Economics, these estimates were adjusted to "future price levels." If all prices were assumed to change in the same proportion, this would not, or ought not to, affect the results. However, shifts in *relative* prices, associated with a shift to an "intermediate level of employment" (much lower than the level of employment in 1948), were assumed. For example, the projected price index for lumber fell from 312 to 145, while that for construction costs declined from 461 to 325. As a consequence, total average annual benefits from the recommended program were written down from $53,355,000 to $26,304,000, and total average annual costs from $23,579,000 to $15,397,000. It should be noted that these were adjustments which put the project in a less favorable light.

This was a commendable effort to use prices which would more nearly reflect the worth of the products that would come from the project and of the resources that would go into it. If future shifts in relative prices can be foreseen, or if more accurate prices than observed ones can be perceived, it is appropriate to make such adjustments. The adjustment described above was probably in the right direction because governmental support programs[25] have presumably exaggerated the worth of agricultural products, as measured by market prices, in comparison with other goods and services. (This was not the reason given for the adjustment, but it is pertinent nonetheless.) However, if it is only pervasive uncertainty that can be foreseen, an attempt to picture this uncertainty would probably be more useful than the introduction of a unique forecast of price changes. In that circumstance, it might be helpful to show how the outcome would be affected if several assumptions about prices were used.

TREATMENT OF TIME

The shape of the time streams was indicated, although not emphasized, in the survey report. On the cost side, the stream was broken down into initial installation costs and subsequent maintenance out-

---

[25] Governmental support of certain prices, as well as a good many other influences both public and private, impair the usefulness of market prices. Only in the case of major influences, such as the support programs, does it seem practicable and worthwhile to try to use adjusted prices.

lays. No time horizon was ever specified, but installation costs were converted to their "average annual equivalent" by taking 2½ per cent of initial public outlays and 4 per cent of initial private outlays. Future costs were never discounted to their present values.

On the benefit side, the survey report dealt mostly with the average annual benefit that might be expected *after the program became fully effective.* However, in an Appendix, the time path and the discounting of delayed benefits were discussed briefly.[26] In this discussion

it was assumed that open-land conservation benefits and floodwater damage reduction benefits will, on an average, be delayed about five years in reaching their maximum and that woodland conservation benefits will not be at the maximum until after thirty years. It was also assumed that each type of benefit would start at zero and uniformly build up to the maximum over the period of delay. The benefits would then level off and remain constant thereafter.

The procedure in discounting benefits was not made clear—for example, the discount rate, time horizon, and precise steps in calculating annual benefits were never stated—but this procedure reduced "the ratio of total benefits to total costs for all measures from 1.7 to 1 to 1.5 to 1."[27]

SUGGESTED CHANGES IN COST-BENEFIT ANALYSIS WITH REFERENCE TO GREEN RIVER WATERSHED

As stated at the outset, the purpose of the study is to offer suggestions that might make analyses more useful in the future than they have been in the past, not merely to criticize past analyses. However, it will help to summarize and clarify those suggestions if we ask how they would affect the case study that has been examined.

The General Criterion

For purposes of evaluating projects, it is assumed here that changes in national well-being are some function of (1) increases in present worth, reflecting increases in the country's real income with changes in the distribution of wealth neglected, (2) the time paths of expected benefits and costs, (3) the variability of the outcome in terms of present worth, (4) changes in the personal distribution of wealth, (5) changes in the regional distribution of wealth, and (6) other vari-

[26] *Green River Watershed* . . . , Appendix D, at the bottom of p. 109 and the top of p. 110.
[27] *Ibid.*

ables. It is assumed that information about the effect of each project on the first five variables would be useful to decision-makers. If it is permissible in this situation to talk about a "main criterion," it is suggested that the principal test be the maximization, for a given budget, of present worth—that is, of the present value of the benefit stream minus the present value of the cost stream—when the amounts are discounted at the marginal internal rate of return.[28] Perhaps it should be re-emphasized, however, that the analyst has no criterion that will by itself reveal the preferred set of projects to Congress or voters or government Agencies. Any "test" for preferred measures, then, can really be no more than information that is pertinent to the final decision.

It is not certain, of course, that estimates of some (but not all) factors on which well-being depends will cause better projects to be chosen. The existence of such estimates may result in the neglect of other non-quantified factors and lead to worse rather than better courses of action in particular cases. But this appears to be a chance worth taking. We must assume that more or "better" information is usually conducive to the improvement of decisions.

The Scope of the Analysis

No modification of the present analysis in this respect is suggested. The use of the watershed as the context does direct attention to a host of spillover effects that are far removed from the location of the installations. Ideally, of course, the impact on floods further down the Ohio and Mississippi valleys, and possible effects on physical production possibilities outside the watershed, should be counted. As a practical matter, however, the context cannot include the whole economy, and it is believed that the scope chosen in this analysis is a suitable compromise. The benefit categories that were included— reduction of flood damages, reduction of sedimentation damages, increases of farm output—appear to include all major gains. It seems unlikely that a larger context would reveal additional costs of major significance. In general, it is assumed that in this case a larger system would not help much to make the criterion more nearly consistent with higher-level aims.

Unfortunately, neither this case study nor the one in Chapter 12 brings out the importance of choosing the context carefully. The selection of relatively small and uncomplicated cases was deliberate. As a consequence, however, these examples underemphasize the possi-

[28] The criterion for ranking independent ventures, if this is to be done, is described below.

bilities of error caused by examining too small a region or too narrow a context.

Projects as Lumps vs. Projects as Small Increments

It would probably cost more than it would be worth to analyze each project by breaking it down into hundreds of small increments and presenting the analysis to Congress in this form. But it might help a good deal, and at little expense, to analyze two or three scales of each project. It would be interesting to see the estimates for a more modest, and a more ambitious, program than the present Green River Watershed program. After all, several scales presumably were considered in the preliminary survey within the Agency; the scale finally proposed for each project is not chosen haphazardly. Enough data probably exist to make reasonable, yet inexpensive, benefit-cost estimates for two or three program sizes.

Along the same line, more component measures could usefully be examined as separable parts of the project. The existing report does present separate figures for channel improvement and the combined program (the former being a relatively unattractive component in terms of the conventional benefit-cost ratio). The advisability of including other components in the project was no doubt considered within the Agency, but formal analyses of roadbank stabilization, fire control, and the like might be worth the attention of the Budget Bureau, Congress, and the general public.

Time Streams

In the treatment of time streams, it would be better to state explicitly the time period that is deemed relevant (that is, the time horizon), to present clearly the time path of expected costs and benefits, to state the rate at which future amounts are discounted, and to calculate the present worth of the streams. An illustrative presentation, with reference to the Green River program, is shown in Table 14. In accordance with the earlier argument that a range of discount rates should be used, present worths at 2½ per cent, 5 per cent, and 8 per cent (with a 50-year time horizon in each case) are shown.[29]

Also the time paths of the undiscounted outlays and benefits are presented in Table 14. This case study brings out rather sharply the need for showing the undiscounted outlays, for the costs that would

---

[29] In order to make available the basic data for the calculations, Table 16 at the end of this chapter shows the cost and benefit estimates programmed through time.

have to be covered by an over-all national water-resources budget (i.e., outgo not covered by benefits up to that time) are markedly different from the outlays that are scheduled for the government. Benefits to whomsoever they accrue would exceed costs after the first three years, but *Treasury* receipts might never outrun governmental disbursements! In these circumstances it is not really clear what budget is to be allocated or what costs are to be covered by that budget. In general, the exhibits reflect the assumption that a water-resource budget for the whole nation is the appropriate concept; but the time path of actual outlays is regarded as a vital supplementary exhibit.

Uncertainty and Ranges

As emphasized earlier, it is hardly sufficient to compare projects solely on the basis of single "best" estimates. If there is a fairly good chance that the Green River project would be, on the one hand, a complete flop or, on the other hand, a smash hit, this information is important—perhaps fully as important as estimates of the "average" outcome. Table 14 presents some illustrative ranges in which the outcome of the Green River program might fall. These ranges would be arrived at "subjectively" and defined imprecisely, yet they might assist a good deal in reflecting our uncertainty. It must be emphasized that the numbers shown are purely illustrative. The writer has little basis for gaging the variability of results under this watershed-treatment program. However, the Agencies which work up specific analyses might appreciate the uncertainties well enough to put down meaningful ranges.

Sensitivity of results to factors about which there is great uncertainty, e.g., crop yields with the project, might also be indicated. More sophisticated techniques for reflecting, or dealing with, uncertainty were not believed to be practicable in this analysis. A case in point would be "Monte Carlo" calculations—repeated "plays" to learn the outcome when uncertain events are determined, within limits, by the use of random numbers. As mentioned previously, such calculations might be helpful in an exhaustive comparison of a few specific projects, but they are too time-consuming for use in the evaluation of a whole shelf of water-resource projects.

Estimation Procedures

A few modifications of estimation procedures were suggested earlier when the Green River model was examined in detail. One of the more important possibilities is the use of "degradation factors" in estimating benefits. Things seldom turn out as well as the physical potentialities may suggest. Some "slippage" should be anticipated, and past experience may give some clue to its "normal" extent. Allowing for this slippage, it should be noted, is a different matter from allowing for uncertainty: to reflect the latter, estimates of average outcomes should be supplemented with other possible, though less likely, results. To allow for slippage, however, *all* benefit-cost calculations—average results and also any supplementary ones—should be downgraded. Because it would require close familiarity with the project, the attempt to apply this suggestion (the use of degradation factors) to the Green River estimates was not made here. In practice, however, it might be one of the most important improvements which could be made.

The published analysis does not mention any allowances for taxes in estimating the increase in farm income. Ideally, costs should include whatever drains on governmental services result from the project. In the Green River proposal, taxes that would be levied on the farmers (or on the project, if it were regarded as a business) would probably not be closely correlated with such costs. Therefore in Table 14, results are shown without any allowance for taxes. The exhibit is accompanied, however, by a warning that the estimates are not applicable to a comparison of the project with private investment. If such comparison is to be made, for example, in connection with deciding upon the size of the water-resources budget, the estimates of present worth in the table should be cut in half. This would make a rough allowance for the following facts: about 45 per cent of the benefit from corporations' investments is siphoned off by the income tax (on the average), and a small percentage is siphoned off by the property tax.[30]

Some of this tax may be shifted by private business, resulting in lower wages and/or an altered price structure. However, the cost and gain from new private investment will be estimated on the basis of that altered price structure, and taxes will then be counted. If public projects are to be compared with private investment, the same procedure should be followed.

---

[30] The effective property rate seems to be about 1.5% of property value, and if the property produces an income of 6%, the effective tax rate would be 25% of annual income. However, in the calculation of the combined rate, each tax should be deducted before figuring the other, and the combined rate works out to be about 50%.

TABLE 14

Suggested Form of Cost-Benefit Exhibits—Green River Program as Illustration

(Amounts in 1948 dollars)

1. Present worth (present value of outputs minus present value of costs) 2½%, 50-year horizon ... $550 million
   5 %, 50-year horizon ... 310 million
   8 %, 50-year horizon ... 151 million

   Note: If the exhibits are to be used for the comparison of this project with private investment, property and income taxes paid on private ventures should be allowed for; in this illustration, a rough allowance could be made by reducing the present-worth estimates by 50%.*

2. Cost that would have to be covered by a national water-resources budget:
   Present value of the nation's investment stream† 2½% discount rate ... 7.3 million
   5 % discount rate ... 7.1 million
   8 % discount rate ... 6.8 million

3. Time paths of undiscounted benefits and costs (millions of 1948 dollars):

Streams	1–5	6–10	11–15	16–20	21–25	26–30	31–35	36–40	41–45	46–50
Total Benefits	29	98	166	233	262	265	267	267	267	267
Total Costs	33	60	88	115	105	105	105	105	105	105
Installation Costs	22	22	22	21	...	...	...	...	...	...
Federal Costs	14	14	14	14	2	2	2	2	2	2

4. Variability of outcome
   Present worth "not likely"‡ to fall outside this range ... $100 to $400 (million)‡
   Present worth "extremely unlikely"‡ to fall outside this range ... −$100 to $600 (million)‡

5. Effect on personal wealth distribution§
   Average value of land and buildings per farm-owner in watershed (1950) ... $5,000
   Average net benefit per principal beneficiary (in this case, per farm-owner) ... $4,900

TABLE 14 (*Continued*)

SUGGESTED FORM OF COST-BENEFIT EXHIBITS—GREEN RIVER PROGRAM AS ILLUSTRATION

(Amounts in 1948 dollars)

6. Effect on regional wealth distribution§

   Average income per family in watershed (1950) $1,300‖

   Percentage increase of income in watershed due to project   20%‖

7. Basis for ranking, if required, to facilitate allocation of national water-resources budget:¶

   Internal rate of return (rate of discount which reduces present worth to zero)   55%

---

* In the estimation of this figure, the venture is looked upon as though it were a large corporation. The corporate income tax, on the average, has been about 45% of net profits in recent years. The effective property tax rate has been about 1.5% of the market value of assets, which amounts to 25% of annual profit if property income is assumed to be 6%. Each tax should be deducted from income before the other is figured; and the combined rate is approximately 50%.

† The nation's investment stream is the net excesses, in the periods in which they occur, of costs over benefits. In this case, these excesses occur in years 1 through 3. It is not clear just what budget is to be allocated, or what costs must therefore be covered by the budget; here it is assumed to be these investment costs from the nation's standpoint.

‡ Such ranges are believed to be useful supplements to "best estimates" even though precise "probabilities" cannot be associated with them. If one insists on precision, the first range might be defined as that in which results would fall 75% of the time (if we could imagine repeated trial-runs), the second range as that in which results would fall 90% of the time. These ranges are solely for illustrative purposes; the writer has not dealt with details of the Green River Program enough to have any "feel" for the variability of possible outcomes.

§ These indicators of wealth distribution and effects of project on wealth distribution are merely illustrative. Present worth of benefits at 5% was used in estimating those subsidy effects.

‖ It is assumed that the increase in *local* income would be 1.2 × the net benefits that are expected to accrue locally from the project itself.

¶ The internal rate should not be used as a basis for ranking interdependent projects, such as several possible sizes of a proposal. This figure (55%) was derived by plotting present worth as a function of the discount rate and then by interpolating to find the rate at which present worth appeared to become zero.

Secondary Benefits

No modification with respect to the inclusion of "secondary benefits" is recommended here. They are correctly omitted from the benefit-cost calculus in the existing analysis of the Green River Watershed program. "Secondary benefit," it will be recalled, is the name applied to increased incomes, chiefly to local producers, resulting from the project. The local expansion draws resources from the uses and regions in which they would otherwise have been employed. The expansion, therefore, although pertinent to the regional distribution of wealth and therefore to the final decision, should not be counted as part of the benefit to the whole country (i.e., the value of incremental output due to the project).

Distribution of Wealth

Another important consideration, regarded as an intangible here because it cannot readily be priced, is the effect of the project on the personal distribution of wealth. Although it is difficult even conceptually to measure the distribution of wealth, or changes in it, a few rough clues may in some cases be very useful to the Agencies, the Congress, or the public. For instance, the Green River program bestows benefits upon persons who neither buy the services from the government nor pay for the installation;[31] it may make a difference whether the recipients are 50,000 comparatively poor farmers or 50 wealthy ranchers. Table 14, using rough numbers, illustrates the presentation of such clues.

Also, whether one likes it or not, projects will be judged partly by their impact on *regional* wealth distribution. It is not clear what sort of concise data would be most useful in this connection. As a possibility, Table 14 offers the percentage increase in income for the Green River Watershed, with income per family in 1950 shown as a benchmark. These items would help to indicate the impact of different projects on relative well-being in their respective localities.

The Criterion for Ranking Projects

The principal drawbacks of the conventional benefit-cost ratio as a criterion of rank have been described. Table 15 serves to re-emphasize some of these shortcomings with reference to the Green River project. The first four ratios in Table 15 are ratios of gross

---

[31] The possibilities of levying taxes or charges for these benefits are worth intensive exploration, but the matter is outside the scope of this study.

TABLE 15

MISLEADING BENEFIT-COST RATIOS, AND THEIR VARIABILITY:
GREEN RIVER WATERSHED PROGRAM

Description*	Computed Ratio
1. Ratio of present value of total benefits (discount rate 5%, time-horizon 50 years) to present value of total costs	2.1 to 1
2. Ratio of present value of total benefits (discount rate 5%, time-horizon 30 years) to present value of total costs	1.9 to 1
3. Ratio of present value of total benefits (4%, 30 years) to present value of total costs	2.0 to 1
4. Ratio of present value of total benefits (4%, 50 years) to present value of total costs	2.1 to 1
5. Ratio of present value of net operating benefits† (5%, 50 years) to first year's investment	72.5 to 1
6. Ratio of present value of net operating benefits‡ (5%, 50 years) to "Federal share" of investment§ (summed but not discounted)	6.5 to 1
7. Ratio of present value of net operating benefits‡ (5%, 50 years) to investment cost (summed but not discounted)	4.2 to 1

* In these computations, there were no adjustments for projected shifts in relative prices.

† In this case "net operating benefits" means "total benefits" minus "all costs" except first-year installation cost.

‡ Net operating benefits are "total benefits minus costs of operation" (i.e., exclusive of installation costs).

§ "Federal share" is defined as that percentage which "Federal installation costs" are in relation to "total installation costs."

benefits to gross costs, with different time horizons and discount rates. Note that this type of ratio is comparatively insensitive to the indicated variations of time horizon and discount rate.[32] But the ratio and its insensitivity to the treatment of distant time periods are without much significance, for the ratio will vary capriciously according to the volume of annual operating expenses and annual benefits.

The fifth ratio in Table 15 is the present value of net operating benefits divided by the first year's investment. If this ratio could be used, it would be unnecessary for the given budget to be the present value of amounts to be expended over several years. It could be simply the budget for the coming year. But this ratio pretends that the benefit stream, after deduction of subsequent investment as well as operating costs, can be attributed to the first year's installation.

[32] Moreover, results in general are less sensitive to variations of the discount rate than would be the results of many other projects: for, in the Green River program, heavy costs as well as benefits would occur throughout the project's life.

TABLE 16

TIME PATHS USED IN CALCULATION OF RATIOS*

(Thousands of 1948 dollars)

Item	1	2	3	4	5	6	7	8	9	10	11	12	13	14	15	16
Benefits																
Land Treatment:																
Crop Increase and Flood Abatement†	0	2561	5123	7684	10245	12807	15368	17929	20490	23052	25613	28174	30736	33297	35858	38420
Land Treatment:																
Timber Increase	0	134	268	402	536	670	804	938	1072	1206	1340	1474	1608	1742	1876	2010
Channel Improvement	0	200	400	601	801	→										
Total	0	2895	5791	8687	11582	14278	16973	19668	22363	25059	27754	30449	33145	35840	38535	41231
Costs																
Installation	4330	→														
Operation	0	1104	2208	3312	4416	5520	6624	7728	8832	9936	11040	12144	13248	14352	15456	16560
Total	4330	5434	6538	7642	8746	9850	10954	12058	13162	14266	15370	16474	17578	18682	19786	20890

* These are the estimates (in *Green River Watershed* . . .) spread over time in accordance with certain statements that were made in the Report. Such time paths must be projected before the amounts can be discounted to their present values. These estimates pertain to the proposed program in its entirety—that is, including the parts to be financed by Federal, local, and private funds.

† In the Survey Report it was assumed that the benefits of land treatment would reach their maximum in 5 years. In the calculations here, however, it was assumed that since the installations were to be built over a 20-year period, the benefits would not reach their peak for 20 years.

TABLE 16 (*Continued*)

TIME PATHS USED IN CALCULATION OF RATIOS*
(Thousands of 1948 dollars)

Item	17	18	19	20	21	22	23	24	25	26	27	28	29	30	31–50
Benefits															
Land Treatment:															
Crop Increase and Flood Abatement†	40981	43542	46103	48666	48666										→
Land Treatment:															
Timber Increase	2144	2278	2412	2546	2680	2814	2948	3082	3216	3350	3484	3618	3753	3888	→
Channel Improvement															→
Total	43926	46621	49316	52013	52147	52281	52415	52549	52683	52817	52951	53085	53220	53355	→
Costs															
Installation	17664	18768	19872	20979	0										→
Operation				20979	20979	20979	20979	20979	20979	20979	20979	20979	20979	20979	→
Total	21994	23098	24202	25309	20979	20979	20979	20979	20979	20979	20979	20979	20979	20979	→

* These are the estimates presented in the Survey Report spread over time in accordance with certain statements that were made in the Report. Such time paths must be projected before the amounts can be discounted to their present values. These estimates pertain to the proposed program in its entirety—that is, including the parts to be financed by Federal, local, and private funds.

† In the Survey Report it was assumed that the benefits of land treatment would reach their maximum in 5 years. In the calculations here, however, it was assumed that since the installations were to be built over a 20-year period, the benefits would not reach their peak for 20 years.

Thus it would give top ranking to those projects that involved the least investment during the coming year. This ratio is at one extreme, relevant investment costs being excluded from the denominator; consequently, it turns out to be a handsome 72.5 to 1 in the table. The ratio of gross benefits to gross expenses is at the other extreme, irrelevant operating costs being included in the denominator; it ends up as a modest 2 to 1 in our illustration. The absolute size of these ratios is beside the point, of course; the trouble is that both would make some good projects look bad and some bad ones look good.

Ratio number 6 in the table involves an error somewhat like the one just discussed: it attributes the payoff to one portion of the investment—in this case, Federal investment instead of the first year's investment. The use of this ratio would favor those projects which involved the most local or private investment in cooperation with the Federal government.

Ratio 7 relates benefits to total investment cost—the simple sum of successive years' installation cost, not discounted to its present value. If this ratio could be used, again it would be unnecessary for the given budget to be the present value of proposed outlays over several years. It could be simply the sum of undiscounted amounts to be spent over those years. But the use of this ratio would definitely give wrong answers. If Projects A and B yield the same benefits and entail the same undiscounted outlays, but A involves smaller outlays in the first year, A is preferred, because part of the capital for A can be put to some other productive use in the first year. According to Ratio 7, however, A would be no better than B.

In this study, in accordance with the argument presented in Chapter 7, the internal rate of return is chosen as the test of rank (whenever an independent ranking is meaningful). This internal rate is shown as part of the main exhibit (Table 14 again). Now, the mechanical use of any ranking device is hazardous, and this one is offered rather reluctantly. All relevant considerations in the comparison of water-resource projects cannot be reduced to a single number on the basis of which they can be correctly ranked. It must be remembered that a unique internal rate of return leaves out of account intangibles and uncertainties. It should be kept in mind that this criterion of rank is useful only in selecting projects for a *given* budget; for it would be foolish to determine the size of the budget in such a way as to maximize the internal rate. Also the relevance of this ranking device depends upon *what* investment budget is given and what outlays it should cover. Nonetheless, if handled with care and if intangibles and uncertainty are recognized and considered in the final decision, this test of rank can be helpful. If independent projects are to be compared and it is appropriate to seek the best set of investments to which a national water-resources budget should be devoted, the internal rate is a suitable ranking device. That is, its use will point to the set which yields the greatest expected present worth for a given amount invested by the nation when the streams are discounted at the marginal internal rate of return.

Chapter 12

CASE STUDY II:
SANTA MARIA PROJECT

T HE SECOND CASE STUDY is the Santa Maria project,[1] which would provide water for irrigation and protection from floods in the Santa Maria Valley of California. This valley comprises the lower 250 square miles of the Santa Maria basin, the mouth of which is about 130 miles northwest of Los Angeles. This locality presents the same problem that is posed by much of the West—a rainy season which often brings serious floods, and a dry season which keeps unirrigated land from being very productive.

The principal works that are proposed in this project are (1) the Vaquero Dam and Reservoir, designed to provide water for irrigation and also some flood protection, and (2) a system of levees and channel improvements, intended to afford additional flood protection. The study of this proposal has several interesting features that set it apart from the previous case study and, indeed, from analyses of most other projects.

First, the official report on the project was prepared jointly by the Bureau of Reclamation and the Corps of Engineers. The two agencies worked in close cooperation in comparing alternative plans for the Santa Maria Valley, in designing the works so as to complement each other, and in evaluating the plan that was finally adopted. Second, in this proposal irrigation is to be accomplished solely by recharging the

[1] Sources were the Bureau of Reclamation's *Santa Maria Project, California,* House Document No. 217, 83rd Congress, 1st Session (Washington, D.C.: U.S. Government Printing Office, 1953); the Corps of Engineers' "Report on Survey Flood Control, Santa Maria River and Tributaries, California" (mimeographed), February 10, 1953; and the Corps of Engineers' "Appendixes to Accompany Report on Survey" (mimeographed), February 10, 1953.

underground water supply, not by surface-water delivery to irrigators. Third, the nature of the project, its context, and the models used in working out the estimates are quite different from those in the Green River analysis.

The Santa Maria project would be about a $25 million investment; and, if the published data are used in the calculations, it would yield present worths of $24 million at a 2½ per cent discount rate and of $4 million at a 5 per cent rate. Its internal rate of return would be 6 per cent. Again, let us examine some of the details of the cost-and-benefit measurements.

MODELS THAT DESCRIBE THE PROJECT'S BENEFITS

The relationships which underlie the estimates will be described in installments. As in the previous case study, a few comments on details of the models will be included in these descriptive sections of the chapter, but major methodological suggestions will be taken up in a separate final section.

Effect of Reservoir on Water Supply

The prospect faced by the people of the Santa Maria Valley at present is a rapidly lowering water table. Industrial plants, farms, and municipalities use deep wells to get their water, and they are running into trouble. Annual consumption in the project area averaged, during the years 1929–1948, about 64,000 acre feet,[2] comprising 57,000 acre feet for irrigation, 2,600 acre feet for cities,[3] and 4,400 acre feet for industry.[4] The safe annual yield, the amount by which the underground store is replenished, is about 50,000 acre feet. This overdraft of 14,000 acre feet per year will probably cause some 8,000 acres of presently irrigated land to be returned to dry farms very soon. In that eventuality, about 26,800 acres would be under irrigation, and annual consumption would be offset by average annual replenishment.

The proposed Vaquero Reservoir would make it possible, on the average, to recharge the underground supply with an additional 18,500 acre feet per year.[5] (Actually the amount would vary, not only on

---

[2] In the last few years consumption has apparently been higher.

[3] Santa Maria, Guadalupe, Betteravia, Orcutt, and Garey.

[4] Sugar refinery, oil refineries, gravel processing plant, and others.

[5] An alternative possibility, getting water by sinking deeper wells, is ignored. This may be justified, however, because salt-water intrusion is already beginning to occur.

account of year-to-year fluctuations in rainfall, but also because of gradual sedimentation and loss of storage capacity.) The reservoir would function in the following way. Of the total storage space of 214,000 acre feet, 89,000 acre feet would be reserved for flood control. That is, outflow would be controlled so as to maximize the recharge of the underground store until the first 125,000 acre feet of storage space were filled. After that, water would be released so as to get the most flood protection out of the remaining 89,000 acre feet of space.[6]

The calculations allowed for depletion of the reservoir's capacity due to sedimentation at a rate of 900 acre feet per annum. This figure was based on experience with the Gibraltar Reservoir in the Santa Ynez watershed and on United States Forest Service estimates which related sedimentation to flood frequencies, watershed cover, and erodibility. Incidentally, sedimentation in the Gibraltar, completed in 1920, far exceeded the original estimates for that project; in the present analysis, the average concentration of sediment in the Santa Maria runoff was assumed to be twice that in the waters that poured into Gibraltar Reservoir. However, the rate at which Vaquero's space would be depleted in this model is still not high in comparison with experience in some reservoirs.

The calculations also took into account evaporation losses, which were estimated to be, on the average, 1,300 acre feet annually. Such losses would be relatively low in this project, because storage in the reservoir "would be only for a few months following each rainy season, while releases for percolation into the riverbed are made. The remainder of the year, and all during dry years, the reservoir would be empty."[7]

Allowance for other wastage was apparently also made. The maximum flow, if the water is to be absorbed by the riverbed before reaching the ocean, is about 300 cubic feet per second, according to stream-flow records for the watershed. The aim would be to maintain this flow, except under flood conditions, by coordinating the releases from the reservoir with those of the Sisquoc River. In this way, wastage into the ocean would be minimized.

Unfortunately, the amount of water that would percolate down to the water table is expressed simply as an average—18,500 acre feet per year—and the precise formulae used to derive the estimates are

[6] The scheduled rates of release, at different water-surface elevations, are shown in Corps of Engineers, "Appendixes to Report on Survey," Appendix 3, pp. 3–4.

[7] *Santa Maria Project*, p. 47.

not shown. A rough check shows that this figure is certainly within a plausible range: at present, average wastage of Santa Maria waters into the ocean appears to be about 35,000 acre feet per year;[8] hence, the project is supposed to capture slightly over 50 per cent of current losses to the ocean, the remainder still being lost as a result of evaporation and occasional flood conditions—that is, situations in which more than 125,000 acre feet of the reservoir's space is filled and flows must exceed 300 cubic feet per second.

In this connection, the following point may be fairly important. Suppose all of the 18,500 acre feet attributed to the project would not be a net addition to the underground water supply. Instead of capturing that amount of water from currently wasted flood waters, the project might take part of it from the present annual "recharge" (50,000 acre feet). It seems likely that *some* of the extra 18,500 acre feet credited to the project would also percolate into the riverbed without the project. This is a "spillover effect"—almost literally— on physical production possibilities from resources other than the dam. Perhaps the effect would not be great, but it may deserve mention in analyses of irrigation projects.

These are engineering aspects of the model, however, a subject to which this review of the Santa Maria analysis is not primarily directed. We shall turn therefore to the next set of relationships, those designed to translate the physical effects into economic effects.

Effect of Reservoir on Net Farm Incomes

The upshot of the increased water supply just discussed is the irrigation of more acres with the project than in its absence. The final projections are shown in Table 17. The total acreage rises at first because some of the irrigable bench lands, which are less productive than the valley floors, are not developed initially. The amount declines later, because sedimentation reduces the amount of water made available by the reservoir.[9]

In the preparation of these estimates, consideration was given to land characteristics and general agricultural practices. For example, 7 per cent of the total irrigable acreage was estimated to be non-

[8] About 40 per cent of 91,800 acre feet. See Corps of Engineers, "Report on Survey . . . ," p. 14. However, the 1941–51 average was about 26,000 acre feet per year, according to the comments of the California Department of Natural Resources, *Santa Maria Project*, p. 113.

[9] Municipal-industrial growth reduces the amount of water available for irrigation both with and without the project.

TABLE 17

ADDITIONAL ACREAGE IRRIGATED WITH PROJECT

(thousands of acres)

Years of Project Operation	Total	In Flood Plain	In Bench Land
1 to 10	10.0	8.8	1.2
11 to 20	12.0	10.0	2.0
21 to 30	11.6	10.1	1.5
31 to 40	11.2	10.3	0.9
41 to 50	10.5	10.4	0.1

agricultural, i.e., used for houses, roads, and so on. Moreover, only 60 to 80 per cent of suitable bench land was assumed to be irrigated in any one year, the remainder being dry-farmed or left fallow. All irrigable flood plain was supposed to be farmed intensively each year. These assumptions are in accord with current cropping procedures.

Current practices are also the basis for assuming that 20 per cent of the water pumped for irrigation gets back into the underground supply, and that irrigation of an acre "requires" about 2 acre feet of water annually. In this connection, "irrigation" is taken to mean the way farmers apply water to their land currently, that is, at a low incremental cost to the users. With the introduction of the project, they would probably continue to consume water in about the same way. That is, once the pumps were installed, the cost of another acre foot would be chiefly the cost of power for the pumping, since project repayment would *not* be accomplished by charges per unit of water consumed. Thus the gains sacrificed by not applying another acre foot to unirrigated lands would not enter the calculations of many users. Indeed, the gains sacrificed by not applying the water to domestic or industrial use would not enter their calculations. As a consequence, use of the additional water, along with the existing supply, might be far from optimal. If the number of pumps could be limited, and the water charged for by the unit, it might be used more effectively, and the gain might be greater, than is projected. Unless some such arrangement is introduced, it seems likely that consumption per acre will continue at the current rate.

These pieces fit together somewhat as follows.[10] The extra acre feet of water go first to the irrigation of the flood plain, making it possible, in the second decade of the project, to irrigate 36,800 acres

[10] Without the *exact* estimates of underground water supplies created by the project, the model and the calculations cannot be reproduced precisely.

(39,600 gross irrigable acres minus 7 per cent of that number, thus allowing for non-agricultural uses). This is an *additional* 10,000 acres of bottomland, requiring 2.05 acre feet of water for each acre or 20,500 acre feet in all. At first glance, this seems to be an overdraft, since the project is supposed to increase the supply in each of the early years by about 20,000 acre feet. It is to be recalled, however, that 20 per cent of the water pumped becomes available again. As an approximation of the total increase in the annual supply, let us allow for one cycle during each year. Accordingly, 20 per cent of 20,000 (4,000 acre feet) becomes available a second time.

All told, then, 24,000 acre feet of water could be used each year during the first two decades without overdraft, making it possible to irrigate some of the upland also. In this calculation, about 1,800 acres of bench land, which takes 1.90 acre feet of water per acre, could be irrigated. The acreage officially projected during the second decade is slightly higher, partly because the water table would actually have been built up a bit during the first decade's operations. Nonetheless, this sample calculation shows roughly how this part of the model works.

The next step was to translate the increase in irrigated acreage into increased income. Without the project, this acreage would be dry-farmed; and its net income[11] per acre was assumed to be the same amount, $32 annually, that could be obtained from dry-bean production.[12] This net income per acre from dry-farming was used for both flood plain and upland.

With the project, the picture is quite different. The anticipated crop patterns, yields, prices, operating expenses and net income per irrigated acre are shown in Table 18. The crop yields "represent average yields under good farming practice. They are based on past production records and estimates made by individual farmers in the area and by the county agricultural commissioner." Estimates were made in terms of a farm price level of 215 (1910–1914=100), prices being approximately representative of the year 1949.[13]

---

[11] Income net of the farmer's operating costs.

[12] Amounts are those presented in section on "Revised Benefit and Cost Data," *Santa Maria Project,* pp. 4–11. These numbers differ from those given in the main portion of the Report because different price levels were used.

[13] In the original estimates (*ibid.,* pp. 59–64), the prices used were "representative of the State average for the base period 1939–44 with adjustment wherever deemed necessary to more nearly reflect long-term outlook" (p. 62). These estimates were later revised, in the process of coordinating the two agencies' analyses, by using a price level comparable to that used by the Engineers in calculating flood-control benefits.

TABLE 18
CROPS, EXPENSES, AND NET INCOME PER IRRIGATED ACRE, WITH THE PROJECT (1939–1944 PRICES)*

	Annual Yield	Price per Unit	Annual Gross Income	Total Operating Expenses	Annual Net Income	Weighting Factor: Percentage Distribution of Total Acreage among Crops
Flood Plain Areas						
Vegetables	...	...	$820†	$683	$137	50
Sugar Beets	18 tons	$9.70	175	140	35	15
Alfalfa and other forage	6 tons	...	237‡	209	28	8
Vegetable and flower seed	...	...	450§	319	131	7
Potatoes	225 hundred-weight	1.50	338	265	73	5
Beans	20 hundred-weight	6.00	120	70	50	15
Weighted average net income per acre based on above amounts					$ 96	
Weighted average net income per acre revised to reflect "1949" prices					157	
Bench Land Areas						
Vegetables	...	...	$597‖	$487	$110	30
Sugar Beets	16 tons	$9.70	155	123	32	5
Alfalfa and other forage	5 tons	...	237	213¶	24	20
Vegetable and flower seed	...	...	380	291	89	5
Potatoes	200 hundred-weight	1.50	300	243	57	10
Beans	18 hundred-weight	6.00	108	64	44	30
Weighted average net income per acre based on above amounts					$ 63	
Weighted average net income per acre revised to reflect "1949" prices					105	

* Source: *Santa Maria Project*, Table 6, p. 62.
† Based on proportionate weighting of income from lettuce, cauliflower, broccoli, and carrots with 100 per cent double-cropping assumed.
‡ Based on gross returns from a 50-cow dairy, assuming 325 pounds of butterfat per cow.
§ Taken from Santa Barbara County crop reports.
‖ Based on proportionate weighting of income from lettuce, cauliflower, broccoli, and carrots with 67 per cent double-cropping assumed.
¶ Increased over flood-plain costs on account of purchased hay.

Table 18 shows the steps that were taken in making the calculations. On the basis of the numbers shown there, the annual net income
from a "composite acre" of flood plain is $96; from an acre of bench
land, $63. However, later revisions in terms of a higher price level
changed these amounts to $157 and $105 respectively. Since these
acres, if dry-farmed, would yield $32 annually (after the above
mentioned revision of price levels), the net gain due to the project is
$125 for every extra acre of bottomland and $73 for every extra acre
of upland that can be irrigated. Multiplication of these amounts by
the number of extra acres to be irrigated gives total irrigation benefits as shown in Table 19.[14]

TABLE 19

ANNUAL IRRIGATION BENEFITS, SANTA MARIA*

(Thousands of "1949" dollars)

Years of Project Operation	Total	On Flood Plain	On Bench Land
1 to 10	$1188	$1100	$ 88
11 to 20	1396	1250	146
21 to 30	1372	1263	109
31 to 40	1353	1287	66
41 to 50	1307	1300	7

*Source: *Santa Maria Project*, Table 1, p 9.

It is noteworthy that these benefits are net of all farmers' operating
costs[15] (which average almost 80 per cent of gross income). Had we
counted gross income as the benefits, and included farmers' operating
expenses as costs, of the project—making the procedure more nearly
consistent with that in the Green River analysis—the conventional
benefit-cost ratio would have been much lower. But, as has been
indicated several times, this ratio does not provide an acceptable basis
for choosing among projects in any event.

By and large, this model appears to be a reasonable one. Only two
comments are offered at this point. The first comment pertains to the

---

[14] There are minor discrepancies, caused chiefly by rounding and the tabular
presentation of averages, between these estimates and those which can be computed with the aid of Table 17.

[15] One operating cost was ignored; although the value of all manual labor
was included, no allowance was made for the earnings of management. This
would tend to overstate slightly the returns attributable to the project.

introduction of long-term forecasts of price levels.[16]   In this connection, the use of special "refined" projections[17] may aggravate the difficulty of comparing projects.   It would be preferable to put all analyses in terms of a common price level.   For as soon as the defects of the conventional ratio are recognized, the absolute dollar estimates are seen to be highly significant; yet these, too, will be meaningless unless all are in the same monetary unit at the time of comparison. What happened in the Santa Maria analysis points up this difficulty. Initially the Bureau of Reclamation used 1939–1944 prices to calculate irrigation benefits, and the Engineers used a projection that was roughly the equivalent of 1949 prices to calculate flood-damage reduction. When the two parts were put together, it seemed more important to use comparable price levels than for each agency to adhere to its particular projection.   And to use comparable price levels is surely as important with respect to different projects as it is with respect to different parts of a single project.

But perhaps the use of a common price level is too much to hope for in the preparation of such analyses.   Next best, in the writer's view, would be the use of current prices—those of the year in which an analysis is made.   If current prices were used, it would generally be recognized that different price levels were used in various analyses; then, at the time a decision is to be reached, benefits and costs could be deflated to a common base year by means of the most suitable price indexes.   Presumably such adjustments could be made if each analysis was in terms of its own special forecast instead of current prices, but the adjustments would be more complicated and more likely to be neglected or handled improperly at the time of decision.   It might well be better to use garden variety current price levels in each analysis.

The second comment relates to the reasonableness of the final estimates of irrigation benefits.   A crude check suggests that the numbers may be a little high.   We can compare gross income per acre as estimated for this project with the corresponding figure (actual) for other projects.   Over the 50-year period, the weighted average gross income attributed to irrigation from the Vaquero Reservoir is over $700 per acre in "1949" prices.[18]   Now such gross crop values per acre are

[16] So far as the adjustment of *relative* prices is concerned, the comments made with respect to the Green River analysis are applicable again.

[17] The use of any prices at all constitutes a forecast.   The term "special forecast" refers to the use of prices other than those of a common base year, or those of the "current" year—that is, the one in which an analysis is made.

[18] Estimated on the basis of the data in *Santa Maria Project*.

not unheard of; in 1949, the Coachella Division of the All-American Canal Project in California grossed $658 ("1949" prices). But such figures are not often encountered. No Federally constructed project could report such a gross during the three years 1949–1951; in 1950, only five out of the sixty-three ventures had gross crop values in excess of $200 per acre (1950 prices), the top being $433 for the Coachella Division and the next being $260 for the Yuma, Arizona, project.[19]

Since, in general, the better lands were supposedly brought under irrigation first, the comparison suggests that the Santa Maria income estimates may be on the high side, so far as the *average* acre and *average* year are concerned. It should go without saying that such bits of evidence do not show anything conclusively. They are introduced here solely to suggest that this part of any cost-benefit model deserves close attention and that estimates all along the line should be subjected to a few checks.

Effect of Reservoir and Channel-Levee Works on Flood Damage

In describing the magnitude of floods, one usually talks about areas covered, depths of inundation, and duration. In describing the effects of flood-control works, however, one thinks, at least initially, of their impact on flows, that is, on the cubic feet discharged per second at designated points. In this analysis, it was convenient to relate the magnitude of floods (and of damage) to such flows—the relationship appears to be a close one—and, in particular, to orient the whole model around peak discharge at Fugler's Point, the confluence of the Cuyama and Sisquoc rivers.

First, from past records, a discharge-frequency curve was derived, showing the number of times one could expect various peak discharges[20] to occur during a period of a hundred years. This curve, of course, pertained to the situation as it would be without the project. Next, a discharge-damage curve was prepared, showing the way average monetary damage over the coming decades was expected to vary with flood size, measured as before by peak flow. (The derivation of this curve will be discussed a little later.)

From these two curves, a damage-frequency relationship was obtained. Since the discharge-damage curve showed an estimate of monetary damage for each peak discharge, one could be substituted

[19] *Interior Department Appropriations for 1953* . . . , House of Representatives, Part 3, pp. 1122–1123.
[20] At Fugler's Point.

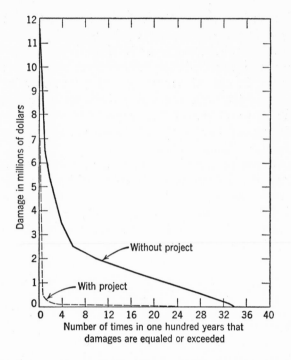

Figure 4. Damage-frequency curves, Santa Maria River.*

* Source: U.S. Army Corps of Engineers, "Appendixes to Accompany Report on Survey, Flood Control, Santa Maria River and Tributaries, California" (mimeographed), February 10, 1953, Appendix 5, Plate 4, following p. 19.

for the other. Hence the discharge-frequency curve could be translated into a damage-frequency curve. The last named curve (in cumulative form, which shows the number of times that each damage figure would be equaled or exceeded) is presented in Figure 4 to illustrate the product of the procedure so far. The area under this curve represents total damage over a 100-year period. This amount could be approximated by multiplying by one the damage expected to occur one time, multiplying by two the amount expected to occur two times, and so on, and then by summing up all these products. Average damage per year is simply the total projected for the entire period divided by 100, which turns out to be $630,000 in this analysis of the Santa Maria Valley.

A similar procedure yielded estimates of annual flood damage with the project. The Vaquero reservoir, with 89,000 acre feet of storage space reserved for flood-control, is supposed to be capable of reducing a storm of 230,000 cubic feet per second to a discharge of 150,000 cubic feet per second (to be called "second feet" hereafter).[21] The levees and channel improvements are supposed to make the Santa Maria River capable of handling 150,000 second feet with no damage (except for small losses below Guadalupe). Speaking very roughly, then, we may say that with the project, significant damage would begin when storms exceeded 230,000 second feet. Moreover, storms larger than 230,000 second feet would cause less damage than the amounts indicated by the original discharge-damage curve: a flood of 250,000 second feet would be shrunk to an "excess" of only 20,000, loosely equivalent to a flood of 50,000 second feet without the project. (The unimproved channel of the Santa Maria can at present cope with discharges of about 30,000 second feet.)

The impact of all this begins to be apparent when it is realized that a flood as large as 230,000 second feet is expected to occur only once in 400 years. This particular size was entitled the standard project flood, which was defined as "a large hypothetical flood that would be exceeded only on rare occasions," and which figured considerably in the design of the project.[22] The "maximum probable flood," defined as the one which "would result from the most severe combination of meteorological and ground conditions considered possible of attainment in the drainage area," is stated to be 380,000 second feet.

The effect of the reservoir and channel works on the damage-frequency relationship is presented in Figure 4. As suggested above, anticipated damage with the project is negligible except in storms larger than 230,000 second feet, which can be expected only once in several hundred years. Again, the area under this curve—that is, the sum of the products of the damage figures times the frequencies of recurrence—is the total expected damage over a 100-year period. Average annual damage is this total divided by 100, or $30,000 in this analysis of the Santa Maria project. Hence the average annual reduction of flood damage attributed to the project was $630,000 minus $30,000, or $600,000.[23]

[21] It will be recognized that these relationships are oversimplified, because several factors (intensity of rainfall, specific channel conditions) which affect these numbers in particular storms are left out of the picture.

[22] However, the Agencies considered formally several other reservoirs and levee systems, differing in both size and location from the finally recommended project. They will be discussed briefly in later paragraphs.

[23] These are the figures given in the Corps of Engineers' "Report on Survey . . . ," pp. 23–24, 41; in House Document No. 217, average annual damage reduction is stated to be $670,000 (pp. 65–66), revised later to $600,000 (p. 5).

Our aim has been to present a fairly compact, though rough, sketch of the damage reduction model. The only details that will be presented here[24] are some points about the derivation of the discharge-damage curve and some data on damage. In gaging the physical consequences of various peak discharges, the analysts considered probable depth and duration of inundation, velocity of flow, and, of course, the antic-ipated location and physical characteristics of various assets. They reviewed the behavior of past floods and studied maps and aerial photo-graphs of the areas which would be inundated in floods of various sizes. In order to estimate the economic consequences, it was then necessary to attach values to both "direct damage," the physical destruction due to overflow and erosion, and "indirect damage," which "includes losses from (1) interruptions to railroad and highway traffic, communications, and industry; (2) emergency expenditure for the care of flood victims; and (3) losses from the general disruption of community activity."[25]

The precise steps in valuing damage are not given, but the nature of the procedure is indicated by the following quotation:

Valuation and production figures were obtained principally from field surveys. The data submitted at the public hearing were supplemented by information obtained in the field and by reports compiled by local interests and by other State and Federal agencies. Estimates of damage under average future conditions were made under assumptions of average future development over the next 50-year period and by using projected price levels as recommended by the Federal Inter-Agency River Basin Committee. The population and property values of the City of Santa Maria have increased steadily since 1920. . . . On the basis of past growth, the average future population and the average future development in the overflow area within the city of Santa Maria during the next 50 years are estimated at 20 per cent greater than the 1949 population and development.[26]

The price forecast recommended by the Inter-Agency River Basin Committee is presumably the Department of Agriculture's long range projection for an intermediate level of economic activity (58,000,000 employed and 8,000,000 jobless).[27] This evidently turned out to ap-proximate the 1949 price level and structure.[28]

---

[24] Considerable detail is available—especially about hydrologic records and relationships, overflow areas from river-mile 1 to river-mile 20 (Fugler's Point), and the physical features of the project—in Corps of Engineers' "Report on Survey . . ." and "Appendixes to Report on Survey."

[25] "Appendixes to Report on Survey," Appendix 5, p. 7.

[26] *Ibid.*, pp. 7–7a.

[27] *Proposed Practices for Economic Analysis* . . . , pp. 16–21. Actually, the

TABLE 20

ESTIMATED DAMAGE FROM FUTURE FLOODS OF VARIOUS MAGNITUDES,
OVERFLOW AREA ALONG SANTA MARIA RIVER*
(Average future conditions; thousands of dollars)

| Type of Property | Average Future Value† | Damage from Floods of Different Magnitude† | | | |
| | | 230,000 second-feet‡ | | 60,000 second-feet‡ | |
		Direct	Indirect	Direct	Indirect
Residential	$18,100	$1,000	$ 190	$ 40	$ 8
Business and industrial	33,500	1,940	680	180	40
Public	8,100	100	20	0	0
Agricultural	17,400	4,760	930	990	200
Irrigation and drainage works	740	70	0	5	0
Highways and roads	770	380	50	20	2
Railroads	900	370	200	5	0
Utilities	160	20	0	0	0
Total	79,670	8,640	2,070	1,240	250
Total Direct and Indirect Damage		$10,710		$1,490	

* Taken from Corps of Engineers' "Appendixes to Accompany Report on Survey Flood Control, Santa Maria River and Tributaries, California" (mimeographed), February 10, 1953, Appendix 5, Table 6, p. 16.

† Average over 50-year period 1953–2002.

‡ Peak discharges at Fugler's Point.

Table 20 shows a few points on the discharge-damage curve. There are two breakdowns of the damage estimates—into the categories of property damaged and into direct and indirect damage.

Damage to agricultural property is one of the more important

---

recommendation is somewhat ambiguous: "All things considered, the most satisfactory approach would result from using prices estimated as they are expected to be at the time when costs are incurred and benefits received" (p. 17); "The most practicable procedure is to estimate the average price level expected over the life of the project. . . . This requires consideration of population growth, technological developments, changes in consumption patterns, levels of employment, amount of foreign trade, possibilities of substitutes and alternative sources of supply, and monetary and fiscal policy" (p. 18). "Finally, it is suggested that where agricultural benefits and costs are involved in benefit-cost analyses, the projections used by the Department of Agriculture in its watershed treatment program with such adaptations thereto as the agencies may need to make in practice, be used as the most appropriate at this time, until longer range projections as recommended above become available" (pp. 20–21).

[28] See *Santa Maria Project*, p. 4.

categories. The general procedures that were used in this connection are described as follows:

Damage to land that would not be permanently destroyed was computed as equal to the cost of restoration, including such items as leveling and re-ditching. Damage to the stored contents of farm buildings would vary greatly according to the season of the year and the quantity of farm produce stored.

. . . The extent of crop damage by a flood of given magnitude would depend on the season in which the flood occurred, because the acreage planted to crops and the value of growing crops vary greatly throughout the year. In general, floods that have occurred on Santa Maria River have occurred in the winter season, from December to March, with most of the floods occurring during the months of January and February. The factors con-sidered in the calculation of crop damage include the variable value of crops on the ground, the probability of flood occurrence at different times of the year, and the estimated depth and velocity of flow. Damage was computed as the reduction in yield, or—for complete destruction of a crop—as the value of the crop at the time of flooding. The crop value on the ground at the time of any flood was assumed to be equal to the cumulative expense to the farmer in overhead, labor, and material from the beginning of ground preparation to the time of the flood, plus a reasonable portion of antici-pated profit. If the analysis showed that a crop would be destroyed too late in the season for another crop to be grown, all the fixed charges for land and operations for the entire crop year were included in the estimate of crop damage. If the analysis showed that another crop could be grown successfully after a flood, only the fixed charges for the part of the crop year before the flood were included.

. . . Damage to livestock would consist of the value of livestock destroyed and the decrease in value because of decrease in weight or grade as a result of the flood. Many of the dairy cows and young stock are pastured in the river channel and adjoining submarginal land. This land is fenced and the animals could not escape without aid. In addition, much of the poultry and many of the smaller animals would be drowned.[29]

Indirect damage, it might be observed, was based on

loss of use of dwellings, cost of renting temporary quarters and of moving, . . . emergency expenditures for sanitation, treatment and prevention of sickness, . . . relief of distress . . . nonrecoverable parts of such items as loss of income from interrupting consumers' purchases, . . . additional operat-ing costs, . . . emergency construction, flood fighting, and policing.[30]

Secondary Benefits

The Corps of Engineers does not count secondary benefits, but the Bureau of Reclamation does.[31] Consequently, in the joint report on

---

[29] Corps of Engineers, "Appendixes to Report on Survey," Appendix 5, pp. 12–13.

[30] *Ibid.*, Appendix 5, p. 11.

the Santa Maria project, the estimate of total gains is shown both with and without secondary benefits. These gains, "as construed by the Bureau of Reclamation, represent increased net income from processing, transporting, and merchandising products of the area and from the projected increase in the sale of consumers' goods and services to local farmers."[32]

These secondary benefits were measured as follows. First, the increase, due to the project, in the annual gross value of each crop was estimated. Next, secondary-benefit factors like the ones described earlier—supposed to be the annual income generated by processing, transporting, and merchandising as a percentage of gross crop value —were applied to the gross value of the various crops. These factors were based on studies which indicated, for example, that sugar beets induce more processing and transporting, in relation to crop value, than do beans or potatoes. Next, another factor was applied so as to give credit to the Federal government for only *part* of these secondary benefits. It was decided to attribute 18.5 per cent—the increase in annual net farm income as a percentage of gross—to the project, the remainder evidently being attributed to the farmers themselves on account of their increased operating outlays. A look at the numbers in Table 21 may further clarify this procedure. (These factors are more recent, and considerably higher than those from the 1952 "Bureau of Reclamation Manual" which were shown in Chapter 9.)

But this was not the end of the calculation. Also included among secondary benefits was the expansion in sales of local goods and services to the farmers. The method of estimation was one provided by the Bureau Manual: simply the multiplication of the estimated direct benefits from a project by 19 per cent. Average annual irrigation benefits, in the 1939–1944 prices used for all the original calculations, were $811,300.[33] Hence the estimated secondary benefits in the form of expanded local sales were 19 per cent of $811,300, or $154,100.

Total annual secondary benefits, thus, were $585,000 plus $154,100, or $739,100, in 1939–1944 prices, amounting to 91 per cent of the direct irrigation benefits of $811,300. When the parts done by the Bureau and the Corps were brought together, these secondary benefits were blown up in the same proportion that direct irrigation benefits were

---

[31] The Corps does include indirect benefits as described above, but these are entirely different from "secondary" benefits.

[32] *Santa Maria Project*, p. 71.

[33] *Santa Maria Project*, Table 7, p. 63.

TABLE 21

THE ESTIMATION OF SECONDARY BENEFITS, SANTA MARIA PROJECT*

(Amounts in 1939–1944 prices)

Crop	Increase in Annual Gross	Secondary-Benefit Factor (per cent)	Secondary Benefits
Vegetables	$2,430,140	74	$1,798,300
Sugar beets	721,470	72	519,460
Alfalfa and other forage	417,600	71	296,500
Seeds	341,730	* 65	222,120
Potatoes	256,260	65	166,570
Beans	245,000	65	159,250
Total			$3,162,200
Percentage attributable to project			18.5%†
Amount attributable to project			585,000

* Source: *Santa Maria Project*, pp. 72–73.

† Increase in net annual farm income ($4,412,200 increased gross minus $3,597,800 increased operating costs, or $814,400) as a percentage of the increase in annual gross ($4,412,200).

blown up in order to put all estimates in terms of a farm price level of 215. Average annual secondary benefits then became $1,204,100.[34]

The only comment on the model is that the apparent refinement of these estimates may be misleading. Actually, the concepts and data are so rough that applying factors like 71 per cent or 18.5 per cent and estimating amounts to the nearest hundred dollars seem, at best, like unwarranted refinements. In this case, however, this point is relatively unimportant; the real issue is whether or not to include secondary benefits at all. According to the reasoning in Chapter 9, the Corps of Engineers is correct in their practice of omitting secondary benefits. Although local growth is pertinent to the regional distribution of wealth and hence to Congressmen's final decisions, it is not properly a "net benefit" to the nation.

MODEL THAT DESCRIBES PROJECT'S COSTS

The aim in this section is merely to summarize the estimate of costs for the time periods in which they would be incurred. (The

[34] *Santa Maria Project*, pp. 5, 9. Amount given is simple average before conversion to present worth and then to annual equivalent.

discounting of future costs and benefits will be taken up separately.) In Table 22 the estimated outlays are shown, broken down by component works and by years.

The construction cost is spread over the period of installation, 4 years for Vaquero, 2 years for the levees along the Santa Maria River, and 1 year for a leveed channel to divert flows from Bradley Canyon to the Santa Maria River. The estimates allow for the dam and appurtenant works; camp construction; land, easements, and rights-of-way; clearing the reservoir area; relocation of railroads, highways, and utilities; levee and channel construction; clearing the

TABLE 22

EXPENDITURES PROGRAMMED THROUGH TIME*

(Thousands of 1952 dollars)

Works	Years of Construction					Years of Operation (each year)
	1	2	3	4	Total	
Vaquero Reservoir	$4,245.5	$4,245.5	$4,245.5	$4,245.5	$16,982	$25.4
Santa Maria Levees	5,248.0	5,248.0			10,496	44.0
Bradley Canyon Levees	902.0				902	2.4

* Taken from Corps of Engineers, "Report on Survey . . . ," p. 39.

floodway; contingencies, engineering, and overhead. A good deal of detail, from the cost of drilling weep holes to outlays for installing grout pipe, is available.[35]

The 3,400 acres devoted to the reservoir would be mostly a canyon-like valley, with only about 300 irrigated acres and a little dry-farmed land being inundated. Even the cost of this area might be reduced "if the Bureau of Reclamation, instead of acquiring the reservoir area in fee, were to obtain a flowage easement up to the maximum flow line of the reservoir. Property owners could then use the reservoir area for livestock grazing. . . . [except while water is stored during and after the rainy season]."[36] It might be pointed out, however, that such a cost reduction would be small, since in any event only

[35] Corps of Engineers, "Appendixes to Report on Survey," Appendix 4, pp. 3–8.

[36] *Santa Maria Project,* pp. 47–48.

$56,000 was allowed for land and rights-of-way in connection with Vaquero.

In preparing these estimates, naturally, local circumstances were taken into account, e.g., the cost of labor and materials in view of their nearest sources. For instance, it was assumed that "coarse aggregates" would have to be transported 25–50 miles, and "non-reactive concrete aggregates" would have to be hauled by rail from Los Angeles, unless a deposit in the Salinas River, at present undeveloped, could be tapped at less expense.

The figures shown in Table 22 include both Federal and non-Federal outlays, the latter being about 10 per cent of the first cost of the Santa Maria levees, about 20 per cent of the first cost of the Bradley Canyon levees, and 100 per cent of the maintenance and operation expense in connection with the two levee systems. Legislation governing the construction of flood-control works by the Corps of Engineers requires that in most cases the cost of land, easements, rights-of-way, maintenance, and operation be borne by local groups.

In Table 22 operating expenses are shown to begin after construction is complete. They do not include interest on investment, interest during construction, or amortization of investment, all of which will be discussed in the next section.

TREATMENT OF TIME

In its initial calculations,[37] the Bureau followed its regular practice of using a 100-year time horizon, but in the revised figures of the joint report, a 50-year time horizon was adopted, in accordance with the customary procedure of the Corps. However, a substantial salvage value was deducted from investment costs to allow for the remainder of the reservoir's useful life at the end of 50 years. In the calculation of salvage value, it was estimated that 45 per cent of the reservoir's usable yield would be left (140 years was its estimated total life, at least in providing water for irrigation). The value of this leftover capacity was assumed to be 45 per cent of the $16,982,000 cost of construction, or $7,641,900. In the project report, the present worth of this amount, at a 2½ per cent discount rate, is stated to be $2,223,000.

The benefit-cost time streams were then reduced to annual equivalents in a straightforward manner: the present worths of the streams were calculated and then amortized over the 50-year period. The results were the amounts which, if received or paid out each year,

[37] *Santa Maria Project*, pp. 61–63, 71–77.

would be equivalent to the present worth of the benefit stream and the cost stream respectively. It should be noted that in all manipulations the discount rate was 2½ per cent.

With this treatment of time, the numbers turned out to be those shown in Tables 23 and 24.

THE CRITERION

The ultimate result of devising these models and making all these calculations pertaining to the Santa Maria project was a benefit-cost ratio of 1.87 to 1.[38] The project was deemed to be economically justified, since benefits, discounted at 2½ per cent, were in excess of costs. It was not stated, of course, that this ratio is, or should be, the *sole* consideration in comparing the project with others. Nonetheless, as is customary in the analysis of water-resource measures, a good deal of emphasis was put on the ratio: for example, in connection with the Santa Maria project, the ratio was stressed in Secretary McKay's report to the President through the Bureau of the Budget.[39] And most persons feel, naturally enough, that the higher the ratio, the better the project. In brief, conventional benefit-cost ratios are regarded as proper criteria by many persons, and for them the measure of the Santa Maria project's worth is 1.87 to 1 (or, if secondary benefits are included, 3 to 1).

SUGGESTED CHANGES IN COST-BENEFIT ANALYSIS WITH REFERENCE TO SANTA MARIA PROJECT

The General Criterion

What was said about criteria in connection with the Green River Program applies to other water-resource measures. Too little is known about several things to permit the prescription of a definitive criterion —too little about the appropriate governmental attitude toward uncertain outcomes, too little about the basic reasons for Congressional intervention in water-resource development. But it is urged that data on incremental present worth to the nation (measured as described), on the time paths of benefits and costs, on the variability of the estimates, and on changes in the distribution of wealth would be highly pertinent to the final decisions. And if any single test must be

[38] Annual equivalent direct benefits of $1,910,700 divided by annual equivalent project costs of $1,024,100.

[39] *Santa Maria Project*, p. 3.

TABLE 23

DERIVATION OF ANNUAL EQUIVALENT COSTS,*
SANTA MARIA PROJECT
(Thousands of 1952 dollars)

Investment

Vaquero Reservoir	$16,982
Levees and channel improvement	11,398
Interest during construction of Reservoir	849
Subtotal	$29,229
Less salvage value of Reservoir	−2,223
Present worth of investment as of first year of operation	27,006

Annual charges

Amortization of investment, 50 years at 2½ per cent†	952.3
Average annual maintenance, operation:	
Vaquero Reservoir	25.4
Levees and channel improvement	46.4
Total annual equivalent	1024.1

* Sources: *Santa Maria Project*, pp. 4–12, 47–48, 74–77; "Report on Survey . . .,"
pp. 38–40.
† This is the annual equivalent, with a 2½ per cent interest rate and a time
period of 50 years, of the present worth of investment ($27,006,000). Interest
on investment is allowed for in this annual equivalent.

TABLE 24

DERIVATION OF ANNUAL EQUIVALENT BENEFITS,*
SANTA MARIA PROJECT
(In projected future prices)†

	Benefits		
Years of Project Operation	Direct	Secondary	Total
1 to 10	$1,187.6	$1,080.7	$2,268.3
11 to 20	1,396.0	1,270.4	2,666.4
21 to 30	1,372.0	1,248.5	2,620.5
31 to 40	1,353.2	1,231.4	2,584.6
41 to 50	1,307.3	1,189.6	2,496.9
Present value of streams (2½%)‡	37,173.7		71,001.4
"Amortization" of present value (50 years, 2½%); i.e. annual equivalent	1,310.7		2,503.4
Average annual flood-control benefits	600.0		600.0
Total annual equivalent	$1,910.7		$3,103.4

* Source: *Santa Maria Project*, Table 2, p. 9.
† The amounts are in terms of a long-term projection in which farm price level
is 215 and prices are roughly representative of 1949.
‡ Present worth factors can be obtained from any set of interest tables or from
Santa Maria Project, p. 9.

used in order to choose the projects for which a given budget is to be spent, maximum present worth (when the streams are discounted at the marginal internal rate of return) is surely superior, for that purpose, to the ratio of benefits to cost.

The Scope of the Analysis

If it were costless, it would be desirable to expand the context of the analysis until all the consequences of the project could be perceived and taken into account. But possible improvements in the analysis from expanding the context have to be weighed against the costs of doing so. In the analysis of the Santa Maria project, a reasonable scope appears to have been adopted. The geographical context, the Santa Maria Basin, includes the area that is likely to be most affected. Effects of the project on the production possibilities of power, fish, wildlife, and recreation would be virtually nil: use of the rivers for power would not be economical with or without the project;[40] fishing in these streams has never amounted to much; wildlife losses would be negligible; and recreation potentialities would not be improved particularly by the Reservoir's temporary storage of water.[41] There would be little impact on the physical production possibilities, so to speak, of water purification and "vector control," the latter referring to the efforts of the Public Health Service to control carriers of malaria, encephalitis, and other diseases. Finally, any influence on physical production possibilities in local industry—for example, sugar-beet processing and oil refining—would be minor in magnitude and uncertain as to direction.

The scope of the analysis also seems to be correct in ignoring any effect on prices received by other farmers. What matters in evaluating the project is the price of the incremental output, not the decline of other farmers' incomes as a result of the increased output and lower price of vegetables, sugar beets, alfalfa, potatoes, and beans.

In general, then, the analysis did allow for the major consequences which are relevant. There are, however, a couple of spillover effects which may have deserved closer attention. One of these, channel aggradation, was clearly recognized, but no increase in cost (or reduction in benefit) was introduced into the model:

Several changes in channel regimen would result from the construction of

[40] Comments, Federal Power Commission, *ibid.*, p. 121.

[41] *Ibid.*, pp. 69–70. The California State Division of Water Resources and other State agencies have disagreed with some of these statements (*ibid.*, pp. 103–116).

the storage reservoir. The channel would aggrade above the reservoir due to deposition of the coarsest part of the bed load immediately with velocity reduction. The channel would degrade immediately below the reservoir due to the capacity of the clear-water outflow to entrain the bed material through turbulent energy. General aggradation of the main channel may occur farther downstream due to the lack of carrying capacity of the reduced flows. This effect would probably be eliminated by the higher velocities resulting from the flow constriction afforded by the levees proposed by the Corps of Engineers . . .

. . . Channel observation ranges should be established to continuously study any changes.[42]

Perhaps, as suggested above, these influences would offset each other, but with the discharge at Fugler's Point limited most of the time to 300 cubic feet per second, it seems to the writer that deposits are likely to build up in the Santa Maria channel; and sometimes it is expensive to cope with such deposition. An extra allowance for this aspect of annual maintenance might have been made.

Another "spillover," the possible impact of the Reservoir's operation on the present annual replenishment of the ground-water supply, was mentioned previously. If significant, this influence might have been taken into account explicitly in the analysis. A related point was brought up by the State Division of Water Resources: would increased irrigation in the Cuyama Valley, "by using additional amounts of ground-water and surface flow, affect the inflow to the Vaquero Reservoir and thereby reduce the estimated yield of that reservoir now estimated at 18,500 acre-feet per annum"?[43]

Project as Lump vs. Project as Increments

The analysis was better than many others in its treatment of separable increments, for alternative project sizes were not only analyzed in preliminary work but were also discussed in the report. "Alternate plans of development employing reservoirs of various capacities at the Round Corral site 12 miles upstream from the mouth of the Sisquoc River were investigated in conjunction with reservoirs of various capacities at the Vaquero site."[44] For some of the possibilities, only qualitative or partial analysis is presented in the report. Thus in the case of Vaquero, the average annual yields of *water* from three alternative sizes were compared, the conclusion being that the smallest spilled too often, allowing too much water to escape into the ocean, while the largest conserved scarcely any more water than the middle-

[42] *Santa Maria Project*, p. 68.
[43] *Ibid.*, p. 106.
[44] *Ibid.*, p. 42.

sized dam (the one with 214,000 acre feet capacity, which was the final selection).[45]   Although dollar gains and costs were not shown, the intended implication was that the increment in size expanded benefits more than costs up to the 214,000 acre feet capacity, but that the next increment, from 214,000 to 234,000 acre feet, raised costs more than benefits.

Moreover, for three other plans, calculations of benefits and costs were actually presented.[46] These plans were (1) the levee and channel improvements alone; (2) channel improvements and levees, without any reservoir, sufficient to cope with a flood of 230,000 second feet; and (3) a reservoir at Fugler's Point, supplemented only by the Bradley Canyon levees. The Vaquero Reservoir plus channel works was recommended because its benefit-cost ratio was the highest.[47] Fortunately, this recommended plan also yielded the greatest benefit[48] and was dominant so far as tangibles were concerned, so the use of the ratio did no harm.

Thus considerable attention was given to the effect of increments— that is, to the gains from, and costs of, tacking on or removing portions of projects. Still more effort of this sort, however, was probably warranted. For example, it would have been in order to exhibit the consequences of adding the levee system, *given* the Vaquero Reservoir. The extra costs due to including this feature amount, on an annual basis, to $448,000.[49] What is the extra benefit attributable to the channel improvements? This benefit arises solely from the reduction of flood damage. The reservoir and the channel improvements together produce gains, on an annual basis, of $600,000. The reservoir by itself would yield annual gains, i.e., flood-damage reduction, of at least $200,000.[50] Hence the addition of the channel improvement would lead to extra annual benefits of at most $400,000. It is worth

---

[45] *Ibid.*, p. 54. The State of California disagreed, not with respect to the over-all size of the project, but with respect to the "mix" of purposes. Since the proposed levee system would cope with floods 50 per cent larger than any recorded flood in the Santa Maria Valley, it was argued that more of the reservoir should be used for irrigation, less for flood control. *Ibid.*, p. 115.

[46] Corps of Engineers, "Report on Survey . . . ," pp. 28–45.

[47] *Ibid.*, pp. 44–45.

[48] According to the writer's estimates.

[49] *Santa Maria Project*, pp. 4–10. This cost is stated to be $576,000 in the "Report on Survey . . . ," pp. 44–45.

[50] This amount comes from a damage-frequency curve, given the reservoir alone, that was derived by the writer from some very rough estimates. If this new damage-frequency curve were shown in Figure 4, it would lie between the two curves that are now presented there.

noting that this benefit is less than the annual gain that channel improvement *alone* would produce ($500,000),[51] because if this feature is added onto the reservoir, the operation of the reservoir already does part of the flood-control job. As a part of this package, this feature does not pay its way according to these rough estimates; yet it is the package that is analyzed in the official project report, and the channel improvements are not examined as a separable feature.

Now, it is not suggested that such component parts can somehow be analyzed outside of the system of water-resource measures. It *is* necessary to fit the alternatives into the system and to recognize interdependencies in calculating benefits and costs. But—and the point is worth this repetition—the alternatives that are being considered should embrace *several* combinations of the components, such as reservoir capacity for irrigation alone, reservoir capacity for irrigation *and* flood control, reservoir capacity for irrigation *and* flood control *plus* channel improvements. Also, the alternatives that are being considered should embrace several sizes, such as a reservoir that would cost $15 million, one that would cost $20 million, one that would cost $25 million. Thus in the context of the system, and given the other components, we should ask: what are the extra costs and extra benefits attributable to each major feature or to each major increment in size?

Time Streams

The treatment of time in the Santa Maria analysis was excellent in that the time paths of benefits and costs were shown, the streams were discounted, and the procedure was made completely clear. However, in final presentation, the principal emphasis should not be on the ratio of the discounted time streams but rather on the present worths of the project at several discount rates. In addition, time paths as such should be a part of the main exhibit, explicitly pointed to as data that are pertinent to final decisions. Table 25 is an illustrative exhibit that is drawn up along the above lines, showing present worths at 2½, 5, and 8 per cent, the same rates which were used in making similar calculations for the Green River program.[52] Note that at discount rates larger than 6 per cent the present value of the Santa Maria project's cost exceeds the present value of the benefits. If the budget can be devoted to projects which yield a posi-

---

[51] "Report on Survey . . . ," pp. 44–45.

[52] Again the Agencies' estimates of costs and benefits are taken as given, for the purpose of making these calculations, even though certain types of modification have been recommended.

tive present worth at 6 per cent, there is a presumption that this one should not be undertaken. Note also that the costs of this project, unlike those of the Green River program, are almost all incurred during the first years, while benefits are spread over many future years; as a consequence, the outcome of the Santa Maria project is extremely sensitive to the discount rate. The contrast between the two projects in this respect underlines the significance of portraying the way results vary with changes in the discount rate.

Uncertainty and Ranges

Table 25 also presents some ranges within which the results of the Santa Maria project might fall. Again it must be stressed that the numbers are used mainly to indicate a form in which such information might be presented. Also it is hoped that these examples point up the reasons that information about variability is relevant, since the numbers illustrate the possibility of differing degrees of uncertainty about the two projects. Such a difference is not altogether implausible, since there may well be less uncertainty about the technology of irrigation than about the technology of soil conservation. There are probably more complete records, for instance, concerning the effect of irrigation upon crop yields than there are concerning the impact of an integrated conservation program upon such yields. Of course, in both cases there are similar degrees of uncertainty about such matters as relative prices in the future.

Estimation Procedures

Most of the comments that might be included under this heading are fully discussed elsewhere. By way of partial recapitulation, however, the customary procedure of using special price-level projections that differ from one analysis to the next calls for some attention. The use of a common price level in all analyses would facilitate comparisons or modifications of all estimates at the time of comparison. If it is not feasible to use prices as of a common base year, then "current prices," as of the year of analysis, are suggested. Their use would leave our uncertainty about future prices open to inspection and would make revision at the time of comparison somewhat easier than would the use of special price-level projections.

Another comment on estimation procedure seems to be worth restatement. As in the Green River analysis, degradation factors might be considered. The outcome of the Santa Maria project did not seem to hinge on a sudden burst of efficiency on the part of the farmers, as

TABLE 25

Suggested Form of Cost-Benefit Exhibit—Santa Maria Project as Illustration

(Amounts in "1949" dollars)

1. Present worth (present value of outputs minus present value of costs) 2½%, 50-year horizon ... $24 million
   5%, 50-year horizon ... 4 million
   8%, 50-year horizon ... −6.5 million

Note: if the exhibits are to be used for the comparison of this project with private investment, property and income taxes paid on private ventures should be allowed for; in this illustration, a rough allowance could be made by reducing the positive present-worth estimates by 45%.*

2. Cost that would have to be covered by a national water-resources budget:
Present value of the nation's investment stream:† 2½% discount rate ... $25 million
   5% discount rate ... 24 million
   8% discount rate ... 23 million

3. Time paths of undiscounted benefits and costs

Streams	Construction (4 years)	1-5	6-10	11-15	16-20	21-25	26-30	31-35	36-40	41-45	46-50
Total Benefits	...	8.9	9.0	10.0	10.0	9.9	9.8	9.8	9.7	9.6	9.5
Total Costs	26.7	.3	.4	.4	.3	.4	.4	.3	.4	.4	.3
Installation Costs	26.7	...	...	...	...	...	...	...	...	...	...
Federal Costs	25.5	.1	.1	.2	.1	.1	.2	.1	.1	.2	.1

4. Variability of outcome
Present worth "not likely" to fall outside this range ... −$2 to +$4 million†
Present worth "extremely unlikely" to fall outside this range ... −$6 to +$10 million‡

5. Effect on personal wealth distribution§
Number of land ownerships (farms, not city lots) ... 458
Average value of land and buildings per farm-owner in watershed (1950) ... $100,000‖
Average net benefit to farmers (as distinct from nation) per farm-owner ... 8,000¶

TABLE 25 (*Continued*)

6. Effect on regional wealth distribution
   Average income per family in Basin (assumed to be same as entire county)   3,500
   Percentage increase of income in Basin due to project   3%**
7. Basis for ranking, if required, to facilitate allocation of national water-resources budget††
   Internal rate of return (rate of discount which reduces present worth to zero)   6%

* In the estimation of this figure, the venture is looked upon as though it were a large corporation. The corporate income tax, on the average, has been about 45% of net profits in recent years. An allowance for higher property taxes after the project has been allowed for in the estimation of net farm income after the project. No further allowance for property tax on the project is suggested in this case.

† The nation's investment stream is the net excesses, in the periods in which they occur, of costs over benefits. In this case, these excesses occur only during the construction period, i.e., during years 1 through 4. It is not clear just what budget is to be allocated, or what costs must therefore be covered by the budget; here it is assumed to be these investment costs from the nation's standpoint.

‡ Such ranges are believed to be useful supplements to "best estimates" even though precise "probabilities" cannot be associated with them. If one insists on precision, the first range might be defined as that in which results would fall 75% of the time (if we could imagine repeated trial-runs), the second range as that in which results would fall 90% of the time. These ranges are solely for illustrative purposes; the writer has not dealt with the project enough to have much "feel" for the variability of possible outcomes.

§ These indicators of wealth distribution and effects of project on wealth distribution are merely illustrative. Present worth of benefits at 5% was used in estimating these subsidy effects.

‖ Assumed to be the same in watershed as in entire county; figure (rounded) taken from *County and City Data Book 1952*, p. 112.

¶ This amount is positive, even if net benefits to the nation are negative, chiefly because farmers do not pay costs that are allocated to flood control.

** Increase in local income assumed to be 1.2 × gross benefits attributed to project.

†† The internal rate should not be used as a basis for ranking interdependent projects, such as several possible sizes of a proposal. This figure (6%) was derived by plotting present worth as a function of the discount rate and then by interpolating to find the rate at which present worth appeared to become zero.

the outcome of the Green River program appeared to do; nonetheless gross benefits seemed high according to the rough checks described earlier.

As for taxes, the analysis of the Santa Maria project explicitly allowed for a tax on acreage in the estimation of future costs of, and net income from, farm operations. Without a more detailed study of the project, it is impossible to say whether these charges represent real costs or transfer payments. This tax allowance, which is in any case a relatively small deduction from the benefit stream, is reflected in the present worth estimates in Table 25. Again, the exhibit is accompanied by a warning that the numbers are not pertinent to a comparison of this proposal with private investments. It is suggested that, in order for the present-worth estimates to be relevant to such comparison, they should (where positive) be reduced by 45 per cent (the average tax on corporations' net incomes).

Distribution of Wealth

While it is contended here that "secondary benefits"—increased local incomes due to induced local expansion—should not be included among the benefits to the whole economy, the impacts of expansion near the project on the distribution of wealth may be a significant consideration. The clues to such impacts that are shown in Table 25 are crude, but they may suggest the type of information which ought to be presented in each analysis. Thus it is probably of some moment that the project's benefits to farmers would, for the most part, go to less than 500 owners. (Competitive forces would presumably cause those gains to "trickle up" to present landowners, since farm labor or loans of capital would not get more than they could earn elsewhere.)

It is also relevant to note a few clues to those owners' present financial status and to the windfall which the project would bestow upon them. Incidentally, the windfall would be positive even if net benefits to the nation were negative, e.g., if benefits were discounted at 8 per cent, because about half the cost of the project would be allocated to flood control and financed by the general taxpayer.

It is not argued here that the effects on regional wealth distribution *ought* to be an important consideration, but it is believed that those effects will nonetheless be given a great deal of attention. If so, indicators of those effects should be explicitly stated. Accordingly crude indicators of the wealth of the Basin, as an area, with and without the project—the same indicators presented in connection with the Green River program—are included in Table 25.

The Criterion for Ranking Projects

The same remarks about ranking projects that were made in the study of the Green River program are applicable to the Santa Maria project. Again, the internal rate of return is presented as the criterion of rank (Item 7 in Table 25). The same troublesome difficulties with a definitive ranking that were described before should be kept in mind; and attention should not be focused on the internal rate of return to such an extent that its limitations or the other items in the Table are ignored.

The Santa Maria Project vs. the Green River Program

The analyses of the two projects produce exhibits that differ from each other greatly. If the estimates were taken at face value, the Green River project would be an attractive candidate under most water-resource budgets. For a relatively small social investment, it would yield handsome present worths even at fairly high discount rates. The Santa Maria, on the other hand, would require a larger social investment and yield comparatively small present worths. This difference is suggested most vividly by the contrast between the two internal rates of return: 55 per cent on the Green River program and 6 per cent on the Santa Maria project. Moreover, the redistribution of wealth under the Green River program would probably be preferred by most persons to that which would occur under the Santa Maria proposal. The latter, in comparison with the Green River program, would provide large subsidies to a few who seem to be relatively well off anyway, and would stimulate the development of an area which already has an average income per family higher than that in the Green River watershed.

On the other hand, the variability of the outcome—the chance of an outcome much poorer than is indicated by these estimates—is probably greater for the Green River project. Knowledge of the effect of conservation measures on yields in an entire watershed is none too firm. Also, while the social investment is estimated to be comparatively small for the Green River proposal because benefits exceed costs after the first three years, the net outlays *by government units* would be higher than for the Santa Maria project. The actual time paths of costs and benefits should be carefully inspected in the two cases.

The foregoing remarks are intended to illustrate the way such exhibits could be used. The numbers shown in these particular case studies, however, should not be used as a basis for a definitive ranking of the Green River and Santa Maria projects. In this connection, the following warnings must be posted. First, while the estimation procedures have been criticized, the estimates in the suggested exhibits (Tables 14 and 25) have not always been revised in accordance with those criticisms. Moreover, new numbers that are rough illustrative estimates have sometimes been introduced. Precision was not necessary for the purpose here, which was to suggest revised *procedures,* not to prepare a revised, and authoritative, comparison of these two projects. If the new numbers were refined, and all the "old" estimates were revised in line with the methodological suggestions offered in this study (e.g., by the application of degradation factors), the two exhibits would be affected differently. Second, the two projects differ quite a bit with regard to scale of investment. Except in the context of additional projects and a specified budget, one cannot conclude that one should be accepted and the other rejected. For a particular budget, it might be that both should be accepted—or both rejected.

Part 5

*Other Potential Uses
of Analysis to Increase
Governmental Efficiency*

Chapter 13

ANALYSIS FOR PERFORMANCE BUDGETS: AN ILLUSTRATION

EARLY IN THIS STUDY, the need for analyses to help government economize was stressed. And in Part II the *general* problems of analyzing alternative courses of action were studied. The results of studying these methodological problems, however, have been applied so far only to the comparison of water-resource projects. What about the need by government in general for more and better analysis, the need that was emphasized at the outset? Can this study of methods—can the suggestions that have been presented—help us use analysis to increase efficiency in other government activities? The answer is surely yes. This concluding Part is an attempt to indicate some other governmental choices where quantitative analysis, and these methodological suggestions, should be helpful. Chapter 13 illustrates another application of these techniques, this time to the comparison of alternative allocations of expenditures among government programs. Chapter 14 is a survey of the opportunities for using these analytical aids in government, both to compare different allocations among programs and to compare different ways of carrying out given tasks.

To compare alternative allocations of funds is to compare the effects of increments (or decrements) in programs A, B, C, and so on. In most cases, we ought not to choose, for example, between the entire medical-care program and the whole of the crime-control program as an all-or-none proposition, but between increases and decreases in the scale of the various activities. To make this sort of comparison is part of the budgeting process, so, as its title indicates, the chapter pertains to the potential use of analysis in connection with budgeting.

Now, quantitative analysis for this purpose can hardly be couched in terms of a definitive criterion; it is bound to be like "consumers' research," simply tracing out costs and selected indicators of gain from alternative programs to assist the policy-maker in exercising his judgment. However, this is neither a new nor an insignificant role, but is a familiar and honorable one, in fact the customary role, for analysis to play. For instance, it seems perfectly clear that cost-benefit analysis too serves in this capacity.

PERFORMANCE BUDGETS AND THEIR POSSIBILITIES

As in the case of any other problem of choice, the first and most important thing to do, before anyone need bother with quantitative estimates, is to think about the problem in the right way. In the determination of the budget, this means considering not just "lower-level" alternatives—e.g., different machines for carrying out a specific operation—but also certain "higher-level" alternatives, that is, different sizes of the various programs. To examine the full range of activities[1] and to choose appropriate scales is usually regarded as the main purpose of budgeting, other tools being used to help economize *within* each activity. Note that this appears to be the view in private industry. A firm's budget is ordinarily used for the purpose of co-ordinating and controlling various programs, for example, to see that expenditures for expansion are in line with the plans of the sales department. Special analyses and constant effort rather than any budgeting procedure are called upon to achieve economies within departments. Accordingly, manuals on business budgeting recommend that budgets be based on *expected* or current performance rather than some *standard* performance for particular departments.[2]

Thinking about the problem correctly also means asking, not "Do we 'need' or 'require' one million units of low-rent housing?" but rather, "What are the gains and costs of having an increase (or decrease) in each activity?" Then, when the right alternatives are considered and the right questions are asked about them, it becomes possible to take a further step and use quantitative aids to advantage. Also it becomes clear that present budgetary forms are probably not the most useful quantitative aids that can be devised. A modification which is often urged is the adoption of some form of "performance

---

[1] The terms "activity," "program," and "function" will be used here as synonyms, all referring to tasks like forest-fire control rather than to objects of expenditure like trucks.

[2] See, for example, J. B. Heckert, *Business Budgeting and Control* (New York: Ronald Press, 1946), p. 10.

budget,"[3] which would entail, at minimum, a revised breakdown of proposed expenditures according to activities. Beyond this revised breakdown of outlays, performance budgeting might involve the estimation of the achievement that could be bought with the indicated outlay for each activity.

Possibilities of Improved Breakdowns of Cost

At present, the main emphasis in the Federal budget is on the classification of obligations and expenditures by "object class," that is, by such categories as personal services, travel, transportation of things, printing and reproduction, and communication services. Observing the relationship between travel outlays and other categories may help point to grossly inefficient methods of carrying out particular tasks. A Congressional subcommittee might well scrutinize at *any* time of the year, or continuously, the previous year's expenditures by object class, along with other evidence as to the internal efficiency of particular programs. But this breakdown of expenditures contributes little so far as the *main* purpose of budgeting, the choice of activity levels, is concerned.

Some attention is given in the present budget to the classification of proposed expenditures according to broad functions.[4] But the categories in the present functional budget are a little too broad. Activities such as the promotion of education or conservation and development of land and water resources (which are broken down further *according to department or agency making the expenditure*) do not help us enough in perceiving what activities and what accomplishments are being purchased.

Portions of the main budget are in terms of activities that are not as broad, but the exhibits are confusing, particularly because of the

---

[3] See "Performance Budgeting: Selected References," Revised, U. S. Bureau of the Budget Library (April, 1951), pp. 1–5. The idea of performance budgeting is not new. Many state and local governments, and parts of the Federal government, have taken steps in this direction. Some of the history of performance budgeting is given by the following quotation: "An old idea revived by the Hoover Report, it was part of [Frederick] Cleveland's thinking in 1910–1912 and was tried in the Borough of Richmond, City of New York, in 1913–1915" ("Symposium on Budget Theory," *Public Administration Review*, Winter, 1950, p. 26). See also Jesse Burkhead, *Government Budgeting* (New York: John Wiley and Sons, 1956), pp. 133–181.

[4] See *Budget of the U. S. Government* for the Fiscal Year Ending June 30, 1953 (Washington, D.C.: U. S. Government Printing Office, 1952), pp. 1144–1157 (Special Analysis B). The budget will hereafter be identified simply as *Budget of the U. S., 1953* (or whatever year is applicable).

TABLE

Portion* of Actual Budget, Fiscal Year 1953,
Salaries and Expenses,
Obligations by Activities

Description	1951 Actual	1952 Estimate	1953 Estimate
1. Nat'l forest protection & management:			
(a) Resource protection and use	$25,689,086	$26,916,425	$28,133,000
(b) Resource development	1,761,187	1,897,600	1,885,000
2. Fighting forest fires:			
Fire suppression	6,096,221	5,408,571	6,000,000
3. Forest research:			
(a) Forest & range management investigations	3,013,742	3,249,037	3,249,834
(b) Forest products investigations	1,291,255	1,261,168	1,249,268
(c) Forest resources investigations	854,259	906,398	897,898
4. Obligations under reimbursements from non-Federal sources	269,584	111,355	111,455
Total direct obligations	38,975,334	39,750,554	41,526,455

Obligations Payable Out of Reimbursements from Other Accounts

	1951 Actual	1952 Estimate	1953 Estimate
5. Rental of equipment to & repair of equipment for other activities of Forest Service & other Federal agencies	3,612,275	3,785,080	3,785,680
6. Sale of supplies, materials, & equipment to other activities of Forest Service & to Federal agencies	288,445	252,500	252,550
7. Construction & maintenance of improvements	90,426	105,000	105,075
8. Protection of intermingled & adjacent forest lands	19,197	26,500	26,520
9. Surveys, land appraisals, mapping, cruising timber, & preparation of timber management plans, snow scale readings, etc., on national forest and other lands	27,727	31,800	31,830
10. Fire suppression on intermingled & adjacent lands under administration other agencies	121,556	125,000	125,000
11. Investigations at experimental forests & ranges	23,968	26,500	26,520
12. Investigations at forest products laboratory	37,186	53,000	53,050
13. Special economic investigations	55,407	63,500	63,555
Total obligations payable out of reimbursements from other accounts	4,276,187	4,468,880	4,469,780
Total obligations	43,251,521	44,219,434	45,996,235

* This is roughly half of the exhibits devoted to Salaries and Expenses. In addition, there are detailed tables on "Amounts Available for Obligation," "Obligations by Objects," and "Analysis of Expenditures." Sections other than Salaries and Expenses pertain to Forest Development Roads and Trails, Smoke Jumper Facilities, Acquisition of Lands for National Forests (Weeks Act), Acquisition of Lands for National Forests (Superior National Forest), Acquisition of Lands for National Forests (Special Acts), State and Private Forestry Cooperation, Cooperative Range Improvements, Miscellaneous, and, completely outside the Forest Service, Control of Forest Pests. In all, there are about 10 pages of the 1953 Budget pertaining to these activities within the Department of Agriculture.

26

FOREST SERVICE, DEPARTMENT OF AGRICULTURE
FOREST SERVICE

Program and Performance

1. *National forest protection and management—(a) Resource protection and use.*—The national forests are protected from fire, and their resources are managed in such ways as to bring about maximum sustained production.

Main Workload Factors

Description	1951 Actual	1952 Estimate	1953 Estimate
Area administered & protected—acres	181,255,449	181,350,000	181,450,000
Timber managed & protected—1000 bd.-ft.	600,000,000	600,000,000	600,000,000
Timber harvested—1000 bd.-ft.	4,600,000	4,600,000	5,000,000
Forest fires controlled—no., cal. yr.	10,103	11,000	11,000
Area burned—acres, calendar yr.	371,743	425,000	350,000
Grazing use—no. of permits	26,708	26,700	26,700
Special use permits—no.	49,806	51,300	52,800
Visitors to nat'l forests	27,367,000	28,500,000	29,500,000
Important watershed lands protected—acres	160,000,000	160,000,000	160,000,000
Big-game animals—no.	2,500,000	2,500,000	2,500,000
Receipts (by fiscal years):			
Timber sales	$52,511,511	$56,550,000	$62,675,000
Grazing	4,165,573	4,450,000	4,500,000
Land use & power	883,203	880,000	880,000
Total receipts	57,560,287	61,880,000	68,055,000

(b) *Resource development.*—Main factors are shown in following table:

Main Workload Factors (In Acres)

	1951 Actual	1952 Estimate	1953 Estimate
Planted to trees (annual)	25,576	25,500	27,500
Planted to trees (cumulative)	1,304,662	1,330,162	1,357,662
Still to be planted (total)	4,056,276	4,030,776	4,003,276
Reseeded to range grasses (annual)	60,000	60,000	70,000
Reseeded to range grasses (cumulative)	400,000	460,000	530,000
Still to be reseeded (total)	3,600,000	3,540,000	3,470,000

2. *Fighting forest fires.*—This provides for employment of additional manpower and other facilities to suppress forest fires which cannot be controlled by the fire control organization provided for under the activity "National forest protection and management."

3. *Forest research—(a) Forest and range management investigations.*—Research is conducted at forest experimental stations and elsewhere to provide private and public land managers and owners with a sound basis for protection and management of timber, range, and watershed lands.

(b) *Forest products investigations.*—These studies, carried out by the Forest Products Laboratory, aid in protecting and enhancing the value and utility of forest products.

(c) *Forest resources investigations.*—These investigations are conducted to inventory and appraise the condition of forest lands and to furnish other information on supply, production, and utilization.

Main Workload Factors (In Acres)

	1951 Actual	1952 Estimate	1953 Estimate
Initial surveys (annual)	9,542,000	13,000,000	14,000,000
Initial surveys (cumulative)	428,155,000	441,155,000	455,155,000
To be surveyed (total)	195,845,000	182,845,000	168,845,000
Resurveys (annual)	19,516,000	22,000,000	23,000,000
Resurveys (cumulative)	120,504,000	142,504,000	165,504,000
To be resurveyed (total)	181,496,000	159,496,000	136,496,000

presentation of "Obligations Payable Out of Reimbursements from Other Accounts." Table 26 shows how proposed expenditures are classified in terms of activities in one of the best presentations that the budget contains. Note that this excerpt does not show any classification by object of expenditure, although the main emphasis of the present budget is on such breakdowns. It does not even show *all* of the breakdown by activities for the Forest Service. Only part of the latter is presented, but it is perhaps enough to suggest that, if it is feasible, a simpler, shorter, and more informative set of budgetary materials is much to be desired.

Finally, in the materials which are sent to Congress to justify the budget, expenditures are sometimes broken down by narrower functions. Indeed these functional categories—such as sanitation and care of public camp grounds, maintenance of improvements, construction of roads and trails, and smoke-jumper facilities for forest fire protection[5]—are often too detailed. Many of these activities simply service others. Besides, it is too great an intellectual task to juggle so many categories.

The breakdowns that are shown in the budget and in the justification materials are apparently patterned after the sample performance budget for the Forest Service that was drawn up by the first Hoover Commission.[6] This sample budget contained many excellent concrete suggestions, but there is no reason to believe that its classification of expenditures is the best that can be devised. The fact that this classification was not drawn up with a view to using indicators of performance may have been a shortcoming, for this may have led to categories which are too numerous and too difficult to compare. In any event, further explorations are surely in order. Clearly there is no unique budgetary breakdown which can be associated with a performance budget. Rather there are many possible breakdowns, and our choice among them depends upon their prospective usefulness to Congress and the Executive Branch and upon the expense of preparation.

In this part of the study, an attempt is made to devise an improved performance budget for the same part of the Federal government, the

[5] *Budget of the U. S., 1953*, pp. 434–442, and "Explanatory Notes for Department of Agriculture, Fiscal Year 1953," Vol. 1 (mimeographed), pp. 286–373. Hereafter, this volume will be identified as the "Justification Statement, 1953." *Hearings on Department of Agriculture Appropriations* for any year will be identified simply as *Senate Hearings* or *House Hearings* for that year.

[6] Commission on Organization of the Executive Branch of the Government, *Budgeting and Accounting,* A Report to the Congress by the Commission (Washington, D.C.: U. S. Government Printing Office, 1949), pp. 78–84.

Forest Service, to which the Commission's sample budget pertained. The one devised here is in terms of fewer activities than were listed in the sample budget presented by the Commission—one-tenth as many, in fact. The revised activity-categories are suggested as ones which might facilitate either the subjective appraisal of performance by policy-makers or, if desired, the provision of meaningful measures of performance by analysts.

Possibilities of Improved Indicators of Performance

It does not contribute much to the primary usefulness of the budget if one attempts to estimate the performance attributable to outlays for object classes, such as transportation of things or printing and reproduction. We are anxious, of course, to find cheaper combinations of these objects with which to carry out each program, and to do this we must estimate the effect *on each program's accomplishment* of using various combinations of transportation, printing, and personal services. But this is different from attaching a measure of performance to quantities of paper clips or printer's ink that are used up in diverse activities. In any event, it is assumed here that special analysis, not the annual budget, should be the mainstay in achieving economy *within* programs.

So, naturally enough, indicators of performance that are designed to aid in the selection of program levels must relate to programs. Some indicators of this sort are employed at present, but their usefulness is rather limited. First, the Budget Bureau's instructions for the preparation and submission of annual budget estimates call for "narrative statements" on program and performance, but these statements are frequently too vague to help much. For example, under the item "cooperative range improvements" in the Forest Service, the statement reads: "On the basis of a statutory formula, part of the grazing fees from the national forests are used to protect or improve the productivity of the range, mainly by construction and maintenance of fences, stock watering facilities, bridges, corrals, and driveways."[7] Such descriptions of the expected accomplishments probably do not help Congressmen much to reach better decisions. Second, in some instances, particularly in the budget of the Department of Agriculture, workload factors or other quantitative indicators of performance are presented. Table 26 shows a number of data which are currently used to describe performance; it should be kept in mind that, in this respect too, this excerpt is one of the best exhibits in the budget. Notice the

[7] *Budget of the U. S., 1953,* p. 441.

mass of numbers generated by showing the amount of planting (reseeding, etc.) done annually, done cumulatively, and still to be done. Such indicators of performance—e.g., the reduction of water runoff due to the reforestation of a thousand acres—usually, and quite understandably, fall far short of describing the achievement which ultimately is of value. The reduction of runoff per se is not what we want. It is not even the decreased size of floods due to the decreased runoff, though this is a step closer. Such clues to the gains may be of some help, but it must be exceedingly difficult for Congressmen or others to evaluate programs on the basis of them. Similarly, it would be difficult for a businessman to evaluate the use of expansible gasoline tanks on the basis of the estimated reduction in gasoline evaporation.

What can be done about it? With reference to the businessman's choice, the reduction in gasoline evaporation can be translated into effects on cost or, better yet, on profits. Government may be able to do something along the same line—that is, to translate proximate clues into measures of performance closer to the achievements which are ultimately valued. It may be possible in a good many cases to effect translations that go at least a little further "down the line." It may be feasible, in some instances, to make a more ambitious translation, one which converts proximate clues into estimates of the present value of gains from the program. The calculations in this chapter constitute an experiment in the more ambitious type of translation. Thus the illustrative budget in the next section shows, alongside the proposed outlays, the present value of the benefit stream that those outlays would purchase.

AN ILLUSTRATIVE PERFORMANCE BUDGET

Tables 27 and 28 constitute a revised performance budget for the Forest Service. Obligations are broken down into three activities: Development and Management of Forests, Forest-Fire Control, and Forest Research. Each of these activities as such yields "direct" benefits, in contrast to a supporting activity like "maintenance of roads and trails" in the conventional breakdown of activities. Obligations are shown for three years, fiscal 1951, 1952, and 1953. Obligations which current proposals entail for several subsequent years should be shown for some programs (as will be explained later), but the column for this purpose is left blank in Table 27. For the first two categories, the indicator of accomplishment is the present value of tangible gains. For forest research, no indicator of accomplishment is presented.

TABLE 27

ILLUSTRATIVE PERFORMANCE BUDGET, FISCAL YEAR 1953, FOREST SERVICE, DEPARTMENT OF AGRICULTURE

Activity	Obligations (millions of current dollars)				Indicators of Expected Accomplishment			
	1951 (Actual)	1952 (Estimated)	1953 (Proposed)	1954–1956 (Entailed by 1953 Proposals)	Description of Indicators	1951	1952	1953	Reduction of Accomplishment if 1953 Activity Reduced $1,000,000
Development and Management of Forests	$44.9*	$53.8*	$53.1*						
					Present Value of Tangible Gains (millions of current dollars)	$76.5	$88.7	$95.6	$4.
					Timber Sales (billions of bd.-ft.)	4.7	4.6	5.0	.4
					Campers', Sportsmen's Visits (millions of man-days)	60	63	66	..
					New Forest Land Acquired (thousands of acres)	33	47	41	..
					Other Gains†	[no indicators]			
Forest-Fire Control	$25.0	$24.5	$26.2						
					Present Value of Tangible Gains (millions of current dollars)	$74.2	$74.2	$74.6	$0.4‡
					No. Initial-Action Fire-fighters	6,000	6,000	6,310	310
Forest Research	5.2	5.4	5.4		[No indicators used—see qualitative description of projects]			
Total, Forest Service	$75.1	$83.7	$84.7						

* Note that no rental charge for the 180,000,000 acres is covered by these Appropriations. Nor is rent imputed in these calculations—on the assumption that the lands have no (relevant) alternative uses. If in fact the value of these lands *in alternative uses* were $3 per acre, we would have to charge interest (i.e., rent) amounting to, say, $27,000,000 (5%)—which would mean that the National Forests were just barely profitable. However, this would *not* affect the costs or gains from marginal changes in the program.

† Other gains for which estimates of present value were prepared include receipts from water and grazing permits, "share" of "receipts" from range cooperatively maintained, contribution to flood control, share of increased productivity of forests and range, and land rentals and miscellaneous receipts. Many of the last-named gains (e.g., from mining permits) are smaller than the costs that are entailed to the government and to the country. (See *House Hearings, 1914,* Part 3, p. 1268, and also B. Davidson, "How to Grab 20 Acres for $1.25," *Reader's Digest,* July, 1953, pp. 141–144.) No attempt was made to attach a value to wild-life conservation.

‡ Rounded to nearest tenth of a million dollars. Lower confidence, and greater variability for any particular year, should be associated with this estimate than with the estimate for "Development and Management of Forests."

TABLE 28

PRESENT VALUE OF TANGIBLE GAINS: SUMMARY*

Activity According to Illustrative Performance Budget	Source of Gains	1951	1952	1953	Reduction of Present Value if 1953 Activity Reduced by $1 Million (millions of current dollars)
Development and Management of Forests	Timber sales, net of depletion†	$51.0	$61.0	$67.0	$4.0†
	Campers', sportsmen's visits to forests§	15.0	16.0	17.0	...
	Grazing and water permits‖	4.0	5.0	5.0	...
	Land rentals, other receipts¶	2.0	2.0	2.0	...
	Share of gains from range cooperatively maintained**	1.0	1.0	1.0	...
	Reforestation national forests**	0.7	0.7	0.7	...
	Share of reforestation and better methods, state and private forests**	1.5	1.5	1.5	...
	Revegetation of range in national forests**	.2	.2	.2	...
	Share of increased productivity, state and private range**	.1	.1	.1	...
	Acquisition of lands for national forests††	.4	.6	.5	...
	Value of flood-prevention aspects**	.5	.5	.5	...
	Value of reduced siltation of reservoirs**	.1	.1	.1	...
	Total	76.5	88.7	95.6	$4.0
Forest Fire Control	Savings of saleable timber, national forests**	48.0	48.0	48.3	0.3
	Share of savings of saleable timber, state and private forests**	12.3	12.3	12.3	...
	Share of savings due to flood control**	10.9	10.9	11.0	0.05
	Share of savings due to silt control**	3.0	3.0	3.0	0.02
	Total	74.2	74.2	74.6	$0.37 or $0.4
Forest Research					[No estimates prepared]

TABLE 28 (*Continued*)

PRESENT VALUE OF TANGIBLE GAINS: SUMMARY*

* Such an exhibit might be part of the published budget, or might be part of the "Justification Statement," published in the Hearings before the Subcommittees on Appropriations.

† Present value due to a particular year's expenditures is assumed to be simply expected receipts during that year. (Of course, some of the outlays are not for handling the current year's cut, but are for the preparation of timber for sale in future years, and some of the previous years' outlays were for the preparation of this year's cut.) Sources were the "Justification Statement, 1953," and the Subcommittee Hearings on the *Department of Agriculture Appropriations for 1953*. Estimates of receipts are net of depletion because cuts are on at least a "sustained-yield" basis and often on a "harvest-improvement" basis.

‡ This is just an illustrative exhibit of *marginal* losses (or gains) associated with small changes in proposed outlays. Here it was assumed that the budget reduction would simply reduce the major "output." Given this assumption, the estimate (based on data pertaining to marginal budgetary changes presented in *Senate Hearings, 1953*, p. 334) is subject to less uncertainty than the estimates of gains associated with the full expenditures.

§ The present value of managing the forests on account of campers' and sportsmen's visits was estimated in the following crude fashion. It is assumed that a charge of $0.50 per man-day would not cut attendance to less than half the present estimate (60 million man-days in 1951). If so, the use of the forests must be worth 30,000,000 times $0.50 or $15 million to the users in 1951. This is not to suggest that it would be a simple costless operation to collect such fees. The chief cost might be that campers would then use the forests surreptitiously, increasing vandalism and fire hazards.

‖ Source was "Justification Statement, 1953," (pp. 302–305), *House Hearings, 1954* (p. 1257).

¶ Source was "Justification Statement, 1953," (p. 302), with same amount assumed to apply to 1953. The Bureau of Land Management collects another $2 million annually from mineral leases on public domain national forest lands. Because of uncertainties about the extent to which these receipts could be attributed to the Forest Service's current activities, such receipts were left out of consideration.

** See supporting Tables 31 to 38 for the derivation of these estimates.

†† Cost per acre ran about $4 to $5 prior to 1943 ($7.65 in 1928). See Bureau of the Census, *Historical Statistics of the U. S., 1789–1945* (Washington, D.C.: U. S. Government Printing Office, 1949), p. 123. It is assumed that the value would be 25% greater than cost because of by-product benefits through integration with other national forests for watershed protection, timber production, and elimination of much surveying, fencing, or even guarding. Finally the value is assumed to have doubled due to inflation, yielding a value of $12.50 per acre acquired. See Table 27 for number of acres acquired.

Research in general has had great value, but the present value of *particular* research programs, such as that in the Forest Service or that in any other specific field, is extremely uncertain. The descriptions of the various research projects, available in current justification materials, may be as good an "indicator" of expected accomplishment as can be devised. In any event, Forest Research serves here to illustrate those activities for which proposed costs (obligational authority) can be segregated but for which no quantitative indicator can be given.

In order to show the sources of gain and just a little about the derivation of the numbers, Table 28 is offered as part of the main exhibit. In order to facilitate appraisal of the suggested exhibits, Table 27 includes, below the present values, some less direct indicators pertaining to these activities. As pointed out earlier, it helps only a little to learn that the 1953 budget for "Forest-Fire Control" would provide 6,310 initial-action firefighters while the outlays for "Development and Management of Forests" would make possible 5 billion board feet of timber sales, 66 million man-days of usage by campers and sportsmen, and 41,000 additional acres of national forest. It might be better not to burden the *main* budget with the less direct measures of performance. The most significant indicators are the changes in accomplishment with identical reductions in the budgets of forest management and forest-fire control. These indicators suggest that forest management, i.e., activities that result in more timber sales, might well be expanded—so far as these estimates of expected performance are concerned. However, in connection with these particular estimates, which are not intended to support definitive conclusions about program levels, several qualifications and special points must be kept in mind.

Major Comments on the Sample Budget

First, the budget is called illustrative for good reason. It is essentially exploratory in nature, and it, too, has numerous shortcomings. For instance, overhead (undoubtedly including some "unallocable" cost) has been allocated among the three activities (Table 29 in the Appendix to this chapter). In fact, the Department of Agriculture had already allocated overhead, other than the expenses of the Office of the Secretary, among the activity categories in the "Justification Statement." Admittedly, the resulting amounts do not coincide precisely with the real incremental costs due to each program, particularly with present accounting procedures. That is, the abandonment of, say, Forest Research, other things remaining the same, would probably not reduce obligations for fiscal 1953 in precisely the amount shown. This retrenchment would have some effect on overhead but not exactly in accordance with these estimates. Moreover, persons in the Budget Bureau or the Department of Agriculture could no doubt point out ways in which the numbers go astray. However, the estimates are believed to be sufficiently accurate to serve their real purpose—to explore the future feasibility and usefulness of this type of budget.

Second, it should be stressed that the most useful indicators of performance are surely those which pertain to comparable and to incremental changes in various activity levels. Thus the present values of expected tangible gains from the *full* programs do not help much, because *average* benefit per dollar obligated (or the ratio of benefits to costs) does not reveal which program should be expanded or contracted. For example, in Table 27, Forest-Fire Control has the higher average benefit, as this program yields approximately the same benefits (present value) as Development and Management of Forests yet costs half as much. Nevertheless, a million dollars taken from Forest-Fire Control would reduce expected benefits less than would a million dollars taken from the other program. Because they might be useful in considering large changes, estimated benefits from the *full* programs are presented in Table 27; but in most situations they would not help department officials or Congress greatly.

In the hearings, the subcommittees quite properly give close attention to incremental changes in various programs, but these changes are usually the proposed decreases and increases, for each category of expenditure, *over last year's outlays*. Such increments, e.g., the difference between the present value of 1952's program and that of 1953's program, may not be very revealing. First, the rest of the economy does not remain the same from one year to the next. Second, it would be a remarkable coincidence if even a few programs increased or decreased their scales by about the same amount from one year to the next. The scale of many programs does not change between budgets, while the scale of some changes drastically. Hence even if benefits could be measured with great precision, we could make only the following type of comparison:

Activity	Change in Obligational Authority from 1951 to 1952	Change in Benefits from 1951 to 1952
A	+$1 million	+$2 million
B	+$50 million	+$200 million
C	0	−$2 million
D	−$5 million	0

C and D illustrate possible effects of the economy's development such as an altered threat of forest fires or an altered relative price of timber. In one case there is a change in benefit without a change in the program; in the other, a shift in program without a change in benefit. Thus variations as between years even with excellent measures of performance are not well designed to help Congress decide which programs should in the future be expanded or contracted.

The indicators that would be most helpful are the changes in the present value of expected gains associated with *identical increments* (or decrements) in the budget proposed for each program. Thus the variations would be comparable from one program to the next and they would not mislead anyone into making all-or-none comparisons. Also it is less hazardous to estimate the worth of a few more (or less) policemen than to evaluate our position on the assumption that all policemen are eliminated. Similarly, we can estimate the value of a few thousand gallons of water, but what would happen to its price if 75 per cent of the annual water supply were eliminated?

Therefore, the principal emphasis must be placed on the marginal changes in the present value of expected gains. According to Table 27, a million-dollar reduction in Development and Management of Forests would shrink the present value of expected gains by four million dollars, while a million-dollar cut in Forest-Fire Control would sacrifice only four-tenths of a million dollars (present value of expected gains). Naturally, if the programs were adjusted upward or downward, these numbers would be altered. That is, further increases or cuts would affect gains by different amounts than those mentioned.

Third among these special points, we would not want to look only at *expected* gains. A small chance of huge gains or of disastrous losses under one policy might be more important to us than the difference between two policies with respect to their outcomes on the average. Wherever this consideration seems particularly important, information about the variability of the outcome should be considered. The activities in our illustration constitute an example of such a case. The estimated benefits sacrificed by cutting one million dollars from "Development and Management of Forests" are probably less variable than the benefits sacrificed by cutting one million from "Forest-Fire Control." The inherent variability about the mean from year to year is less, and the uncertainty due to imperfect estimation procedures is less. In such situations, we would not want to base decisions solely on average or expected values—to choose *mechanically* the larger expected gains that could be achieved through timber sales rather than a lower probability of catastrophic forest fires that could be achieved through forest-fire control.

Fourth, note that, even aside from uncertainty, the present value of tangible gains as an indicator of performance does not tell anyone exactly what should be done. It includes no estimate of intangible gains or costs—those which cannot be put in terms of the common denominator—yet these will sometimes be important considerations. It includes no estimate of the present value of tangible gains for *many* of the alternative programs. (Imagine, for instance, an attempt to make such estimates in the case of most State Department activities.) There may be legitimate differences of opinion about the real purpose of some government interventions or programs. Finally, these indicators include no estimates of the effects of changes other than the flat marginal ones that have been described. Nonetheless, these indicators, wherever calculable, go further than other indicators of performance in pointing toward "correct" policies. They would provide administrators and Congressmen with clues which would *help* them to decide which programs should be cut, if a budget reduction is to be achieved, or which programs should be cut and which expanded.

Fifth, some comments on the treatment of time streams should be made. In these illustrative calculations, future gains (net of operating costs) were discounted at 5 per cent. The discount rate should in principle reflect the rate of return in the marginal alternative opportunity. If the problem of choice is whether to put another $1,000,000 into a government program or leave it in the private sector of the economy, the marginal rate of return in the private sector is the proper rate of discount. If the problem is the allocation of a given budget among programs, the marginal internal rate of return is the proper discount rate. The former problem is the one posed here, whether or not to devote an extra million dollars to "management of forests," so 5 per cent seemed to be a reasonable representation of the opportunities foregone.

Note, in connection with the treatment of time, that the use of present values brings the time stream of costs and benefits into comprehensible form but conceals the year-by-year programming of costs and gains. By and large, the budget is bound to pertain to proposed obligational authority for the coming fiscal year. For some programs or individual projects, Congress may look at several years' costs, but it is unlikely to do so for all activities. Hence, in general, the budget probably ought to emphasize what the *coming year's* obligational authority will buy, assuming that work is carried on to its completion, not abandoned prematurely.[8] But what it will buy may include gains that occur only if certain expenditures are made in subsequent years. Strictly speaking, one cannot attribute part of the gains to this year's expenditure, though this may be better than any practicable alternative procedure. Anyway, wherever present values are contingent upon substantial future outlays, this fact ought to be indicated, for example, by showing the costs entailed in several subsequent years. This would help Congress and/or the Executive Branch take into account the dependence of the estimated current performance upon future capital and operating outlays and the risk of premature abandonment of the program. (These considerations are over and above the inherent variability of costs and benefits due to imperfect foresight and estimation procedures.)

Sixth, it might not be desirable—or, in any case, feasible—to include any estimated present values in the official budget, for it is difficult to imagine acceptance of such controversial estimates as part of the main document. These estimates, however, might serve equally well as (1) supplementary exhibits prepared by researchers working for Congress and the Budget Bureau or even by outside research groups hoping to improve budgetary decisions; (2) a type of justification exhibit prepared each year by the departments. Such estimates would thus not have to be in the main document in order to serve as part of a performance budget. The important thing is that officials ought to (indeed, *have* to) think in terms of the gains associated with proposed programs in order to reach decisions. *Systematic* thinking in these terms might be encouraged if improved estimates of programs' achievements were discussed in the hearings.

Derivation of the Estimates

Tables 30 to 38 in the Appendix to Chapter 13 explain the derivation of the numbers. If estimates of present values were to be introduced, such supporting tables would presumably have to be discussed in the hearings as justification materials. The models used to estimate the present value of expected benefits were rough aggregative ones. For instance, in Tables 37 and 38, an exponential equation was used to estimate the effect of diminishing returns to scale as more or less money was devoted to forest-fire control.

---

[8] This does not mean the programs should never be abandoned. It may be economical, in view of the situation at one time, to undertake Program A, taking into account the likelihood that it will pay off when completed. It may later be economical, in view of altered circumstances, to abandon Program A.

It should be observed that the illustrative budget deals with the coming year's obligations rather than with the coming year's disbursements. Our interest in comparing different programs is in their relative "profitableness," not in their comparative impacts on the cash position or the fiscal-monetary situation. In recent years, much emphasis has rightly been put on the "cash budget," because total cash disbursements and receipts indicate the extent to which the government is exerting inflationary or deflationary pressure. However, if we are asking which activities should be cut or which should be expanded, the emphasis should be on future costs that are still subject to change. It is assumed that obligational authority is a closer approximation to proposed costs than the cash outlays which are anticipated during the coming year. Either figure is bound to represent imperfectly the cost of resources taken for the government's activities.

In preparing the estimates, it was assumed that budget cuts would have the effect of slashing the major outputs of the programs—timber sales in the Development and Management of National Forests, fire-damage-prevented in the Fire Control Program. If the departments estimated the effects of marginal cuts, they could no doubt allocate the cuts so as to keep up performance somewhat better than is shown. However, it is probably more accurate to assume that the cuts would reduce the output of the program than to assume that they would have no effects other than the miraculous elimination of waste. In order to get the same task performed at less cost, it takes a good deal of special effort, careful analysis, and earnest cooperation in addition to the pressure of a budget cut.

In connection with Development and Management of National Forests, no rent was charged on the assumption that the lands have no valuable (or politically acceptable) alternative uses. Congressmen do not always accept this assumption, as they occasionally assert that *anybody* could make a nice profit if he was given the land and trees for nothing. Indeed, the Department of Agriculture states that our national forests are worth $200 million.[9] If this represents sale value or value in alternative uses, then a rental should certainly be charged. The whole program would then appear much less profitable, and it might even appear that some lands should be sold or put to those alternative uses. As long as the lands are to be held as national forest, however, the gain (loss) *from an expansion (cut)* in the timber program will not be affected, even if rent is charged and the *average* profitability of the operation is reduced.

[9] *Senate Hearings, 1953*, p. 377.

A final comment on procedure: the programs as segregated here are composed entirely of Department of Agriculture activities. In actuality, there are activities in several departments which carry out related tasks or have similar by-product benefits. Perhaps those activities that are most closely related ought to be formally brought under the same department or agency. Such reorganization is frequently recommended.[10] In any event, indicators of performance ought in principle to reflect spillover effects on production possibilities in other governmental (or private) operations. In this exploration of a revised budgetary exhibit, it should be noted that little attention was given to spillovers outside the Department of Agriculture.

RELATION TO OTHER BUDGETARY REFORMS

It may be worth noting that the preceding suggestions with respect to performance budgeting appear to be compatible with other budgetary reforms that have been emphasized in recent years.

THE NEED FOR BETTER COST ACCOUNTING. Many persons have pressed for more extensive adoption of accrual accounting and of account classifications that would facilitate better costing of activities.[11] If accounting procedures were improved, performance budgets along the lines suggested would be increasingly useful. Indeed, budgeting in terms of missions or activities is naturally associated with costing by activities, and those who have recommended the latter have usually recommended both. Of course, the revamping of accounting systems will take many years, and even then the treatment of incremental overhead costs in such a huge multi-product "firm" will be

---

[10] E.g., *House Hearings, 1954*, p. 1239. Of course, there will always be some overlap and spillover because it will never be possible to look at all the pieces of the budgetary problem simultaneously.

[11] Cost accounting, and better use of costs as management tools in government, have been discussed for a long time—e.g., by Carl W. Tiller, *Government Cost Accounting*, (Chicago: Municipal Finance Officers' Association of the U. S. and Canada, 1940). On the other hand, even recent textbooks often give the impression that the need for cost accounting is less in government than in business because the main objective of a governmental unit is not to make a "profit" but to guard its cash and obligational-authority positions. See L. Morey and R. P. Hackett, *Fundamentals of Governmental Accounting*, 2nd ed. (New York: John Wiley and Sons, 1951), pp. 20–46. The notion that government is not out to make a profit for us, i.e., to yield benefits that are worth more than they cost, is an unfortunate one. I am indebted to David Novick of The RAND Corporation for the use of unpublished materials on the improvement of cost accounting and budgeting in government.

rough. Budgeting by activities might help even without these accounting reforms, but is, to say the least, compatible with them.

THE NEED TO SHORTEN THE BUDGET CYCLE. Professor Arthur Smithies is particularly persuasive on the need to shorten the budget cycle.[12] At present, the preparation of one year's budget—from the first steps that are taken within the departments to the submission of the budget to Congress—takes about two years. Although this makes it possible to give attention to detail, the reliability of the estimates is impaired by inconsistencies that develop over the two-year budget cycle. Records of past expenditures should be examined carefully in order to derive statistical and cost factors, but estimates of *future* expenditures seem likely to be more accurate and more consistent internally if prepared over a much shorter cycle (through the use of these factors). To a considerable extent, such factors are used at present,[13] but extension of this practice seems desirable. Performance budgets of this type discussed in this chapter would readily fit in with this procedure. They would be improved by the careful examination of past outlays in order to derive factors, but they would not have to be tied to detailed programming of future outlays.

THE NEED TO PRESENT A SINGLE APPROPRIATIONS BILL. Numerous experts would prefer to have Congress consider all major activities and decide upon their appropriations "simultaneously" rather than determine those appropriations one at a time. An over-all budget that is less massive than the current one would be essential to the consideration of a single bill. A budget broken down by activities and accompanied by better quantitative indicators of achievement is not only consistent with but perhaps prerequisite to the use of a single appropriations bill.

THE NEED FOR "CEILINGS" AND "B-LISTS." Some observers urge that departmental estimates should be presented, to an increasing extent, under the constraint of a preliminary ceiling assigned by the President, with a separate exhibit of "B-priority" outlays—that is, ones which would be made if the ceiling was raised. The term "B-priority" probably serves to confuse matters. In these circumstances, departments would in effect submit alternative budgets based on two

[12] Arthur Smithies, *The Budgetary Process in the United States* (New York: McGraw-Hill, 1955), pp. 240–257.

[13] Major Sidney Miller, "Sample Procedures in Computing Air Force Budget Estimates," a paper presented at the annual meeting of the Operations Research Society of America, May 15–16, 1953 (abstract published in *The Journal of the Operations Research Society of America,* May, 1953, p. 147).

different ceilings (one of which would not be clearly specified). Perhaps a more straightforward arrangement would be to call for, and send on to Congress, estimates based on two specific ceilings. This would give a better idea of the effect of changes than would a request by the appropriations committee for "priorities." Such a request at best leads the department to reply that it has done its utmost to secure equal benefits from incremental outlays on all programs and prefers to apportion a cut among its programs on the basis of further analysis. At worst, such a request for "priorities" leads either to a reply that every proposed outlay is indispensable or to a listing of "priorities" in reverse order. (The latter procedure is sometimes adopted by a department for tactical reasons—because most sensible persons may then conclude that even the item bearing the *lowest* priority is clearly "indispensable.") Performance budgeting of the type illustrated in this paper would certainly be compatible with the use of two ceilings.

FOREST SERVICE: ALLOCATION OF OBLIGATIONS AMONG ACTIVITIES IN ILLUSTRATIVE PERFORMANCE BUDGET*

	Development, Management of Forests			Forest-Fire Control			Forest Research		
	1951	1952	1953	1951	1952	1953	1951	1952	1953
1. Direct obligations									
Resource protection and use	17,843	18,726	19,642	7,846	8,190	8,491			
Resource development	1,761	1,898	1,885						
Fighting forest fires: suppression				6,096	5,409	6,000			
Forest research							5,159	5,416	5,397
Under reimbursement from non-federal sources	—	—	—						
Construction of roads and trails	4,000	8,419	5,500	270	111	111			
Maintenance of roads and trails	7,318	8,150	7,500						
Obligations under reimbursement from non-federal sources						970			
Smoke-jumper facilities				27	1	1			
Acquisition—Weeks Act	249	75	75						
Acquisition—Superior	76	207	150						
Acquisition—Special Acts	64	142	142						
State and private forestry cooperation	469	1,348	1,343	9,450	9,450	9,450			
Cooperative range improvements	46	931	700						
Emergency Reconstruction	69	25							
Forest roads and trails		16							
Acquisition—Coronado									
Brush disposal		318	500						
Payments to states and counties (omitted)†									
Roads and trails for states	3,035	5,638	6,038						
2. Obligations under reimbursement from other accounts									
Control of forest pests	1,774	1,750	2,213						
Surveys, appraisals	28	32	32						
Investigations at forest products lab	37	53	53						

267

TABLE 29 (*Continued*)

FOREST SERVICE: ALLOCATION OF OBLIGATIONS AMONG ACTIVITIES
IN ILLUSTRATIVE PERFORMANCE BUDGET*

Special economic investigations	55	64	64						
Remainder of such obligations under salaries and expenses‡				1,191	1,285	1,054	1,191	1,285	1,054
Construction and maintenance of roads and trails	19	47	47						
Sale of supplies, materials, equipment‡				58	73	73	58	72	73
State and private forestry cooperation	1,324			9,483					
Cooperative range improvements	3								
Forest roads and trails, emergency	189	305	305						
Roads and trails for states	—								
3. Obligations of other programs§ allocated to forest service									
Control of forest pests (remainder not shown above)	5,339	4,250	5,787						
Grand totals	44,947	53,754	53,103	24,971	24,518	26,150	5,159	5,416	5,397

* Allocations were based largely on information in the "Justification Statement, 1953." The Department of Agriculture has already allocated overhead (except for the "Office of the Secretary") among the activities. Of course, this is not a "correct" solution to these allocation problems. For example, the "adjudication of mining claims consumes many man-years of work by mineral examiners, rangers, supervisors, and regional office personnel" (*Ibid.*, p. 309). These costs may not properly belong to Forest Service, but to, say, the Justice Department. On the other hand, good maps appear to be essential to national forest administration, and their cost seems to be shared with the U.S. Geological Survey. *Note, too, that no rent is covered by these Appropriations or imputed in these calculations on the ground that the lands have no relevant alternative uses.* There are many other kinds of problems. One of the most important that has to be faced is to cross not only intradepartmental lines but also departmental lines in allocating costs and allowing for benefits.

† Treated as transfer payments, not as real costs of these activities.

‡ Arbitrarily allocated equally between Development and Management of Forests, on the one hand, and Forest-Fire Control, on the other.

§ Payments to counties by the Bureau of Land Management, Department of Interior, are included in "Conservation and Development of Forest Resources" (Category 402) in the official functional budget (Special Analysis B, *Budget of the U.S., 1953*, p. 1151). Here they are treated as transfer payments, not as real costs of these activities.

TABLE 30

RECONCILIATION OF TOTAL OBLIGATIONS BY ACTIVITIES IN
CONVENTIONAL BUDGET WITH THOSE IN PERFORMANCE BUDGET*

(Page references are to the *Budget of the U.S., 1953.*)

	1951	1952	1953
Forest Service: Current (pp. 435–443)			
Salaries and expenses	43,252	44,219	45,996
Forest development, roads and trails	11,480	16,763	13,194
Smoke-jumper facilities	—	—	970
Acquisition, Weeks	249	75	75
Acquisition, Superior	76	207	150
Acquisition, Special Acts	64	142	142
State and private forestry cooperation	10,807	10,798	10,793
Cooperative range improvements	472	931	700
Emergency reconstruction	46		
Forest roads and trails, emergency	70	25	
Forest Service: Permanent (pp. 474–476)			
Acquisition, Coronado		16	
Expenses, brush disposal		318	500
Payments Minnesota, school funds, states (omitted)†			
Roads and trails for states	3,224	5,943	6,343
Control of forest pests (pp. 432–434)	7,113	6,000	8,000
Subtotal	76,853	85,437	86,863
Less amounts in "Control of forest pests" counted also as Forest Service obligations that were reimbursable from Control of forest pests	1,774	1,750	2,213
Total obligations in *Budget of the United States, 1953*, and also in this illustrative performance budget‡	75,079	83,687	84,650

* This reconciles total obligations according to the illustrative performance budget with the sum of "obligations by activities" for the Forest Service (plus Control of Forest Pests) according to the published *Budget of the U.S., 1953*, pp. 432–443, 474–476. It is more difficult to effect a reconciliation (other than for 1953) with the amount allocated to the Forest Service in Special Analysis B, "New Obligational Authority and Expenditures by Function and Agency," *Budget of the U.S., 1953*, p. 1151, on account of numerous small transfers.

† Treated as transfer payments, not as real costs of the programs.

‡ Except for rounding errors.

TABLE 31

Share of Gains from Range Cooperatively Maintained and from Revegetation, State and Private Range

	1951	1952	1953
Expenditures on work in national forests on range management (thousands of current dollars)			
1. Revegetation and improvements	709*	—	—
2. Maintenance of range	1,011*	—	—
Expenditures on cooperation with states on range management (thousands of current dollars)			
1. Revegetation and improvements	204	—	—
2. Maintenance of range	265	—	—
Expenditures on cooperation as percentages of expenditures in national forests			
1. Revegetation and improvements (204÷709) 30%			
2. Maintenance of range (265÷1,011) 25%			

[It is assumed that expenditures on cooperation will be equally productive—i.e., that the gains from expenditures on *cooperation* for revegetation and maintenance would be, in 1951, 30% and 25% respectively of the gains from similar National Forest activities.]

	1951	1952	1953
Present value of gains from range management in national forests (millions of current dollars)			
1. Revegetation and improvements	0.2†	—	—
2. Maintenance of range	4.0‡	—	—
Present value of gains (Federal share) from cooperative range management (millions of current dollars)			
1. Revegetation and improvements (30% of $0.2)	0.1	0.1§	0.1§
2. Maintenance of range (25% of $4.0)	1.0	1.0	1.0

* Source was "Justification Statement, 1953," pp. 290–291.

† Rounded to nearest tenth. See Table 28 or Table 34.

‡ Grazing receipts—see Table 28.

§ No appreciable change in scale of activity is indicated for 1952 or 1953.

TABLE 32

VALUE OF REFORESTATION IN NATIONAL FORESTS

	Without Reforestation	With Reforestation	Increase Due to Reforestation	1951	1952	1953
Allowable annual cut on "sustained-yield" basis (millions of board feet per thousand acres)	0.05*	0.3†	0.25			
Value of annual cut per thousand acres at $10 per thousand board feet‡ (thousands of dollars)	0.5	3.0	2.5			
Amount of reforestation (thousands of acres)				43	43§	43§
Value of *increase* in annual cut due to reforestation (43 times $2.5): Value available annually after, say, 20 years (thousands of dollars)				107.5‖	107.5	107.5
Cost of preparing above increase for sale (12½%)¶				13.4	13.4	13.4
Net value of increase in annual cut 20 years hence				94.1	94.1	94.1
Discounted value 20 years hence of above increase: Discount rate 5% (thousands of current dollars)				1,882.0	1,882.0	1,882.0
Present value of above (.38 times $1,882): Discount rate 5% (thousands of current dollars)				715.0§	715.0§	715.0§

* This number is simply the total allowable cut in our national forests (6,000 million board feet) divided by the number of acres of forest-producing land (120,000 thousand acres). See *Senate Hearings, 1953*. Perhaps it should be noted that 60,000,000 acres of our national forests—e.g., land above the timber line—do not produce merchantable timber. This allowable cut without reforestation seems reasonable in view of other data and statements about the productivity of forest lands in "need" of reforestation. Also, the average private cut is .18 million board feet per thousand acres, but depletion apparently accounts for a great deal of this amount.

† This number is based on an example of allowable cut with good stocking: 48 million board feet from 157 thousand acres ("Justification Statement, 1953," p. 303). Under favorable conditions, allowable annual cut per acre may be twice this estimate (*Ibid.*, p. 294).

‡ Average price during fiscal year 1951 according to "Justification Statement, 1953," p. 303. Price given in *Senate Hearings, 1953*, p. 330, is $14.

§ Budget does not indicate any change in scale of activity—change in appropriation is due to pay-rate increase.

‖ It is assumed that on the average the growth is sufficient in 20 years to permit the full "allowable annual cut" on a "sustained-yield basis." Some cutting, and also extra costs of supervision, would occur prior to the end of this waiting period.

¶ Source was *Senate Hearings, 1953*, p. 334.

TABLE 33

VALUE OF SHARE OF GAINS FROM REFORESTATION AND BETTER METHODS, STATE AND PRIVATE FORESTS*

	Without Reforestation	With Reforestation	Increase Due to Reforestation	Without Improved Practices	With Improved Practices	Increase Due to Improved Practices	1951	1952	1953
Allowable annual cut on "sustained-yield" basis (millions of board feet per thousand acres)	0.05	0.3	0.25	0.1	0.2†	0.1			
Value of annual cut per thousand acres at $10 per thousand board feet (thousands of dollars)	0.5	3.0	2.5	1.0	2.0	1.0			
Amount of reforestation (thousands of acres)									
Extent of improved practices (thousand acres)							300†	300§	300§
Value of increase in annual cut (300×$2.5 plus 2,558×$1)—value available annually after 20 years (thousands of dollars)							2,558†	2,558	2,558
Cost of preparing above increase for sale (12½%)							3,308	3,308	3,308
Net value of increase in annual cut 20 years hence							414	414	414
Discounted value 20 years hence of above increase: Discount rate 5% (thousands of dollars)							2,894	2,894	2,894
Present value of above (.38 times $57,880): Discount rate 5% (thousands of dollars)							57,880	57,880	57,880
Federal share of above present value (Forest Service contributes about 1/15‖ of estimated total State, Private, and Federal outlays on replanting and improved practices)							21,994	21,994	21,994
							1,466	1,466§	1,466§

* See Table 32 for the derivation of most of these numbers.

† "Good practices" would probably double the annual output net of depletion on most farm woodlands. See *Long-Range Agricultural Policy: A Study of Selected Trends and Factors Relating to the Long-Range Prospect for American Agriculture* for the Committee on Agriculture, House of Representatives, 80th Congress, 2nd Session, March 10, 1948.

‡ "Justification Statement," 1953," pp. 345–46.

§ The Budget does not suggest any change in the scale of these activities in 1952 or 1953.

‖ *House Hearings,* 1953, p. 966.

TABLE 34

VALUE OF REVEGETATION OF RANGE IN NATIONAL FORESTS

	1951	1952	1953
Number of acres reseeded (thousands)	60	60*	60*
Allowable increase in grazing without impairing range or aggravating erosion (thousands of animal-unit months)	38	38*	38*
Total allowable grazing (thousands of animal-unit months)	7,620†	—	—
Allowable increase due to reseeding as percentage of total allowable grazing	0.5%		
Receipts from total allowable grazing (thousands of dollars)	4,000†		
Increase in annual receipts due to reseeding (thousands of dollars)	20‡		
Present value of above increase maintained 10 years;§ Discount Rate 5% (thousands of dollars)	154	154*	154*

* Budget does not suggest any change in the scale of activity in 1952 or 1953.

† "Justification Statement, 1953," pp. 304–305.

‡ It is assumed that receipts will increase in the same proportion that allowable grazing (animal-unit months) increases.

§ The assumption is that the extra grazing begins immediately and that the increased productivity lasts 10 years without additional improvements or reseeding.

TABLE 35

VALUE OF FLOOD-PREVENTION ASPECTS OR ACTIVITIES

			1951	1952	1953
Expected tangible losses annually (millions of dollars)		275*			
Estimated acreage contributing excessive run-off of water (millions)					
Acreage that might burn without protection					
State and private forests	10†				
National forests	5†				
Acreage that might be denuded through cutting and overgrazing (about ⅓ of forests and associated range land)	200‡				
Cropland and other range that might be denuded through heavy use (about ½ of acreage)	700†	915			
Estimated tangible losses if above acreage were "protected" through Dept. of Agriculture measures (millions of dollars)		75§			
Acres actually to be "treated" (thousands of acres)					
Development and management of forests					
Reforestation in national forests			43‖	43	43
Share of reforestation in state and private forests			191¶	191	191
Revegetation on range in national forests			60**	60	60
Share of revegetation on state-private range			18††	18	18
Total			312	312	312
Forest-fire control					
Expected acreage protected from fire—national forests			4,700‡‡	4,700	4,730
Share of acreage protected from fire—state, private forests](¼ of 7,000‡‡)			1,750	1,750	1,750
			6,450	6,450	6,480
Percentage of total (915 million) to be "treated"					
Development and management of forests			0.034 of 1%	0.034 of 1%	0.034 of 1%
Forest-fire control			0.705 of 1%	0.705 of 1%	0.708 of 1%

VALUE OF FLOOD-PREVENTION ASPECTS OF ACTIVITIES

Estimated annual reduction of flood losses§§			
Development and management of forests (millions of dollars)	0.07	0.07	0.07
Forest-fire control	1.41	1.41	1.41
Present value of above annual reduction of flood losses (discounted at 5%, gains assumed to persist for only 10 years due to growing threat of fire, probable necessity of reseeding or replanting)			
Development and management of forests (millions of dollars)	0.5	0.5	0.5
Forest-fire control (millions of dollars)	10.9	10.9	11.0

* Annual damage other than silting of reservoirs estimated at $250 million in 1948 prices. See Dr. Hugh H. Bennett, "The Tools of Flood Control," *Yearbook of Agriculture, 1948* (Washington, D.C.: U.S. Government Printing Office, 1948), p. 66; and G. R. Phillips and B. Frank, "To Help Control Floods," *Trees, Yearbook of Agriculture, 1949* (Washington, D.C.: U.S. Government Printing Office, 1949), p. 609. This estimate was multiplied by 110% to allow for inflation and put the figure approximately in terms of 1952–1953 dollars.

† See Tables 37 and 38 for basis of these estimates.

‡ These numbers are simply personal judgments based on reading *House Hearings, 1953,* pertaining to soil conservation and flood control.

§ Runoff of water from watersheds that were burned or denuded was from 22 to 239 times the runoff from similar watersheds that were unburned or replanted. See Carl B. Brown, *The Control of Reservoir Silting,* U. S. Department of Agriculture Miscellaneous Publication No. 521 (Washington, D.C.: U.S. Government Printing Office, 1944). These watersheds, however, were great flood hazards in all likelihood, and the average potential reduction of runoff is probably much smaller. On the other hand, at this early stage in such work, selectivity should enable the program to do somewhat better than average. It was finally assumed that "treatment" could cut *peak* runoff and flood damage to about ¼ of its present magnitude. Note that the more other programs (dams, channel dredging) accomplish, the less the potential damage reduction from extension of this type of measure.

‖ See Table 32.

¶ It is assumed that Federal expenditures—which are about ⅕ of total state, private, and Federal outlays under the cooperative program—have the effect of "treating" ⅕ of the total (2,858 thousand acres) for which improved practice or reforestation is adopted.

** See Table 34.

†† Federal outlays for reseeding under the cooperative program in 1951 were about 30 per cent of Federal outlays for reseeding in the national forests. It was assumed that this made possible the reseeding of 30 per cent of 60, or 18, thousand acres.

‡‡ See Tables 37 and 38.

§§ Numbers are simply the product of potential savings ($275 – $75) and percentages of total acreage to be "treated."

TABLE 36

VALUE OF ACTIVITIES IN REDUCING SILTATION OF RESERVOIRS

		1951	1952	1953
Expected tangible losses annually (millions of dollars)	70*			
Estimated acreage contributing excessive silt (millions)	915†			
Estimated tangible losses annually if above acreage were "protected" through Dept. of Agriculture programs	15‡			
Percentage of total acres (915 million) to be treated†				
Development and management of forests		0.034 of 1%	0.034 of 1%	0.034 of 1%
Forest-fire control		0.705 of 1%	0.705 of 1%	0.708 of 1%
Expected annual reduction of losses from siltation§ (millions of dollars)				
Development and management of forests		0.019	0.019	0.019
Forest-fire control		0.388	0.388	0.389
Present value of above annual reduction of losses (discounted at 5%, gains assumed to persist for only 10 years)				
Development and management of forests (millions of dollars)		0.1	0.1	0.1
Forest-fire control (millions of dollars)		3.0	3.0	3.0

* Annual damage as of 1943–1944 was estimated to be from $10 to $50 million. See Carl B. Brown, *op. cit.*, p. 21. The average of these two figures, or $30 million, was taken as a base, doubled to allow in a rough way for inflation, multiplied by 115% to make a crude allowance for the increased reservoir capacity at risk. (Reservoir capacity was assumed to have grown at about the same rate as population.) The resulting figure, $69 million, was rounded to $70 million.

† See Table 35.

‡ The reduction of erosion is about the same as the reduction of water-runoff when land is given grass or forest coverage. See footnote § in Table 35.

§ $55 million ($70 million minus $15 million) times the percentages of total acres to be treated.

TABLE 37

Value of Savings of Saleable Timber Due to Fire Control: National Forests

	Without Organized Protection	With Present Protection	Saving Due to Protection (1951–1952)	1951	1952	1953	Reduction of Savings if 1953 Activity Curtailed by $1 Million (millions of dollars)
Acres (thousands) expected to be burned annually	5,000*	300†	4,700				
Expected tangible losses (millions of dollars) annually	51	3†	48	48	48	48.3	0.3

Effect of reduction in expenditures

Let percentage of acres at risk that were saved $(94\%)=P$, and the amount spent on fire control ($16 million in 1951–1952)$=Z$

Assume that $P=e^{-K/Z}$, or $94\%=e^{-K/16}$‡

Then $K=.99$

Now let expenditures fall by $1 million

$P=e^{-.99/15}$, or 93.5%

Expected savings due to protection $= 93.5/94$ times $48 million, or $47.7 million

Reduction of savings if 1953 expenditures were curtailed by $1 million

* Total national-forest acreage is 180,000,000. In tracts without organized protection, about 15% is expected to burn over each year. See *Trees, Yearbook of Agriculture, 1949*, p. 485. But this does not mean that a *new* 15% of the total 180,000,000 acres could burn each year. It is probably not too high, with today's traffic in the parks, to assume that 100 million acres (over half) might burn in a 20-year period, with the average *new* acreage expected to burn annually being 5,000,000 acres.

† "Justification Statement, 1953," p. 304. This number is roughly the average loss in 1951 and 1952. The use of earlier years, when the forests were used less extensively, would probably understate expected damage.

‡ The use of this relationship, an "exponential function," is simply a way of approximating the way in which returns (timber saved) diminish as more money is devoted to the program. That is, it seems sensible to assume diminishing returns, and this relationship helps one determine a plausible rate at which those returns might diminish.

TABLE 38

Value of Savings of Saleable Timber Due to Cooperative Fire-Control: State and Private Forests

	Without Organized Protection	With Present Protection	1951	1952	1953
Acres (thousands) expected to be burned annually	10,000*	3,000†			
Saving because of protection (thousands of acres)		7,000			
Expected tangible losses (millions of dollars) annually	70	21†			
Saving because of protection (millions of dollars)		49			
Federal share of saving due to protection (25%)‡		12.3	12.3	12.3	12.3

Effect of reduction in expenditures

Let percentage of acres at risk that were saved (70%) = P, and the amount spent on fire control ($9 million by Federal Government) = Z

Assume that $P = e^{-K/Z}$, or $70\% = e^{-K/9}$

Then $K = 3.24$§

Now let expenditures fall by $1 million

$P = e^{-3.24/8}$, or 67%

Expected savings due to protection = 67/70 times $49 million, or $47 million

Reduction of savings if 1953 outlays were curtailed by $1 million *and states curtailed similarly* (millions)   2.0

Reduction of savings if federal reduction were not matched by state curtailment (25% of $2 million)   0.5

* Total state-private acreage is 361,000,000. In tracts without organized protection, 15% is expected to burn over each year. See E. Pierce, C. A. Gustafson, "Building a Fire Organization," *Trees, Yearbook of Agriculture, 1949,* p. 485. See also *Senate Hearings, 1953,* p. 353. But obviously this does not mean that a new 15% of the total 361,000,000 acres could burn each year. It is probably not too high, however, to assume that 200 million acres (over half) might burn in a 20-year period, with the average *new* acreage expected to burn annually being 10,000,000 acres.

† *Trees, Yearbook of Agriculture, 1949,* p. 485.

‡ *Senate Hearings, 1953,* p. 353.

§ Of course K is not constant over time. The danger increases gradually as more campers, tourists, and traffic enter or pass the wood lands.

Chapter 14

ANALYTICAL AIDS
TO GOVERNMENTAL ECONOMY:
A SURVEY OF OPPORTUNITIES

THE PREVIOUS CHAPTERS have discussed the need for analysis in choosing government courses of action, the general problems and methods of analyzing alternatives, the application of these methods to the comparison of water-resource projects, and the further application to the comparison of alternative government programs. But these applications pertain to only a small portion of the total number of alternatives confronting government. Are these particular comparisons the only ones in which quantitative analysis is feasible? To what further extent might these analytic aids be usefully employed? Naturally, final answers to questions of this sort cannot be given here. The only way to find out for sure whether or not such aids can lead to better choices is to try them out. That would call for the preparation of a host of analyses in full detail, a step that is far beyond the scope of this study. A prior step, and the only one that can be taken here, is to get a tentative answer, or a "feeling" for the answer, by surveying the problems of choice that confront the government. This final chapter reports on the results of such a survey that was made of the non-defense sectors of the budget.[1]

METHODS USED IN SURVEY

The aim of the survey, as just stated, was to help us appraise, in a very rough fashion, the potential contributions of analytical aids to government efficiency. These contributions can be conceived of in terms of the two types of application that have been illustrated:

[1] Virtually all of the defense budget is believed to contain opportunities for using analysis to good advantage.

(1) the use of analysis to help compare alternative program levels (as in the preceding chapter on performance budgets); (2) the use of analysis to seek more efficient ways of accomplishing a designated task or program level (as in the selection of water-resource projects). This second application of analysis embraces a wide variety of comparisons that come under such headings as cost-benefit analysis, operations research, systems analyses, and evaluations in terms of work-measurement units. In the survey, the general procedure was to go through the budget systematically, trying to combine existing categories of expenditure into more meaningful programs, and indicating those programs in which one of these applications appeared to have some promise.

It might be noted that the line of demarcation between the two uses of analysis is by no means a hard and fast one. The distinction between the comparison of programs and the comparison of ways to carry them out obviously depends upon just what activities are designated as "programs." Nonetheless, a distinction of this sort has been made by those who have helped to assign decision-making responsibilities. Such a distinction will continue to be made as long as authority is delegated and decentralized. The distinction, rough though it may be, is therefore pertinent to formulating analyses and to appraising the potential uses of analytical assistance.

Surveying Opportunities for Use of Analysis to Compare Program Levels

The procedure can best be described by means of a sample worksheet, such as that shown in Table 39. This particular sheet summarizes the writer's views on potential applications of analysis in certain programs pertaining to health and medical care. At the left is a suggested breakdown of expenditures by programs—construction of hospitals, operation of hospitals, outpatient services, control of communicable disease, and treatment of special groups. These seemed to be useful programs in terms of which this part of the budget could be recast, for, in these programs, analysis might be able to yield meaningful indicators of performance, such as the ones listed in the middle section of the worksheet.

The dollar amounts shown are the result of breaking down and recombining figures that are given in the original budget. Departmental lines were crossed frequently in order to combine expenditures that belonged in one program, though it was impossible to learn much about the composition of many aggregate figures shown in the budget.

TABLE 39

Sample Worksheet from Survey of Budget

A Possible Breakdown by Programs	Amount in 1954 Budget (millions)	"First Application" Possible Indicators of Performance to Aid in Comparing Program Levels	"Second Application" Possible Quantitative Comparisons to Aid in Economizing Within Programs
Health and Medical Care			
Construction of hospitals			
Hospital-bed-producing projects	157	Present value of manhours lost if program cut§	Alternative locations, subcontracting arrangements, programs for saving lives or improving medical care, designs and methods.
Rehabilitation and modernization	13	Present value of construction, operating costs saved	Same alternatives listed immediately above.
Alterations and repairs	9		Same alternatives listed immediately above.
Operation of hospitals			
Neuropsychiatric hospitals (Veterans' Administration)	166	Present value of manhours lost if program cut	Alternative allocations of patients or of specialists, financing methods (e.g., fees to cover part of cost in certain cases), institutional arrangements, supply arrangements (decentralized procurement), equipment and methods, definitions of eligibles; also work-measurement comparisons among government and private hospitals; also alternative programs for saving lives and providing medical care.
Tuberculosis hospitals (Veterans' Administration)	47	Present value of manhours lost if program cut	
General hospitals: beds for service-connected disabilities	167*	Present value of manhours lost if program cut	
General hospitals: beds for non-service-connected disabilities	166*	Present value of manhours lost if program cut	
Reimbursement to non-V.A. hospitals	21	Present value of manhours lost if program cut	
Hospitals (and other medical outlays) for Indians	22†	Present value of manhours lost if program cut	
Other hospitals (Public Health Service, Freedmen's, St. Elizabeth's)	49	Present value of manhours lost if program cut	
Veterans' homes (including reimbursement of state homes)	26	Present value of manhours lost if program cut	
Administration: hospitals	‡		Work-measurement comparisons; alternative efforts to secure compliance concerning eligibility.

TABLE 39 (*Continued*)
SAMPLE WORKSHEET FROM SURVEY OF BUDGET

A Possible Breakdown by Programs	Amount in 1954 Budget (millions)	*"First Application"* Possible Indicators of Performance to Aid in Comparing Program Levels	*"Second Application"* Possible Quantitative Comparisons to Aid in Economizing Within Programs
Outpatient services			
Outpatient services, Veterans' Administration	105	Present value of manhours lost, and value of future medical and hospital care incurred, if program cut	Work-measurement comparisons; alternative methods, allocations of effort among regions or ailments; equipment, routes to similar amount of health improvement.
Outpatient services, Public Health Service	5		
Control of communicable disease			
Venereal disease (grants and technical aid to states)	8	Present value of manhours lost, and value of future medical and hospital care incurred, if program cut	Alternative allocations among regions and measures, methods and equipment; ways of organizing these activities, efforts to obtain public's cooperation.
Tuberculosis (grants and technical aid to states)	6		
Other special diseases	1		
Treatment of special groups			
Health—maternal and children's	15	Present value of manhours lost, and value of future medical and hospital care incurred, if program cut	Alternative allocations among regions and measures, methods and equipment.
Payments to Hawaii (leprosy)	1		
Rehabilitation of disabled veterans	62		
Rehabilitation of other disabled (care, training, tools): grants to states	10		

* Allocation may be impossible; it is intended here merely as a device to suggest orders of magnitude.
† This item includes amounts (probably small) for preventive medicine, research, and outpatient services.
‡ Included in General Administration.
§ The "manhours lost" would be the time of patients who would recover less rapidly (or not at all) or of persons who would become disabled in the absence of the preventive measures.

The exploratory nature of dollar estimates put together in this way is surely apparent.

Possible indicators of performance are suggested for all of the broad programs listed on this particular worksheet, and all of them in this case are estimated present values of tangible gains. Their inclusion means that estimates sufficiently accurate to be useful are tentatively judged to be feasible. It does not mean that their preparation would be a simple matter, because, for one thing, the estimation of spillovers from medical care would pose some real difficulties. Nor does it mean that policy-makers should pay attention solely to these indicators, for in providing medical care there is more at stake than merely conserving resources which have value as inputs in the productive process. Nevertheless, this value is one of the highly relevant considerations, probably being closely correlated with other desirable effects (e.g., reduction of pain and illness per se).

Surveying Opportunities for Use of Analysis to Economize Within Programs

In the right-hand column of the worksheet are listed some comparisons that might show cheaper ways of achieving a given task or program level. These are only general "types" of comparisons that appear to hold some promise.[2] To list more specific comparisons would require a close acquaintance with each activity. For instance, in connection with the highway program, it would require great familiarity with road construction, and an exceedingly voluminous set of worksheets, to put down specific alternatives like the employment of the "X-100 Road Paver." Or, in the medical-care program, if the alternatives were to be fairly inclusive, e.g., including the encouragement of medical schools as an alternative to the expansion of hospital capacity, a more detailed study would be necessary. Hence these types of special analysis are intended to be merely suggestive, not exhaustive.

Some of the "types" of alternatives that are mentioned in Table 39 need to be defined more clearly. For example, the term "alternative institutional arrangements" means either purchasing the service from private enterprise or producing the service in a government "firm"

[2] The *Task Force Reports* of the Hoover Commission were also drawn upon (see Appendixes A and C through R, *Task Force Reports* on various subjects, prepared for the Commission on Organization of the Executive Branch of the Government, January, 1949, and the *Task Force Reports* prepared for the Second Commission, January–June, 1955).

set up with a stock or industrial fund. These funded governmental businesses, such as the Military Sea Transport Service, are supposed to pay for their materials, charge prices for their products, and keep businesslike records. If they act in this fashion, decisions about such matters as methods of production, price policies, facilities, and scale of output may be made in the light of profits or losses. The aim in putting these activities on a funded basis is to sharpen incentives affecting their conduct, provide better criteria for appraising their performance, and compel customers to take the cost of the product into account instead of getting the product by requisition. Whether or not a funded business achieves these aims depends upon the specific characteristics of the operation and of the rules set up under the fund. But in some situations stock and industrial funds appear to be promising methods of conducting activities. An alternative arrangement that deserves most serious consideration (and is too often ignored) is simply to buy the service from private firms. For example, even some insurance or compensation programs could be contracted for, much as one buys an annuity; eligible recipients would have to be clearly specified, and the contract might have to be renegotiated occasionally, but there would be a powerful incentive to eliminate ineligible recipients and to cut costs. These "alternative institutional arrangements" appear to deserve emphasis, because again and again evidence suggests that a major deterrent to increased efficiency in government is the lack of clear-cut incentives and objectives. Hence changes that might clarify objectives or improve incentives—changes of institutional setups, the variables which determine salaries and promotion, or other aspects of administration—seem fairly promising.

Another term that occurs frequently in the sample worksheet is "work-measurement comparison." In this sort of comparison, work-units (such as cases processed or parcels shipped) are set up, and the performance of different offices or of the same office through time is measured in terms of those work-units. One might also compare work-units performed when different methods, equipment, or organizational arrangements are used. Usually, the objective would not be to maximize the number of work-units, or any ratio like the number of units per manhour. Rather, the aim would be to use these measures in much the same way that business uses ratio analysis—as indicators which signal the observer that something is probably wrong. Businessmen do not ordinarily seek to maximize sales per dollar of selling expense; they would probably not say "the higher this ratio, the better off the firm." Yet such financial ratios may provide valuable tips about where further analysis will be fruitful. Similarly, work-measurement comparisons may yield useful clues; and *sometimes* work-units as such may be suitable criteria in the selection of the "best" policy.

Another term that is used, "alternative programs that achieve the same general objective," suggests something akin to performance budgeting and illustrates the impossibility of drawing a hard-and-fast line between the two general applications of analysis. For, quite apart from performance budgeting, it may well be advisable sometimes to compare the use of different programs to achieve the same general purpose. For example, in addition to comparing alternative methods of carrying out the vocational-education program (different allocations of funds among types of training, or different devices and media like television, motion pictures, cutaway sections, shop models, and so on), one might also compare similar outlays on different programs—apprenticeship vs. vocational education—in terms of the common objective, i.e., greater productivity through increased opportunity to acquire skills.

Finally, for some research programs, the survey suggested that "alternative allocations of effort among research projects" might well be compared. Systematic analysis cannot provide neat solutions to this problem. Judgment must play a major role in deciding upon the extent to which various research proposals are to be supported. Nonetheless, analysis, too, can be brought to bear. A critical examination of plausible criteria for allocating research funds may in itself lead to better decisions. Moreover, in allocating funds for applied research, it may be possible to get some appreciation of both the expected gains from solving certain problems and the chances of solving them with varying levels of expenditure.

Roughly speaking, total non-defense obligations examined in the survey comprise the obligations and applications of funds proposed in the 1954 budget under the following headings:

	Amount	
Agency or Fund	(millions of dollars)	
Funds applied in revolving funds		
Funds Appropriated to the President	13	
Independent Offices	1,640	
Federal Security Agency	5	
General Services Administration	232	
Housing and Home Finance Agency	1,402	
Agriculture	5,361	
Commerce	138	
Defense (Civil Functions)	288	
Interior	53	
Justice	21	
Labor	2	
State		
Treasury	66	9,221
District of Columbia (funds applied from trust)		132
Post Office (funds applied from income)		2,243
Obligations of Departments and Agencies[3] (excluding		
AEC, military functions of Defense Department,		
civil defense, reserve for contingencies)		29,367
Total		40,963

A precise reconciliation with the budget requires a large number of extra adjustments to allow for exceptions and special cases. (For example, the survey omits certain interest payments from one agency to another, includes military medical care, and omits some revolving funds which served no purpose other than bookkeeping.) However, since the aim here is not to set up definitive program categories or to make exact estimates, a precise reconciliation is hardly necessary.

Inclusion of the outlays under most of the revolving funds needs a word of explanation. Our concern is not with the cash budget or with "net" obligations, but rather with any government operation that uses resources and that might be carried out more efficiently. It would not be correct to ignore 80 per cent of postal operations simply because the public pays for them in a special way, e.g., by buying stamps. Activities set apart under a revolving fund should not be ignored simply because the fund is reimbursed by government (or private) purchasers or because the funded activity even makes a profit. Thus the financial statement of the government is partially "deconsolidated." As a result of this deconsolidation, certain amounts are shown twice. If a government agency buys a service from a private firm, the pur-

[3] *Budget of the U.S., 1954,* Table 5, p. A-9.

chase price gets into the budget once; if the agency buys the service from a government "firm" or revolving fund, the amount gets into a "deconsolidated" budget, and into this survey, twice. But this is fitting and proper for purposes of seeking potential economies in government operations, because the government's activities *are* greater if they produce some of their own inputs by means of a funded operation than they would be if the inputs were purchased from private industry.

CONCLUSIONS

Use of Analysis to Compare Program Levels

The survey suggests that perhaps 20 per cent of annual non-defense obligations goes into programs for which present values of tangible gains could be used as indicators of performance. Major programs in this category include certain activities pertaining to resource development, education and training, transportation, and disease and pest control. The survey suggests further that at least an additional 40 per cent of proposed outlays is for programs for which other useful quantitative indicators could be devised. As stated before, the latter would be measures of physical accomplishment translated as far as possible into the achievements that are ultimately of value to us. For example, in programs intended to enforce certain laws or regulations, estimates of the number and type of violations with programs of different sizes, showing their deterrent effects, may be helpful indicators of accomplishment. Or, in programs to give grants and subsidies (such as grants to states for aid to dependent children, payments to retirement and disability funds, compensation to veterans or to the aged), even the average disbursement to ultimate recipients might be a revealing indicator of performance. In activities pertaining to defense, measures of logistic or military capability with programs of different sizes could often be devised.[4] More details and additional programs for which indicators of performance might be developed are shown in the Appendix at the end of this study. With existing legislation and governmental organization, of course, the budget can hardly be presented in terms of those programs. They are intended mainly to suggest future possibilities either in the comparison of particular programs or in the design of budgetary exhibits.

[4] For examples of what can be done in connection with the defense sector of the budget, see Florence N. Trefethen, "A History of Operations Research," in J. F. McCloskey and F. N. Trefethen (eds.), *Operations Research for Management* (Baltimore: The Johns Hopkins Press, 1954), pp. 5–28.

Use of Analysis to Economize Within Programs

Virtually all of the non-defense budget is amenable to analysis for finding cheaper ways to carry out programs. Examination of these activities confirms one's intuitive feeling that there are alternative ways of conducting almost every operation and that some of them appear to merit serious consideration.[4]

Some budgetary sectors appear to be more promising than others. In these sectors, the formal comparison of different methods of carrying out tasks seems especially likely to help officials to effect significant economies. This judgment is based partly on the amount of money involved in these operations, partly on the evidence, small as it may be, that efficiency could be increased in conducting them. A few examples of promising comparisons that might be made in each of these broad sectors are summarized below. (In a number of instances, some study and experimentation along the lines indicated are being carried out at present.)

Natural Resources Sector

Obligations proposed for this sector in the 1954 budget amounted to almost two billion dollars. Examples of promising analyses include comparisons of:

1. Alternative possibilities of measuring performance (e.g., benefits minus costs) to provide a better basis for hiring, firing, promoting, commending, censuring, and paying the management of individual power, irrigation, timber, and park enterprises.

2. The use of present equipment vs. the use of more and different equipment in forest-fire control, forest management, soil and moisture conservation, range management, irrigation, and so on. Budgetary procedures may normally be biased against the authorization of capital items that would cut costs.

3. Individual water-resource projects and individual (regional) soil conservation programs (i.e., improved cost-benefit analysis, the topic to which much of the present study has been devoted). This includes the comparison of alternative combinations of upland moisture-retention measures, upstream reservoirs, and downstream multi-purpose dams for particular watersheds.

4. Costs and gains under alternative means of administration which might eliminate duplication by different agencies in lease management, soil conservation, and land management.

5. The costs and effects of alternative sets of charges for and constraints on the use of mineral and range lands.

6. The effects of alternative sets of power fees, including charges that would reflect incremental costs more accurately.

7. Alternative construction programs that might accomplish the same task if power and transmission facilities were better integrated with private facilities, perhaps through more buying and selling among governmental producers, governmental users, and private producers.

8. The effects of increments in fire-control outlays vs. increments in fire-suppression outlays.

9. Total outlays on the soil conservation program with present administration vs. total outlays with additional expenditures for tighter administration.

10. The operation of various natural resource enterprises by government vs. lease or sale to, and operation by, private concessionaires or owners.

Post Office Department

The 1954 budget for this program amounted to nearly three billion dollars. The examples of analysis that might well be fruitful are comparisons of:

1. Alternative measures of performance (e.g., profits, losses) to provide a better basis for hiring, promoting, and making incentive payments to postmasters. Initially, the hope might be to point up the problem of incentives to bolster the usual recommendations that postmasters be "non-political" appointments. If the postal service were operated by private enterprise—even a big semi-bureaucratic utility firm—management would probably devise (far from perfect) measures of performance and sharpen incentives. Government could surely do something about this also.

2. Alternative combinations of truck, rail, bus, and air transport of the mails.

3. The cost of procuring truck repairs and supplies locally from private enterprise vs. the cost of procurement from central government depots.

4. Ownership of trucks vs. ownership of lighter vehicles vs. lease of vehicles.

5. Outlays for fast service vs. other uses of the resources.

6. The costs of alternative means of dispensing stamps and postal

notes—window service vs. increased use of stamp-vending and note-vending machines.

7. Maintenance of the postal savings system vs. other uses of the resources. Estimates of the cost and benefit reduction due to discontinuance or simplification of the postal savings system might point persuasively to better policies.

8. The provision of current parcel-post services vs. other uses of the resources. One might estimate the cost and benefit reduction due to a restriction of parcel-post service.

9. The cost of operation of parcel-post service by government vs. sale to, and operation by, a "public utility" company.

10. The effects of alternative sets of charges, including ones that reflect incremental costs more accurately. A subsidy to those particular firms and individuals who make heavy use of the mails has little to commend it.

Roads and Highways

Federal outlays have run about 600 million dollars per year, and the total including state and local expenditures has come to approximately 5 billion dollars. The President's highway message in February, 1955, favored a program which would involve total outlays of 101 billion dollars over a 10-year period, though the program adopted was a more modest one. Useful analysis in this connection might compare:

1. Additional purchases of highways, air-transport facilities, and sea-river-harbor navigation aids.

2. Additional construction of freeways in metropolitan areas vs. interstate highways vs. intrastate roads. Specific proposals would have to be examined.

3. Extra highways in one region vs. addition to the networks in other regions.

4. Additional routes vs. extra-lane superhighways.

5. The cost of highway construction by government construction crews vs. that of highway construction by private contractors.

6. The costs of using alternative materials, equipment, and methods in highway construction to meet certain specifications. (A good deal of research has already been done on this and numerous other subjects mentioned here.)

7. The quantitative effects of alternative sets of gasoline taxes, vehicle taxes, and tolls that would reflect costs more accurately, helping to adjust economically the rate of growth of automobile usage.

Health Services

The amount involved here is roughly one and a half billion dollars annually. The employment of analytical aids might include comparisons of:

1. The present value of identical increments (or decrements) in various component activities. The present value of outlays on preventive medicine, research, control of communicable disease, and training might be measured in terms of estimated savings of future costs for hospitalization and treatment plus the value of future manhours that would be saved.

2. The present arrangements vs. operation of parts of the hospital system as a funded enterprise. Under the second arrangement, users would have an incentive to buy hospital space wherever it was cheapest (e.g., from the Army, Navy, Veterans' Administration, private hospitals, public health service), and the hospitals would have an incentive to sell available space (within whatever constraints were set up concerning eligibles). Duplicate construction could perhaps be reduced, and the allocation of doctors and specialists improved, if the system of facilities were operated as if it were a business.

3. Work-measurement systems that might be used to select better methods in hospitals, administration, and auxiliary services. Work-units should be selected carefully, and the measure of overall performance might be something like profits, with appropriate rules for pricing and costing so as to discourage rather than encourage the "length of stay" in government hospitals (abnormally high in comparison with that in private hospitals).

4. The effects of alternative definitions of eligibles, with special reference to non-service-connected disabilities and to dependents of servicemen.

For particular activities, persons who have worked in government or have become familiar with detailed operations could point out many additional possibilities. But this scanning of the *whole* non-defense budget gives a broad picture of the potential role of analytical aids to governmental economy. What evidence there is suggests that the sort of analysis discussed and illustrated in this study *is* capable of helping government achieve significant economies.

APPENDIX ON POSSIBLE CLASSIFICATIONS OF EXPENDITURES BY PROGRAMS, AND INDICATORS OF PERFORMANCE[1]

A Possible Breakdown by Programs[2]	Amount in 1954 Budget (millions)[3]	Useful Indicator of Performance May Be Feasible[4]
I. Development of Natural Resources		
A. Tennessee Valley Authority		
Construction: Hydroelectric Dams	10	X[5]
Construction: Steam Plants	214	X
Construction: Transmission Facilities	53	X
Operations: Power	85	X
Operations: Multi-purpose Reservoirs	3	X
Administration: Construction of Power Facilities	2	
Administration: Operations (Power and Reservoirs)	1	
Plant Protection and Services to Visitors	1	
Construction: Navigation Facilities	1	X
Construction: Chemical Facilities	2	X
Operations: Chemicals (Munitions, Fertilizers)	16	X
Research: Chemicals (Products, Processes)	1	
Demonstrations: Use of Fertilizers	1	X
Administration: Chemicals Program	1	
Development, Management of Tennessee Valley Forests	1	X
Development, Management of Tributary Watersheds	1	X
Acquisition of General Facilities	1	X
General Services (Reimbursable)	12	

[1] The budget for the military services, Atomic Energy Commission, and Civil Defense Administration are excluded, since measurement of performance or analysis of operations would involve classified information. However, the former Mutual Security Administration, which poses similar problems of measurement, is included with certain other programs pertaining to international security and foreign relations.

[2] The aim was to select program categories that would be more useful in performance budgeting than are the existing categories; however, for several sectors of the budget, the breakdowns (or some of the programs) are those already shown in the presentation of "obligations by activities" or "funds applied."

[3] These amounts are the sums of the items that were assigned to these programs from various departments or agencies and various appropriations within departments. Reconciliation with totals shown in the budget is difficult because in some cases the amounts for 1953 had to be used, and intra-government outlays were often included here but not in the budget totals. The estimates are exceedingly rough. Administration and overhead have not been allocated with any precision, and a correct allocation would depend upon the precise problem of choice that was under consideration.

[4] This could mean the performance achieved with the full program, though usually it should refer to the performance that could be achieved with a relatively small increment, or that would be sacrificed with a relatively small decrement, in the program.

[5] An "X" means that "present value sacrificed if the program were cut" is suggested as a possible indicator of performance at the margin. A footnote means that some other measure of performance is suggested and indicates the nature of that other measure.

A Possible Breakdown by Programs[2]	Amount in 1954 Budget (millions)[3]	Useful Indicator of Performance May Be Feasible[4]
I. Development of Natural Resources (*continued*)		
B. Missouri River Basin		
Construction: Missouri River Basin	64[6]	X
Advance Planning and Preparation	9	X
Operation and Maintenance	4	X
C. Other Multiple Purpose Projects,[7] Including Power		
Advance Planning (Army Civil Functions)	4	X
Construction (Army Civil Functions)	327[8]	X
Operation and Maintenance	9	X
D. Flood Control		
Research: Flood Control Studies (Army Civil Functions)[9]	2	
Construction: Local Flood Protection (e.g. levees)	60	X
Construction: Reservoirs for Flood Control (Army CF)	56	X
Operation: Reservoirs for Flood Control (Army CF)	3	X
Operation: Other Flood-Control Measures (Army CF)	1	X
Operation: Emergency Repair, Rescue, Flood Control (Army CF)	14	X
Construction: Mississippi River Flood Control (Army CF)	31	X
Maintenance: Mississippi River Flood Control (Army CF)	13	X
Construction: Mississippi Tributaries Flood Control (Army CF)	17	X
Maintenance: Mississippi Tributaries Flood Control (Army CF)	2	X
Construction: Flood-Prevention Measures (Agriculture)[10]	14	X
Analysis of Flood-Prevention Projects	1	
E. Forest and Land Management		
Soil and Moisture Conservation (Interior and Agriculture; includes soil-building)	325[11]	X
Research: Soil and Moisture Conservation	1	
Development, Management of National Forests	50	X
Forest-Fire Control	34	X
Forest-Pest Control	7	X
Research: Forestry	6	
Development, Management of Grazing Lands	6	X

[6] Program should be broken down at least into types of projects—i.e., such types as power, flood-control, and multi-purpose.

[7] Many of the projects listed under Irrigation are also multiple purpose, but they serve for the present to suggest the magnitude of our efforts in irrigation.

[8] Breakdown by projects is readily available, but our major concern here is with programs rather than with hundreds of individual projects.

[9] Hereafter labeled "Army CF."

[10] These are measures that are primarily for flood prevention, such as the construction of upstream reservoirs. Other measures in Agriculture also affect flood prevention but are primarily for soil conservation, management of the range, or management of the forests.

[11] Breakdown, and comparisons of performance, by regions would probably be helpful.

A Possible Breakdown by Programs[2]	Amount in 1954 Budget (millions)[3]	Useful Indicator of Performance May Be Feasible[4]
I. Development of Natural Resources (*continued*)		
E. Forest and Land Management (*continued*)		
Management of Leases and Disposal	5	X
Weed Control (Halogeton)	1	X
Boundary Survey	1	
Administration: Land Management	1	
Development of Indian Territory: Roads, Trails	8	X
Topographic Surveys and Mapping	15	
Minerals-Resource Surveys and Mapping	7	
Administration: Geological Survey	1	
Expansion of Park Facilities	18	X
Management of Parks	20	X
Administration: National Parks	1	
Emergency Operations, Drought (Bureau of Reclamation)	1	
F. Irrigation[12] and Water Supply		
Construction (chiefly Reclamation)	132[13]	X
Rebuilding and Betterment, Existing Facilities (Reclamation)	4	X
Operation and Maintenance (Reclamation)	21	X
Operation and Maintenance (Indians)	3	X
Analysis of Projects (Reclamation)	3	X
G. Power (other than TVA, Missouri Basin, multi-purpose)		
Construction: Transmission Facilities, S.E.	7	X
Operation: Purchase, Scheduling, Marketing, S.E.	1	X
Administration: S.E. Power Administration	14	
Construction: Transmission Facilities, S.W.	2	X
Operation: Purchase, Scheduling, Marketing, S.W.	7	X
Administration: S.W. Power Administration	1	
Construction: Transmission Facilities, Bonneville	55	X
Maintenance of Facilities, Bonneville	3	X
Operation: Production Scheduling, Marketing, Bonneville	3	X
Administration: Bonneville Power Administration	1	
Operation: Power Installations in Indian Territory	2	X
Research: Niagara Power Development	1	
H. Navigation[15]		
Construction: Channels and Harbors (Army)	26	X
Operation and Maintenance: Channels and Harbors	46	X

[12] These projects are often multi-purpose, but many are primarily for irrigation purposes, and they serve to indicate the magnitude of our irrigation program.

[13] Further breakdown by projects is readily available, but our main concern here is with programs rather than individual projects.

[14] Less than $500,000.

[15] Other navigation aids in section on transportation; projects included here are closely related to other work on development of natural resources.

A Possible Breakdown by Programs[2]	Amount in 1954 Budget (millions)[3]	Useful Indicator of Performance May Be Feasible[4]
I. Development of Natural Resources (*continued*)		
H. Navigation (*continued*)		
Construction: Locks and Dams (Army)	14	X
Operation and Maintenance: Locks and Dams	22	X
Emergency Removal of Obstacles (Army)	1	
Research: Navigation Studies (Army)	1	
I. Conservation of Fish and Wildlife		
Administration of Fish and Game Laws	2	[16]
Propagation, Distribution of Food Fishes	6	X
Mammal and Bird Reservations	18	[16]
Control of Predatory Animals	1	[16]
Construction, Fish and Wildlife Facilities	5	[16]
Research; Fish and Fishery Resources	4	
Research; Birds and Mammals	[17]	
Administration, Departmental and Regional	1	
Administration, Pribilof Islands	2	
J. General Administration and Research		
Research: Regional and Basin Studies	4	
Research: Basic Data and Techniques (e.g., Hydrology, Utilization of Saline Water)	9	
Administration: Unallocable at Present (Army Engineers and Bur. Reclamation)	17	
II. Transportation and Communications		
A. Maritime Activities[18]		
Ship Construction	119	[19]
Operating Subsidies to U.S. Ship Operators	25	[19]
Expenses of Mothballed Fleet of Merchant Vessels	9	[19]
Maintenance of Shipyards and Terminals	1	[19]
Maritime Training	5	[19]
Administration: Maritime Programs	9	[19]
Operation of Reserve Vessels (Revolving Fund)	62	X
Deactivation of Vessels	2	[19]
Administration: Vessels Operations	2	
Sea Navigation Aids	102	X
Search, Rescue, and Law Enforcement	108	[20]
Coast Guard, Port Security	40	

[16] Effect of cut in program on specified fish and game populations.

[17] Less than $500,000.

[18] These programs are closely related to Defense, and relevant analyses of their value would have to use classified information.

[19] Impairment of logistic capability if program cut.

[20] Change in number of rescues, reported violations if program cut.

A Possible Breakdown by Programs[2]	Amount in 1954 Budget (millions)[3]	Useful Indicator of Performance May Be Feasible[4]
II. Transportation and Communications (*continued*)		
B. Post Office Activities[21]		
Parcel Post (and other types of service)	21	24
Mail Handling and Window Service	921	
Collection and Delivery	519	
Local Transportation	92	
Rural Delivery	194	
Mail Handling in Transit	184	
Administration and Services	331	
Water Transportation	19	
Truck Transportation	62	
Rail Transportation	401	
Air Transportation	142	
Terminal and Transportation Charges by Foreign Countries	11	
C. Other Transportation and Communications		
Roads and Highways	671	X
River—Harbor Navigation Aids[22]		
Air Navigation Aids and Facilities	140	X
Washington, D.C., Airports	3	X
Regulation of Air Transportation	29	
Regulation of Interstate Commerce—ICC	12	
Regulation of Communications—FCC	8	
III. Health and Medical Care		
A. Items Unallocated Among Programs[23]		
Medical Care, Maintenance and Operations, Army	198	
Medical Care, Maintenance and Operations, Navy	91	
Medical Care, Maintenance and Operations, Air Force	87	

[21] The budget probably ought to be presented in terms of the incremental costs attributable to such services as parcel post (holding the other services constant) plus other outlays that would be unallocable in this process. However, these data were not developed for this study, and the present budget categories were used here as the "programs."

[22] This item is included in the natural-resources budget because of its close relationship to other work of the Army Engineers in the development of natural resources.

[23] Distribution of these amounts, and of the outlays by the services for construction of medical facilities, among the indicated programs was not attempted for present illustrative purposes.

[24] Physical accomplishment, or possibly present value, sacrificed if programs cut.

A Possible Breakdown by Programs[2]	Amount in 1954 Budget (millions)[3]	Useful Indicator of Performance May Be Feasible[4]
III. Health and Medical Care (*continued*)		
B. Construction of Hospitals		
Hospital-bed-producing Projects	157	X[28]
Rehabilitation and Modernization	13	X
Alterations and Repairs	9	
C. Operation of Hospitals		
Neuropsychiatric Hospitals (Veterans' Administration)	166	X
Tuberculosis Hospitals (V.A.)	47	X
General Hospitals: Beds for Service-Connected Disabilities	167[25]	X
General Hospitals: Beds for Non-Service-Connected Disabilities	166[25]	X
Reimbursement to Non-V.A. Hospitals	21	X
Hospitals (and other Medical Outlays), Indians	22[26]	X
Other Hospitals (Public Health Service, Freedmen's, St. Elizabeth's)	49	X
Veterans Homes (including Reimbursement of State Homes)	26	
Administration: Hospitals	27	
D. Outpatient Services		
Outpatient Services, V.A.	105	X
Outpatient Services, Public Health Service	5	X
E. Control of Communicable Disease		
Venereal Disease (Grants and Technical Aid to States)	8	X
Tuberculosis (Grants and Technical Aid to States)	6	X
Other Special Diseases	1	X
F. Treatment of Special Groups		
Health—Maternal and Children's	15	X
Payments to Hawaii (Leprosy)	1	X
Rehabilitation of Disabled Veterans	62	X
Rehabilitation of Other Disabled (Care, Training, Tools): Grants to States	10	X
Rehabilitation of Other Disabled (Counsel, Placement, Administration)	14	X

[25] Allocation may be impossible; it is intended here merely as a device to suggest orders of magnitude.

[26] This item includes amounts (probably small) for preventive medicine, research, and outpatient services.

[27] Included in General Administration.

[28] These measures of performance in medical-care programs would be present value of the loss of manhours, the increase in future operating costs, or the increase in future outlays for medical care that would be incurred if the programs were cut. Naturally, these estimates of present value would not reflect *all* the accomplishments of these activities.

A Possible Breakdown by Programs[2]	Amount in 1954 Budget (millions)[3]	Useful Indicator of Performance May Be Feasible[4]
III. Health and Medical Care (*continued*)		
G. Policies Affecting Outlays for Future Medical Care		
Preventive Medicine and Measures	39	X
Medical Research	57	X
Medical Training	11	X
Construction: Medical Research Facilities	17	
Administration: Research and Training	3	
Food and Drug Administration	7	
H. General Administration (Unallocated)		
Medical Administration, V.A.	9	
Supply Operations, V.A.	11[29]	
General Administration: Public Health Service	4	
IV. Housing and Community Development		
A. General Administration and Research		
Housing Research	1	
Agency-Wide Coordination and Supervision	1	
Administration: Other Programs	1	
B. FNMA (Revolving Fund: Funds Applied)		
Purchase of FHA and VA Mortgages	719	
Administration: FNMA	5	
Fees for Servicing Mortgages, FNMA	14	
C. Special Housing Loan Programs		
Mortgage Loans, Alaska Housing	8	
Loans to Educational Institutions	40	
Loans for Prefabricated Housing	19	
Administration: Housing Loan Programs	1	
Loans to Public Agencies: RFC	35	
D. Slum Clearance and Urban Development		
Advance Planning Loans	6	X
Temporary Loans (Acquisition, Clearance of Land)	20	X
Capital Grants to Local Public Agencies	20	X
Administration: Slum Clearance	2	
Community Development—Territories (Alaska, Virgin Islands)	16	X[30]
E. Home Loan Bank Board and FSLA		
Administration: Home Loan Bank Board	1	
Examination of Savings and Loan Ass'ns	2	
Expenses: Federal Savings and Loan Insurance Corp.	1	

[29] Also contains whatever the Veterans' Administration proposed to spend on medical research and training.

[30] The present value of such development programs could reflect saleable values created, but could not reflect all of the accomplishments which are aimed at in these programs.

A Possible Breakdown by Programs[2]	Amount in 1954 Budget (millions)[3]	Useful Indicator of Performance May Be Feasible[4]
IV. Housing and Community Development (*continued*)		
F. War Housing		
Acquisition of Mortgages, Real Properties and Stock—		
War Housing	143	
Disposition of War Housing	2	
Operating Expense—War Housing Programs	35	
Administration: War Housing Programs	5	
G. Other Insurance Programs		
Acquisition of Mortgages and Real Property	23	
Operating Expense	26	
Administration	6	
Mortgagors' Share Mutual Insurance Earnings	8	
H. Low-Rent Housing		
Loans to Local Authorities for Low-Rent Housing	258[31]	X[33]
Annual Subsidy for Low-Rent Housing	40	
Operating Expense (Including Inspections) Low-Rent		
Housing	3	
Administration: Low-Rent Housing	11	
I. Miscellaneous		
Homes Conversion Program		
Subsistence Homesteads, Greentowns		
Acquisition of Real Property—Vets' Re-use	32	
Operating Expenses—Vets' Re-use	1	
Administration—Vets' Re-use	32	
V. Subsidies to Special Groups		
A. Disabled or Retired Veterans and Survivors		
Compensation for Total Disability ⎫		34
Compensation for "Serious" Disability ⎪		34
Compensation for "Slight" Disability ⎪		34
Pensions to Veterans Over 65 ⎬	2499	34
Pensions to Other Veterans ⎪		34
Pensions to Remarried Wives ⎪		34
Pensions to Other Dependents ⎭		34
Administration: Compensation, Pensions	37	35

[31] Further breakdown, perhaps by regions, would be desirable.

[32] Less than half a million dollars.

[33] See footnote 30.

[34] Number and percentage of total claims that would be certified with and without cut in program (assumed cuts show in some cases how performance might change if legislation were altered). Also average payment to each type of recipient might be a helpful exhibit.

[35] Savings (or losses) if administration were tightened (or cut).

A Possible Breakdown by Programs[2]	Amount in 1954 Budget (millions)[3]	Useful Indicator of Performance May Be Feasible[4]
V. Subsidies to Special Groups (*continued*)		
B. Veterans Who Seek Education, Training		
Education: Institutions of Higher Learning ⎫		X
Education and Training: Other ⎭	810	X
Administration: Education and Training	45	
C. Veterans Who Buy Homes		
Loan Guaranty: Interest Gratuities, Losses	61	
Loan Guaranty: Loans and Property Acquired	14	
Administration: Loan Guaranty	13	
D. Veterans Who Are Unemployed		
Unemployment Compensation to Veterans	47	
E. Veterans Who Hold Military Insurance		
National Service and Other Military Insurance	51	
Administration: Insurance	29	
F. Miscellaneous Veterans' Assistance		
Indemnities and Allowances for Deaths	30	
Grants to Republic of Philippines	3	
Canteen Service (Revolving Fund)	25	
Miscellaneous Benefits to Disabled Veterans	7	
G. Payments for Benefit of Farm Groups		[36]
Support of Wheat	424	
Support of Corn	176	
Support of Cotton and Cottonseed Products	50	
Support of Wool	24	
Support of Grain Sorghum	17	
Support of Rosin	6	
Support of Oats	3	
Support of Peanuts	2	
Support of Tobacco	2	
Support of Milk (non-dry fat)	5	
Support of Mohair	3	
Holding Down Barley	−1	
Holding Down Beans (dry, edible)	−6	
Holding Down Eggs	−1	
Holding Down Flaxseed	−2	
Holding Down Linseed Oil	−4	
Holding Down Olive Oil	−1	
Holding Down Seeds	−12	
Holding Down Other Commodities	−6	
Removal of Depreciation Allowances Included Above	−7	
Purchase for Foreign Domestic Resale	66	
Storage Facilities Program	3	
School Lunch Program	83	
Restriction of Output (Allotments, Quotas)	6	
H. Payments for Benefit of Other Producers		
Subsidy to Sugar Producers	65	
Import Regulation for Benefit of Various Producers	50	

[36] It would be difficult to devise suitable measures of performance for price-support programs, the aims of which are highly complex. (Perhaps the volume of each commodity moving into or out of storage would be helpful.) This does not mean, of course, that analysis holds no promise here. Tracing out certain consequences of price supports is feasible and extremely useful.

A Possible Breakdown by Programs[2]	Amount in 1954 Budget (millions)[3]	Useful Indicator of Performance May Be Feasible[4]
VI. Social Security (Payments to Aged and Distressed Persons *in General*)		
A. Old Age and Survivors' Insurance		
Federal Old-Age Benefits ⎫		[37]
Federal Survivors' Benefits ⎰	4298	[37]
Processing Initial Claims	30	[38]
Monthly Recertification of Awards	9	
General Administration, OASI	25	
Construction: OASI	2	
State Old-Age Assistance—Federal Grants	875	[37]
Administration: State Old-Age Assistance	43	[38]
B. Unemployment Relief		
Unemployment Compensation—Federal Grants	218	[39]
Work Relief and Direct Federal Relief		
Relief and Welfare Services, Indians	4	
C. Miscellaneous Grants to States		
State Aid to Dependent Children	294	[39]
Administration: State Aid to Dependent Children	25	[40]
State Aid to Blind	33	[39]
Administration: State Aid to Blind	2	[40]
State Aid to Disabled	71	[39]
Administration: State Aid to Disabled	8	[40]
State Services to Crippled Children	12	[39]
State Services for Child Welfare	7	[39]
Administration: Federal Grants	2	
D. Management of Retirement, Disability Insurance		
Payment to RR Retirement Account	695	[41]
Processing Initial Claims	4	[42]
Monthly Recertification of Awards	1	[42]
General Administration: Railroad Fund	1	
Annuities Panama Canal and Lighthouse Employees	3	[41]
Payment to Civil Service—Retirement and Disability Fund	427	[41]
Administration: Retirement and Annuities	1	
VII. Services to, and Development of, Special Sectors		
A. Agricultural Research and Analysis		
Marketing Methods and Costs	1	
Improvement of Product Quality	1	
Improvement of Marketing Organization	2	

[37] Average payment to final recipients with the program and perhaps with changes in the provisions of the law.

[38] Savings (or losses) in payments if Administration and Processing were tightened (or cut).

[39] Average payment, average cost per claim, in various states.

[40] Percentage of claims certified in various states, perhaps with varying amount spent on Administration.

[41] Types of coverage, average payment under the plan.

[42] Number and percentage of claims certified (or recertified) with different amounts devoted to Administration.

A Possible Breakdown by Programs[2]	Amount in 1954 Budget (millions)[3]	Useful Indicator of Performance May Be Feasible[4]
VII. Services to, and Development of, Special Sectors (*continued*)		
A. Agricultural Research and Analysis (*continued*)		
Collection, Dissemination of Market Data	2	
Analysis of Agricultural Techniques, Problems	1	
Data on Farm Prices, Incomes, Population	1	
Crop and Livestock Estimates	3	
Administration and Executive Direction: Agricultural Research	43	
Research at Agricultural Experiment Stations	14	
Research on Strategic and Critical Agricultural Materials	43	
Consumers' Research, with Special Emphasis on Farm Living and Agricultural Products	2	
Research on Animal Husbandry	2	
Research on Animal Diseases, Parasites	2	
Research on Dairy Cattle Management	1	
Research on Uses of Cereal and Forage Crops	1	
Research on Uses of Fruits and Vegetables	2	
Research on Uses of Dairy Products	43	
Research on Uses of Oilseed	1	
Research on Uses of Cotton and Fibers	1	
Research on Uses of Sugar and Special Plants	1	
Research on Uses of Animal Products	1	
Research on Uses of Agricultural Residues	43	
Research on Field Crops	4	
Research on Horticultural Crops	3	
Research on Use of Fertilizers, Soils, Irrigation	3	
Research on Use of Agricultural Equipment	1	
Research on Insects and Pest Control	4	
B. Control of Disease and Pests in Agriculture		
Import-Export Inspection and Quarantine	1	
Supervision over Interstate Movement of Livestock	1	
Control of Tuberculosis, Brucellosis	6	X
Control of Other Animal Disease	1	X
Control of Foot-and-Mouth and Other Highly Contagious Diseases		X
Control of Insects and Plant Disease[44] (Breakdown Shown in Budget)	6	X
Plant Quarantines	3	X
Emergency Control of Insects, Plant Disease	1	
C. Marketing Services for Agriculture		
Meat Inspection	14	
Product Grading and Standardization	6	
Licensing and Regulation of Market Practices	2	
Market News and Other Service	4	
Commodity Exchange Supervision	1	

[43] Less than $500,000.
[44] Other than insects or disease relevant to forest management.

A Possible Breakdown by Programs[2]	Amount in 1954 Budget (millions)[3]	Useful Indicator of Performance May Be Feasible[4]
VII. Services to, and Development of, Special Sectors (*continued*)		
D. General Development and Disaster Relief in Agriculture		
Crop Insurance Indemnities	23	
Crop Insurance Administration	8	
Net Loans for Rural Electrification	135	X
Net Loans for Rural Telephone Program	65	X
Administration: Rural Electrification	6	
Administration: Rural Telephone Program	3	
Loans for Farm Ownership Development	38	
Loans for Production and Subsistence	120	
Loans for Development of Water Facilities	7	X
Administration: Above Loan Programs	29	
Grants, Farmers' Home Administration	45	
Supervision of Farm Credit Banks	2	
Promotion of Farmers' Cooperatives	45	
Extension of Efficient Methods, Payments to States and Territories	32	X
Administration: Extension Service	1	
General Administration, Agriculture	5	
National Arboretum	45	
International Agricultural Trade Relations	45	
Coordination of Agricultural Publications and Information Services	1	
Library and Branches	1	
Disaster Loans (Revolving Fund)	35	
Administration: Disaster Loans	2	
Liquidation of Land Bank Loans	1	
Crop, Livestock, Commodity Loans and Discounts	2498	X
Interest on Borrowed Funds, Federal Intermediate Credit Banks	20	
Administration: Federal Intermediate Credit Banks	2	
E. General Development of Commerce and Industry		
Copyright Office	1	
Patent Office	12	46
Analyses of National Economic Trends	1	
Information to Promote Industry, Trade	5	
Field Offices to Promote Industry, Trade	2	
Anti-monopoly Analyses, Litigation	7	
Anti-deceptive Practices in Commerce	2	
Administration (Incl. Executive Direction) FTC	1	
Administration (Incl. Executive Direction) Commerce	2	
General Weather Services	25	X
Weather Research	1	
Administration: Weather Bureau	2	
Testing Products, Special Research	57	
Regulation of New Security Offerings	1	

[45] Less than $500,000.
[46] Applications processed per year if program cut (or expanded).

A Possible Breakdown by Programs[2]	Amount in 1954 Budget (millions)[3]	Useful Indicator of Performance May Be Feasible[4]
VII. Services to, and Development of, Special Sectors (*continued*)		
E. General Development of Commerce and Industry (*continued*)		
Prevention of Fraud in Securities Transactions	2	
Regulation of Securities Markets and Public Utility Holding Companies	1	
Assistance to Courts in Reorganization	47	
Administration and Central Services: SEC	1	
Administration: RFC	10	
Loans to Business Enterprises: RFC	101	
Acquisition of Assets, Rubber Program	30	
Expenses, Rubber Program	278	
Acquisition of Assets, Tin Program	1	
Expenses, Tin Program	139	
Acquisition of Assets, Fiber Program	2	
Expenses, Fiber Program	7	
Expenses, Liquidation Program	2	
F. General Research and Education		
Vocational Education (Breakdown by Vocations or Regions)	22	X
Apprenticeship Programs	3	X
Assistance to School Districts Overburdened with Federal Activities (Regional Breakdown)	70	X
School Construction in Areas Overburdened with Federal Activities		
Administration: Assistance to Schools Overburdened with Federal Activities	1	
Services to State, Local School Systems	1	
Other Educational Services	1	
Educational Aid to the Blind	1	X
Educational Aid to the Deaf	47	X
Educational Aid: Howard University	5	X
Educational Aid: Indians	27	X
Library of Congress	7	
Smithsonian Institution	4	
National Gallery of Art	1	
Formulation, Servicing of Research Policy	2	
Support of Basic Research Projects	9	
Training of Scientific Personnel	5	X
Current Census Statistics	6	
Census of Agriculture	2	
Census of Business	10	
Census of Transportation	2	
Census of Manufactures	2	
Census of Mineral Industries	1	
Electronic Computing System	1	
Administration: Bureau of Census	1	
Administration and Physical Plant: National Bureau of Standards	1	

[47] Less than $500,000.

A Possible Breakdown by Programs[2]	Amount in 1954 Budget (millions)[3]	Useful Indicator of Performance May Be Feasible[4]
VII. Services to, and Development of, Special Sectors (*continued*)		
F. General Research and Education (*continued*)		
Research, National Bureau of Standards	2	
Development, National Bureau of Standards	2	
Other Scientific Services	2	
Construction of Radio Laboratory	1	
G. General Development of Labor Productivity		
Mediation, Conciliation in Labor Disputes	5	
Investigation of Charges of Unfair Labor Practices	6	
Trial Examiner Hearings and Board Adjudications	2	
Securing of Compliance with Board Orders	2	
Adjustment of Grievances, Rail Employees	1	
Mine Health and Safety	6	X
Importation of Mexican Farm Labor	2	X
Welfare of Women Workers	48	
Wage and Hour Regulations: Administration	1	
Wage and Hour Regulations: Enforcement	7	49
Labor Standards Regulation: Enforcement	1	49
Labor Standards Regulation: Development	1	
Administration: Department of Labor	2	
Data: Manpower and Employment	2	
Data: Prices and Cost of Living	1	
Data: Wages and Related Data	1	
Other Data and Analysis	1	
Administration and Central Services: Bureau of Labor Statistics	1	
VIII. General Government		
A. Legislative Functions		
Senate	12	
Professional and Clerical Assistance to Senate Committees	2	
House of Representatives	24	
Professional and Clerical Assistance to House Committees	2	
Construction (Architect of the Capitol)	9	
Legislative Reference Service	1	
B. Judicial Functions		
Supreme Court	1	
Lower Courts and Other Judicial Services	24	
Special Courts (Claims, Customs, Patents Appeal)	2	
Tax Court	1	

[48] Less than $500,000.
[49] Number and type of violations if program cut.

A Possible Breakdown by Programs[2]	Amount in 1954 Budget (millions)[3]	Useful Indicator of Performance May Be Feasible[4]
VIII. General Government (*continued*)		
C. Executive Functions		
White House Office (Including the President)	2	
Economy in Government—Budget Bureau	2	
Other Budget Bureau Functions	2	
Advisory Councils (Stability, National Security)	2	
Disaster Relief and Emergency Fund	27	
White House Police and Secret Service	1	
D. Management of Receipts, Debt, Disbursements		
Economy in Government: Gen'l Accounting Office	3	
Audit of Federal Transportation Payments	7	[51]
Audit of Other Payments	16	[51]
Settlement of Claims	4	
Administration and Counsel, General Accounting Office	2	
Investigation and Audit of Tax Returns	138	[51]
Processing Returns, Remittances, etc.	67	
Collection of Delinquent Tax Accounts	26	[51]
Taxpayer Conferences and Appeals	14	
Interpretation and Ruling Services	6	
Regulation and Controls (e.g., Beverage Laws)	20	[51]
Statistical Reporting	2	
Executive Direction, Bureau of Internal Revenue	[50]	
Processing of Checks, Deposits, Withheld Taxes	5	
General Banking and Reporting Services	18	
Disbursements (Processing Payments)	12	
Retirement of Currency	1	
Savings Bonds: Issue, Service, Retirement	41	[52]
Savings Bonds: Promotion	5	[53]
Other Securities: Issue, Service, Retirement	7	[52]
Debt Accounts: Maintenance and Audit	1	
Executive Direction: Debt Management	1	
Coinage and Care of Monetary Metals	5	
Engraving and Printing: Currency	15	
Engraving and Printing: Federal Reserve Notes	8	
Engraving and Printing: Securities	3	
E. Other Central Services		
Government Printing Office	84	
Civil Service Commission	19	

[50] Less than $500,000.
[51] Receipts sacrificed if program cut.
[52] Average volume outstanding during the year.
[53] Estimated volume outstanding if program cut.

A Possible Breakdown by Programs[2]	Amount in 1954 Budget (millions)[3]	Useful Indicator of Performance May Be Feasible[4]
VIII. General Government (*continued*)		
E. Other Central Services (*continued*)		
Surplus Property Disposal	1	
Buildings Management	183	
Real Property Acquisition and Assignment	5	
Repairs and Improvement (outside Washington, D.C.)	26	
Other Construction	18	
Construction and Blueprinting Services	5	
Supply Operations	250	
National Archives and Record Service	6	
Administration, General Service Administration	5	
Legal Activities (Taxes, Claims, etc.)	10	
Engraving and Printing: Other	10	
F. Crime Control		
Probation System	2	
Federal Prison System, Custody	11	
Federal Prison System, Care and Treatment	15	
Support of Federal Prisoners in Non-Federal and Alaskan Prisons	3	
Federal Prison System Administration	1	
F.B.I. Criminal Investigations F.B.I. Security Investigations	68	
F.B.I. Central Services and Administration	12	
U.S. Attorneys and Marshals	14	
Control of Narcotics	3	56
Control of Counterfeiting and Forgery	3	57
G. General Administration		
Federal Security Agency	4	
Agriculture	5	
Commerce	2	
Interior	3	
Justice	3	
Labor	2	
Treasury	3	
H. Other General Government		
American Battle Monuments Commission	10	
National Capital Park and Planning Commission	1	
Subversive Activities Control	54	
Canal Zone Government	17[55]	

[54] Less than $500,000 for the Control Board; amount should include part of F.B.I. costs and the expenditures of the Congressional Committees concerned with this problem.

[55] These items can be broken down into various public works and governmental functions; in some cases performance could be measured fairly well, and in most cases analysis of alternative activities or methods might suggest economies.

[56] Value of manhours, medical care, etc. that would be lost (gained) if program were cut (expanded). (As usual, this estimated value could not reflect *all* of the accomplishments that are aimed at in such programs.)

[57] Increased volume of counterfeiting, forgery, if program were cut.

A Possible Breakdown by Programs[2]	Amount in 1954 Budget (millions)[3]	Useful Indicator of Performance May Be Feasible[4]
VIII. General Government *(continued)*		
H. Other General Government *(continued)*		
District of Columbia	144[58]	
Territorial Governments	13[58]	
Governmental Services to Indians	23[58]	
Payment from Tribal Trust Funds to Indians	21	
Immigration Controls and Deportation	34	
Aliens: Records, Investigation	10	
Naturalization	4	
Administration: Immigration, Naturalization	2	
Payment of Customs Duties, Taxes, to Puerto Rico	15	
Interest on Public Debt	6350	
Interest on Refunds of Receipts	65	
IX. International Relations and Security		
Executive Direction and Policy Formation	9	
Conduct of Diplomatic and Consular Relations	84	
International Organizations	42	
Domestic Public Information, Liaison	2	
Central Services and Administration	11	
Boundary, Water, and Claims Commissions	12	
International Information and Educational Activities	156	
Government in Occupied Areas	50	
Economic and Technical Assistance, Europe	4969	
Economic and Technical Assistance, Near East	184	
Economic and Technical Assistance, Asia	329	
Economic and Technical Assistance, American Republics	20	
Military Assistance in Europe		
Ground	1696	59
Naval	539	59
Air	1128	59
NATO and Related Facilities	15	59
Military Assistance—Near East		
Ground	243	59
Naval	31	59
Air	536	59
Military Assistance—Asia and Pacific		
Ground	403	59
Naval	105	59
Air	117	59

[58] See footnote 55.

[59] Estimated reduction in capability (e.g., say the retarding or stopping of a given enemy attack) if the program were cut. Estimates could not be made public, and they would not show the whole picture—e.g., uncertainties, other types of payoff—but they could probably be more useful than estimates of the physical military units.

A Possible Breakdown by Programs[2]	Amount in 1954 Budget (millions)[3]	Useful Indicator of Performance May Be Feasible[4]
IX. International Relations and Security (*continued*)		
Military Assistance—American Republics		
Ground	34	61
Naval	9	61
Air	20	61
Escapees—Europe	5	
Administration—Europe	78	61
X. Special Defense Production Programs[62]		
Strategic and Critical Materials	343	61
Reserve Plants and Tools	5	61
Minerals and Metals Procurement	414	61
Rubber Procurement	9	61
Machine Tools Procurement	46	61
Administration: Defense Materials Procurement	6	61
Agricultural Commodities	10	61
Minerals Exploration, Dept. of Interior	11	61
Other Acquisitions as Reserves	102	61
Defense Production Administration	3	61
Defense Transport Administration	2	
Price Controls	37	
Rent Controls	11	
Wage and Salary Controls	12	
Office of Administrator, ESA	60	
Assistance to Small Defense Plants	4	
Allocation of Materials, NPA	22	61
Allocation of Materials, Field Service	6	61
Miscellaneous Mobilization Activities, Commerce	1	61
Export Controls	4	61
Petroleum Production and Distribution	2	61
Electric Power Expansion	1	61
Miscellaneous Mobilization Activities, Interior	1	61
Agricultural Production Goals	2	61
Miscellaneous Mobilization Activities, Agriculture	3	61
Renegotiation of Contracts	18	
Buildings Management: Defense Production	6	

[60] Less than $500,000.

[61] See footnote 59. This type of indicator would have more relevance with respect to some programs than with respect to others. With all their limitations, however, such indicators of performance might help government to shift funds from less important to more important programs.

[62] Most of these amounts are the 1953 program, since only the total, not the breakdown, was presented (for later transmission) in the 1954 Budget.

BIBLIOGRAPHY

Government Publications

ADAMS, FRANK, AND MARTIN R. HUBERTY, *Value and Cost of Water for Irrigation in the Coastal Plain of Southern California*, Bulletin 43, The South Coastal Basin Investigation, Division of Water Resources, State of California Department of Public Works, 1933.

Annual Report of the Chief of Engineers, U.S. Army, 1951, Vol. 3, *Report of the Federal Civil Works Program as Administered by the Corps of Engineers*, Part I, U.S. Government Printing Office, Washington, 1952.

BROWN, CARL B., *The Control of Reservoir Silting*, U.S. Department of Agriculture Miscellaneous Publication 521, U.S. Government Printing Office, Washington, 1944.

Budget of the United States Government for the Fiscal Year Ending June 30, 1953, U.S. Government Printing Office, Washington, 1952.

Budget of the United States Government for the Fiscal Year Ending June 30, 1954, U.S. Government Printing Office, Washington, 1953.

CLARK, J. M., E. L. GRANT, AND M. M. KELSO, "Secondary or Indirect Benefits of Water-Use Projects," Report of Panel of Consultants to Michael W. Straus, Commissioner, Bureau of Reclamation (mimeographed), June 26, 1952.

COMMISSION ON ORGANIZATION OF THE EXECUTIVE BRANCH OF THE GOVERNMENT (The Hoover Commission), *Budgeting and Accounting*, A Report to the Congress by the Commission, U.S. Government Printing Office, Washington, February, 1949.

COMMISSION ON ORGANIZATION OF THE EXECUTIVE BRANCH OF THE GOVERNMENT (The Hoover Commission), *Task Force Reports* prepared for the Commission, U.S. Government Printing Office, Washington, January, 1949.

COMMISSION ON ORGANIZATION OF THE EXECUTIVE BRANCH OF THE GOVERNMENT (The Second Hoover Commission), *Task Force Reports* prepared for the Commission, U.S. Government Printing Office, Washington, January–June, 1955.

Economic Evaluation of Federal Water Resource Development Projects, Report to the Committee on Public Works, House of Representatives, by Mr. Jones of Alabama, from the Subcommittee to Study Civil Works, 82d Congress, 2d Session, U.S. Government Printing Office, Washington, 1952.

"Explanatory Notes for Department of Agriculture, Fiscal Year 1953," Vols. 1–2, justification statements prepared in the Department of Agriculture (mimeographed).

Green River Watershed, Kentucky and Tennessee, printed as House Document No. 261, 82d Congress, 1st Session, U.S. Government Printing Office, Washington, 1951.

Missouri: Land and Water, The Report of the Missouri Basin Survey Commission, U.S. Government Printing Office, Washington, 1953.

"Performance Budgeting: Selected References," Revised, U.S. Bureau of the Budget Library, April, 1951.

Proposed Practices for Economic Analysis of River Basin Projects, Report to the Federal Inter-Agency River Basin Committee, prepared by the Subcommittee on Benefits and Costs, Washington, May, 1950.

"Report on Survey Flood Control, Santa Maria River and Tributaries, California," prepared by the Los Angeles District Engineer's Office, Corps of Engineers, U.S. Department of the Army (mimeographed), February 10, 1953.

"Revised Statement on Secondary Benefits," Federal Inter-Agency River Basin Committee, Subcommittee on Benefits and Costs, January 8, 1952.

Santa Maria Project, California, printed as House Document No. 217, 83d Congress, 1st Session, U.S. Government Printing Office, Washington, 1953.

Study of Civil Works, Parts 1–3, Hearings before the Subcommittee to Study Civil Works of the Committee on Public Works, House of Representatives, 82d Congress, 2d Session, U.S. Government Printing Office, Washington, 1952.

U.S. BUREAU OF THE BUDGET, "Circular No. A-47," December 31, 1952.

—— *Techniques for the Development of a Work Measurement System,* Management Bulletin, U.S. Government Printing Office, Washington, March, 1950.

—— *A Work Measurement System: Development and Use (A Case Study),* Management Bulletin, U.S. Government Printing Office, Washington, March, 1950.

U.S. BUREAU OF THE CENSUS, *County and City Data Book, 1952,* U.S. Government Printing Office, Washington, 1953.

—— *Historical Statistics of the United States, 1789–1945,* U.S. Government Printing Office, Washington, 1949.

U.S. BUREAU OF RECLAMATION, "Bureau of Reclamation Manual," Vol. XIII, "Benefits and Costs," March, 1952.

—— *The Columbia River,* Vol. 1, published as House Document No. 473, 81st Congress, 2d Session, U.S. Government Printing Office, Washington, 1950.

—— *Hell's Canyon Project Idaho-Oregon,* Bureau of Reclamation, Region 1, Boise, Idaho, Project Planning Report No. 1-5.75-0, April, 1948.

—— "Payette Unit, Mountain Home Project, Idaho," Project Planning Report No. 1-5.5-5 (mimeographed), September, 1945.

U.S. DEPARTMENT OF AGRICULTURE, "Long-Range Agricultural Policy," A Study of Selected Trends and Factors Relating to the Long-Range Prospect for American Agriculture, prepared for the Committee on Agriculture, House of Representatives, 80th Congress, 2d Session, March 10, 1948.

—— *Trees, The Yearbook of Agriculture, 1949,* U.S. Government Printing Office, Washington, 1949.

—— *Yearbook of Agriculture, 1948,* U.S. Government Printing Office, Washington, 1948.

U.S. House of Representatives, *Department of Agriculture Appropriations for 1953*, Parts 1–3, Hearings before the Subcommittee of the Committee on Appropriations, 82d Congress, 2d Session, U.S. Government Printing Office, Washington, 1952.

—— *Department of Agriculture Appropriations for 1954*, Parts 1–5, Hearings before the Subcommittee of the Committee on Appropriations, 83d Congress, 1st Session, U.S. Government Printing Office, Washington, 1953.

—— *Interior Department Appropriations for 1953*, Parts 1–4, Hearings before the Subcommittee of the Committee on Appropriations, 82d Congress, 2d Session, U.S. Government Printing Office, Washington, 1952.

U.S. Senate, *Agricultural Appropriations for 1953*, Hearings before the Subcommittee of the Committee on Appropriations, 82d Congress, 2d Session, U.S. Government Printing Office, Washington, 1952.

—— *Interior Department Appropriations for 1953*, Hearings before a Subcommittee of the Committee on Appropriations, 82d Congress, 2d Session, U.S. Government Printing Office, Washington, 1952.

A Water Policy for the American People, Vol. 1, The Report of the President's Water Resources Policy Commission, U.S. Government Printing Office, Washington, 1950.

"Work-Measurement and Work-Status Reporting System: PMA Commodity Offices," unpublished working papers and exhibits, Production and Marketing Administration, Department of Agriculture, 1952 and 1953.

Other Books and Pamphlets

Alchian, Armen A., *Economic Replacement Policy*, The RAND Corporation, Report R-227, April 12, 1952.

Burkhead, Jesse, *Government Budgeting*, John Wiley and Sons, New York, 1956.

Committee for Economic Development, *Control of Federal Government Expenditures*, A Statement on National Policy by the Research and Policy Committee, January, 1955.

Dean, Joel, *Capital Budgeting: Top-Management Policy on Plant, Equipment, and Product Development*, Columbia University Press, New York, 1951.

DeHaven, James C., Lynn A. Gore, and Jack Hirshleifer, *A Brief Survey of the Technology and Economics of Water Supply*, The RAND Corporation, Report R-258-RC, October, 1953.

Douglas, Paul H., *Economy in the National Government*, University of Chicago Press, Chicago, 1952.

Eckstein, Otto, "Benefits and Costs, Studies in the Economics of Public Works Evaluation," Unpublished Ph.D. thesis, Harvard University, April, 1955.

Friedman, Milton, *Essays in Positive Economics*, University of Chicago Press, Chicago, 1953.

Hart, B. H. Liddell, *Strategy, The Indirect Approach*, Frederick A. Praeger, New York, 1954.

Heckert, J. B., *Business Budgeting and Control*, Ronald Press Company, New York, 1946.

Hicks, J. R., *Value and Capital*, Clarendon Press, Oxford, 1946.

KNIGHT, F. H., *The Economic Organization,* University of Chicago Press, Chicago, 1933.

LERNER, ABBA P., *The Economics of Control,* Macmillan Company, New York, 1944.

LEYS, WAYNE A. R., *Ethics for Policy Decisions,* Prentice-Hall, Englewood Cliffs, N. J., 1952.

LUTZ, FRIEDRICH, AND VERA LUTZ, *The Theory of Investment of the Firm,* Princeton University Press, Princeton, 1951.

MAASS, ARTHUR, *Muddy Waters,* Harvard University Press, Cambridge, Massachusetts, 1951.

MARGOLIS, JULIUS, "External Economies and The Justification of Public Investment," Office of Naval Research Technical Report No. 22, Department of Economics, Stanford University, October 25, 1955.

——— "Welfare Criteria, Efficient Pricing and Decentralization of Public Services: Irrigation, A Case Study," Office of Naval Research Technical Report No. 26, Department of Economics, Stanford University, November 23, 1955.

MILLIS, W. (ed.), *The Forrestal Diaries,* Viking Press, New York, 1951.

MOREY, L., AND R. P. HACKETT, *Fundamentals of Governmental Accounting,* 2nd ed., John Wiley and Sons, New York, 1951.

MOSHER, FREDERICK C., *Program Budgeting: Theory and Practice,* Public Administration Service, New York, 1954.

PETERSON, ELMER T., *Big Dam Foolishness,* Devin-Adair Co., New York, 1954.

PIGOU, A. C., *The Economics of Welfare,* 4th ed., Macmillan and Co., London, 1948.

Principles of a Sound National Water Policy, Prepared under the Auspices of the National Water Policy Panel of the Engineers Joint Council, July, 1951.

RANSMEIER, JOSEPH S., *The Tennessee Valley Authority, A Case Study in the Economics of Multiple Purpose Stream Planning,* Vanderbilt University Press, Nashville, 1942.

SAMUELSON, PAUL A., *Foundations of Economic Analysis,* Harvard University Press, Cambridge, Massachusetts, 1947.

SCITOVSKY, TIBOR, *Welfare and Competition,* George Allen and Unwin, London, 1952.

SMITHIES, ARTHUR, *The Budgetary Process in the United States,* Committee for Economic Development Research Study, McGraw-Hill Book Company, New York, 1955.

STIGLER, GEORGE, *The Theory of Price,* Macmillan Company, New York, 1946.

TILLER, CARL W., *Government Cost Accounting,* Municipal Finance Officers' Association of the U.S. and Canada, Chicago, 1940.

WALKER, MABLE L., *Municipal Expenditures,* The Johns Hopkins Press, Baltimore, 1930.

Articles

ALCHIAN, ARMEN A., "The Rate of Interest, Fisher's Rate of Return Over Costs and Keynes' Internal Rate of Return," *American Economic Review,* Vol. 45, December, 1955, pp. 938–943.

ALCHIAN, ARMEN A., "Uncertainty, Evolution, and Economic Theory," *Journal of Political Economy*, Vol. 58, June, 1950, pp. 211–221.

BERGSON, ABRAM, "On the Concept of Social Welfare," *Quarterly Journal of Economics*, Vol. 68, May, 1954, pp. 233–252.

BUCHANAN, JAMES M., "The Pricing of Highway Services," *National Tax Journal*, Vol. 5, June, 1952, pp. 97–106.

—— "The Pure Theory of Government Finance: A Suggested Approach," *Journal of Political Economy*, Vol. 57, December, 1949, pp. 496–505.

DAVIDSON, B., "How to Grab 20 Acres for $1.25," *Reader's Digest*, July, 1953, pp. 141–144, reprinted from *Collier's*, April 11, 1953, pp. 13–16.

ELLIS, HOWARD S., AND WILLIAM FELLNER, "External Economies and Diseconomies," *American Economic Review*, Vol. 33, September, 1943, pp. 493–511, reprinted in K. E. BOULDING AND G. J. STIGLER (eds.), *Readings in Price Theory*, Richard D. Irwin, Chicago, 1952, pp. 242–263.

ENKE, STEPHEN, "On Maximizing Profits," *American Economic Review*, Vol. 41, September, 1951, pp. 566–578.

FLEMING, MARCUS, "External Economies and the Doctrine of Balanced Growth," *Economic Journal*, Vol. 65, June, 1955, pp. 241–256.

FRIEDMAN, MILTON, "Discussion," *American Economic Review, Papers and Proceedings*, Vol. 39, May, 1949, pp. 196–199.

GOODEVE, SIR CHARLES, "Operational Research As a Science," *Journal of the Operations Research Society of America*, Vol. 1, August, 1953, pp. 166–180.

HITCH, CHARLES J., "Sub-optimization in Operations Problems," *Journal of the Operations Research Society of America*, Vol. 1, May, 1953, pp. 87–99.

"Hot as Hell's Canyon," *The Economist*, August 20, 1955, p. 616.

HOTELLING, H., "The General Welfare in Relation to Problems of Taxation and of Railway and Utility Rates," *Econometrica*, Vol. 6, July, 1938, pp. 242–269.

KEY, V. O., JR., "The Lack of a Budgetary Theory," *American Political Science Review*, Vol. 34, December, 1940, pp. 1137–1144.

KITTEL, CHARLES, "The Nature and Development of Operations Research," *Science*, Vol. 105, February 7, 1947, pp. 150–153.

LESTER, R. A., "Marginalism, Minimum Wages, and Labor Markets," *American Economic Review*, Vol. 37, March, 1947, pp. 135–148.

LEVINSON, HORACE C., "Experiences in Commercial Operations Research," *Journal of the Operations Research Society of America*, Vol. 1, August, 1953, pp. 220–239.

MEADE, J. E., "External Economies and Diseconomies in a Competitive Situation," *Economic Journal*, Vol. 62, March, 1952, pp. 54–67.

MILLER, LESLIE A., "The Battle that Squanders Billions," *Saturday Evening Post*, May 14, 1949, pp. 30–31.

OLIVER, H. M., JR., "Marginal Theory and Business Behavior," *American Economic Review*, Vol. 37, June, 1947, pp. 375–383.

SAVAGE, L. J., AND J. H. LORIE, "Three Problems in Rationing Capital," *Journal of Business*, Vol. 28, October, 1955, pp. 229–239.

SCITOVSKY, TIBOR, "Two Concepts of External Economies," *Journal of Political Economy*, Vol. 62, April, 1954, pp. 143–151.

SIMON, HERBERT A., "Staff and Management Controls," *Annals of the American Academy of Political and Social Science*, Vol. 292, March, 1954, pp. 95–103.

"Symposium on Budget Theory," *Public Administration Review*, Vol. 10, Winter, 1950, pp. 20–31.

TINTNER, G., "The Theory of Choice Under Subjective Risk and Uncertainty," *Econometrica*, Vol. 9, July-October, 1941, pp. 298–304.

TREFETHEN, FLORENCE N., "A History of Operations Research," in J. F. McCLOSKEY AND F. N. TREFETHEN (eds.), *Operations Research for Management*, The Johns Hopkins Press, Baltimore, 1954.

VINER, JACOB, "Cost Curves and Supply Curves," *Zeitschrift für Nationalökonomie*, Vol. 3, 1931, pp. 23–46, reprinted in K. E. BOULDING AND G. J. STIGLER (eds.), *Readings in Price Theory*, Richard D. Irwin, Chicago, 1952, pp. 198–232.

PUBLISHED RAND RESEARCH

Princeton University Press, Princeton, New Jersey

Approximations for Digital Computers, CECIL HASTINGS, JR., 1955.
International Communication and Political Opinion: A Guide to the Literature,
BRUCE LANNES SMITH AND CHITRA M. SMITH, 1956.
Dynamic Programming, RICHARD BELLMAN, 1957.
The Berlin Blockade: A Study in Cold War Politics, W. PHILLIPS DAVISON, 1958.
The French Economy and the State, WARREN C. BAUM, 1958.

Columbia University Press, New York

Soviet National Income and Product, 1940–48, ABRAM BERGSON AND HANS
HEYMANN, JR., 1954.
Soviet National Income and Product in 1928, OLEG HOEFFDING, 1954.
Labor Productivity in Soviet and American Industry, WALTER GALENSON, 1955.

The Free Press, Glencoe, Illinois

Psychosis and Civilization, HERBERT GOLDHAMER AND ANDREW W. MARSHALL, 1949.
Soviet Military Doctrine, RAYMOND L. GARTHOFF, 1953.
A Study of Bolshevism, NATHAN LEITES, 1953.
Ritual of Liquidation: The Case of the Moscow Trials, NATHAN LEITES AND
ELSA BERNAUT, 1954.
*Two Studies in Soviet Controls: Communism and the Russian Peasant, and
Moscow in Crisis*, HERBERT S. DINERSTEIN AND LEON GOURÉ, 1955.
A Million Random Digits with 100,000 Normal Deviates, THE RAND CORPORA-
TION, 1955.

McGraw-Hill Book Company, New York

The Operational Code of the Politburo, NATHAN LEITES, 1951.
*Air War and Emotional Stress: Psychological Studies of Bombing and Civilian
Defense*, IRVING L. JANIS, 1951.
*Soviet Attitudes Toward Authority: An Interdisciplinary Approach to Problems
of Soviet Character*, MARGARET MEAD, 1951.
Mobilizing Resources for War: The Economic Alternatives, TIBOR SCITOVSKY,
EDWARD SHAW, LORIE TARSHIS, 1951.
The Organizational Weapon: A Study of Bolshevik Strategy and Tactics,
PHILIP SELZNICK, 1952.
Introduction to the Theory of Games, J. C. C. MCKINSEY, 1952.
Weight-Strength Analysis of Aircraft Structures, F. R. SHANLEY, 1952.
The Compleat Strategyst: Being a Primer on the Theory of Games of Strategy,
J. D. WILLIAMS, 1954.
Linear Programming and Economic Analysis, ROBERT DORFMAN, PAUL A. SAMUEL-
SON, AND ROBERT M. SOLOW, 1958.

Public Affairs Press, Washington, D.C.

The Rise of Krushchev, MYRON RUSH, 1958.

Behind the Sputniks: A Survey of Soviet Space Science, F. J. KRIEGER, 1958.

Row, Peterson and Company, Evanston, Illinois

German Rearmament and Atomic War: The Views of German Military and Political Leaders, HANS SPEIER, 1957.

West German Leadership and Foreign Policy, EDITED BY HANS SPEIER AND W. PHILLIPS DAVISON, 1957.

Stanford University Press, Stanford, California

Strategic Surrender: The Politics of Victory and Defeat, PAUL KECSKEMETI, 1958.

INDEX

Adams, Frank, 17n
Agencies, and allocation of investment
    budgets, 114, 148
    capital rationing in, 85
    and cost-benefit analysis, 20, 151, 203
    criteria for preferred set of projects
        for, 202
    estimation of time horizons by, 125
    and Federal Power Commission, 19
    flood damage information obtained
        by, 226
    and over-counting, 152
    position of, in regard to duplicate
        facilities, 146–148
    and secondary benefits, 157
    and wealth distribution, 208
    see also Bureau of Reclamation, Corps
        of Engineers, and Department of
        Agriculture
Agricultural Conservation Program, and
    annual cost of crop production,
    198
Alaska, development of, 60, 162n
    see also Regional development
Alchian, Armen A., 10n, 71n, 77n, 86n,
    92n
All-American Canal Project, 223
Alternative institutional arrangements,
    defined, 283–284
"Alternative justifiable expenditure,"
    178–180
Alternatives, appropriate, 97
    designing of, 57, 97
    desirable investigation of, 52–53
    interrelated, 55
    marginal rate of return dependent on,
    88

Alternatives, mutually exclusive, 55
    scales and combinations of, 57
    in water-resource measures, 238
Analysis, operations, use of, 8
    piecemeal, 31–32, 57, 99–100
    quantitative, in comparison of pro-
        gram levels, 280–283, 287
    cost-benefit analysis as example of,
    16
    development of, 5–8
    distinction between uses of, 279–280
    and economy within programs, 253,
    283–287, 288
    in government, 3, 8–9, 16, 247–248,
    279
    in handling of intangibles, 62–64, 69
    necessity for use of, 3
    outlook for use of, 15–16, 96
    private firms' use of, 10
    and theory of choice, 5
    use of, by decision-makers, 8, 133
    see also Cost-benefit analysis
    systematic, and natural selection, 10n
Analyst, and preparation of perform-
        ance budget, 253
    task of, in preparation of exhibits,
    124
Annual turnover, influence of, on bene-
        fit-cost ratio, 108–111, 110n, 199
    see also Benefit-cost ratios
Appropriations bill, single, and per-
        formance budgeting, 265

B-lists, and performance budgeting,
    265–266
Balanced development
    see Regional development

319